# THE FISHERMEN

About the **Translator**: **Marc Linder**, who taught on the social science faculty at Roskilde University Centre in Denmark for three years, has translated two volumes of German fiction—Johannes Bobrowski, *I Taste Bitterness* (Seven Seas Publishers, 1970), and Fred Wander, *The Seventh Well* (Seven Seas Publishers, 1976)—and was certified as a simultaneous interpreter for Danish and German by the United States Department of State. After completing a Ph.D. in political science at Princeton University, he worked at universities in Germany and Mexico. A graduate of Harvard Law School, he represented migrant farmworkers in the Rio Grande Valley for seven years on behalf of Texas Rural Legal Aid before coming to the University of Iowa in 1990, where he is a professor of labor law. Among the more recent of his fifteen books are *Wars of Attrition: Vietnam, the Business Roundtable, and the Decline of Construction Unions* (Fănpìhuà Press, 1999); *Of Cabbages and Kings County: Agriculture and the Formation of Modern Brooklyn* (University of Iowa Press, 1999), which was awarded the Theodore Saloutos Prize for the best book in agricultural history; and *Void Where Prohibited: Rest Breaks and the Right to Urinate on Company Time* (Cornell University Press, 1998).

About the **Second Revised and Enlarged Edition**: The Introduction has been expanded, a Cast of Characters has been added, and several stylistic changes have been made to the text.

About the **Publisher**: **Fănpìhuà Press**, which accepts no revenue from its books, publishes works that increasingly profit-driven university presses refuse to consider. Fănpìhuà Press plans to publish other novels by Hans Kirk. Its books are distributed by Prairie Lights Books, Iowa City, Iowa: (800) 295-BOOK or info@prairielights.com.

# Hans Kirk

# The Fishermen

Second Revised and Enlarged Edition

Translated and with an Introduction and Notes by

Marc Linder

Fănpìhuà Press
Iowa City
2000

Copyright © 1928 by Hans Kirk and Gyldendal
Translation, Introduction, and Notes
Copyright © 1999 and 2000 by Marc Linder
All rights reserved
Printed in the United States of America

Translated from the eighth Tranebog edition of
Hans Kirk, *Fiskerne* (Copenhagen: Gyldendal, 1974).

Cover photograph of Hans Kirk courtesy of Gyldendal.

Map of Limfjord taken from Det Danske Selskab,
*The Limfjord: Its Town and People*, pp. 8-9
(Copenhagen: Det Danske Selskab, 1964),
courtesy of Det Danske Kulturinstitut.

The translations: *Lord Jesus, in Thy name we now*,
*Arise all things that God has made*, and
*Now sin, with reign unbroken*, taken from
*Hymnal for Church and Home*, pp. 350, 322, 153
(Blair, Neb.: Danish Lutheran Publishing House, 1927),
courtesy of Augsburg Fortress Publishers.

Suggested Library of Congress Cataloging
Kirk, Hans, 1898-1962
    The Fishermen/by Hans Kirk. Translated and with an Introduction
and Notes by Marc Linder. 2nd ed., rev. and enl.
    xxxi, 305 p.; map; 21 cm.
    Includes bibliographical references
    ISBN 0-9673899-2-5
    PT8175.K53F513 2000
    Library of Congress Control Number 00-133086

Publication of this edition was made possible in part by grants from the
Office of the Vice President for Research of The University of Iowa and
the Iowa Law School Foundation.

# Contents

| | |
|---|---:|
| Introduction | v |
| Further Reading | xxv |
| Acknowledgments | xxvii |
| Map of the Limfjord | xxviii-xxix |
| Cast of Characters | xxx |
| **The Fishermen** | 1 |
| Notes | 295 |

# Introduction

Hans Kirk's 1928 novel *The Fishermen* is the best-selling Danish book of all time—apart from the Bible and hymnbook, which play such an important part in it. On the strength of this first novel, the author was chosen to receive a stipend for artists from the Danish parliament in 1931.[1] In 1935 Danish radio broadcast a dramatic adaptation co-written by Kirk.[2] The novel attained the peak of its fame in 1977 (and again in 1987) when Danish state television broadcast a six-hour film adaptation.[3] An eleven-hour talking book appeared in 1999.[4] As a staple of the modern Danish literary canon, the book has been required reading in high schools for decades. For immigrants as well as Danish adults and children with reading problems there is even an "easy-to-read" abridged edition accompanied by a workbook.[5] Continuously in print since its original publication—its thirtieth edition was issued in 1998—and translated into twelve languages, *The Fishermen* is perhaps the first "collective novel," in which a group microcosm, rather than an individual main character or hero, is the focus and sharply illuminates social relations.[6]

---

[1] Morten Thing, *Hans Kirks mange ansigter: En biografi* 350, 164 (Copenhagen: Gyldendal, 1997)

[2] Hans Kirk and Sigurd Thomsen, "Ikke ved styrke," in *Omkring Fiskerne* 308-14 (Bo Elbrønd-Bek and Ole Ravn eds.; Copenhagen: Reitzel, 1977) (excerpt).

[3] Thorkild Borup Jensen, "Fra roman til drejbog," in *Omkring Fiskerne* at 332-58; Thorkild Borup Jensen, *Fra bog til skærm: "Fiskerne" som TV-spil* (Copenhagen: Reitzel, 1977). The film was directed by Jens Ravn.

[4] Produced by the Dansk Biblioteks Center.

[5] Hans Kirk, *Fiskerne* (Helle Helmersen ed.; Herning: Special-pædagogisk forlag, 1998); *Opgaver til Fiskerne* (Helle Helmersen ed.; Herning: Special-pædagogisk forlag, 1999).

[6] See Janet Mawby, "The Collective Novel and the Rise of Fascism in the

## Introduction

Yet this novel, like the rest of Kirk's works—including eight other novels, hundreds of novellas and short stories, children's books, radio plays, political tracts, memoirs, travelogues, literary translations, literary and political essays, reviews, and thousands of journalistic pieces—remains unknown to the English-reading world. The indexes to *The New York Times* and *The Times* of London include no obituary for Kirk, although nine of his books have been translated a total of forty-four times into twenty languages.[7]

Penguin Books bought the English-language rights in 1946 and a translation (*The Jutland Fishermen*) was prepared; in 1947 Elias Bredsdorff, whose "Introduction" was to have accompanied the Penguin translation, noted in a British literary magazine that a translation was "shortly to be published in the Penguin Li-

---

1930's," in *Ideas and Ideologies in Scandinavian Literature Since the First World War: Proceedings of the 10th Study Conference of the International Association for Scandinavian Studies, held in Reykjavik, July 22-27, 1974*, at 143-61 (Sveinn Skorri Höskuldsson ed.; Reykjavik: University of Iceland, 1975); Finn Klysner, *Den danske kollektivroman: 1928-1944* (Copenhagen: Vinten, 1976). On the possible relationship between *The Fishermen* and a Polish collective novel that appeared in Danish translation while Kirk was writing his book, see F. J. Billeskov Jansen, *Læsefrugter: Fra et langt livs erfaringer med litteraturen* 222-26 (Copenhagen: Munksgaard, 1995). The Polish novel is Władysław Reymont, *The Peasants: A Tale of Our Own Times* (4 vols; Michael Dziewicki tr.; New York: Knopf, 1924-1925).

[7]Thing, *Hans Kirks mange ansigter* at 377-78. Among other novels, Kirk translated B. Traven, *Death Ship* and *The White Rose*, Howard Fast, *Clarkton*, and Sophus Winther, *Take All to Nebraska*. Some of Kirk's most important essays were posthumously republished in Hans Kirk, *Litteratur og tendens: Essays og artikler* (Copenhagen: Gyldendal, 1974); Hans Kirk, *Det borgerlige frisinds endeligt: Essays og artikler* (Copenhagen: Gyldendal, 1978 [1969]). On Kirk's novellas, most of which he wrote to make ends meet, see Ole Ravn, "Efterskrift," in Hans Kirk, *En plads i verden og andre fortællinger* 163-69 (N.p.: Hovedland, 1987). In 1937 *The New York Times* at least took notice of Kirk, characterizing him as the spokesman for Denmark's "[r]ural proletarianism" in a brief review of *Daglejerne*. Alma Luise Olson, "The Literary Scene in Scandinavia," *The New York Times*, Aug. 22, 1937, sect. 7, at 8, 23.

*Introduction*

brary."[8] Two bibliographies of Danish literature in translation published in 1950 and 1951 still listed the translation as forthcoming.[9] But in 1952 Penguin informed the Danish publisher that rising costs and problems with paper had prompted it to abandon planned publication.[10] Bredsdorff conjectures that the translation may have been discarded as unsatisfactory, and that "[a]nticommunist political bias during the Cold War may also have played a part in keeping any work by Kirk from being published in English."[11] The present translation is an effort to redress this glaring omission in the worldwide dissemination of Scandinavian literature.[12]

An American audience may find it unimaginable that the au-

---

[8]Elias Bredsdorff, "Danish Literature Since 1930," 53 (117) *Life and Letters* 79-91 at 81 (May 1947).

[9]The entry in Elias Bredsdorff, *Danish Literature in English Translation* 88 (Copenhagen: Munksgaard, 1950), read: "Hans Kirk: *The Fishermen*. Translated by Marianne Gilliam. With an Introduction by Elias Bredsdorff. (Shortly to be published Harmondsworth 1950)." The next year P. M. Mitchell, *A Bibliographical Guide to Danish Literature* 44 (Copenhagen: Munksgaard, 1951), carried the same information, adding: "To be published 1951 Harmondsworth Middlesex: Penguin." Marianne (Helweg) Gilliam was the daughter of a Danish professor of Danish at the University of London. Elias Bredsdorff, *Mit engelske liv: Erindringer 1946-1979*, at 13 (1984).

[10]Bo Elbrønd-Bek and Ole Ravn, "Indledning," in *Omkring Fiskerne* 11-43 at 38.

[11]Elias Bredsdorff, "Hans Kirk," in *Twentieth-Century Danish Writers* 245-53 at 248 (Marianne Stecher-Hansen ed.; Detroit: Gale Research, 1999).

[12]A few pages of *Fiskerne*, with historical and linguistic notes, were included in a reader for English-language students of Danish. *Modern Danish Prose: A Selection of Danish Texts for Foreign Students* 77-83, 150-52 (H. A. Koefoed, comp.; Copenhagen: Høst, n.d. [1955]). An extract of a few pages of *Daglejerne* was translated by Marianne Helweg as "The Birth of a New Era," in *Contemporary Danish Prose: An Anthology* 243-50 (Copenhagen: Gyldendal, 1958). An extract of a few pages of *Skyggespil* was translated by Lydia Cranfield as "Exile," in *Norseman*, 14(2): 126-33 (Mar.-Apr. 1956), without revealing its source. See also Carol Schroeder, *A Bibliography of Danish Literature in English Translation: 1950-1980*, at 101 (Copenhagen: Det Danske Selskab, 1982).

*Introduction*

thor of a Western European country's best-selling novel was a high-profile member of the Communist Party. Yet Kirk joined the Danish Communist Party in 1931 and remained an influential member and cultural functionary until his death in 1962; after World War II he became cultural editor of the party newspaper, *Land og Folk*. Despite his prominent position, however, he opposed both socialist realism as a literary genre and party interference with artists' work. Nevertheless, even after Khrushchev's secret speech attacking Stalin in 1956, Kirk continued to defend Stalin's achievements in building socialism, which he was certain would one day be regarded as "the greatest event in the history of the human race till now."[13]

Later that year, in response to an editorial by the editor in chief of Denmark's leading social-democratic newspaper enjoining him to "kneel repentantly and beg for forgiveness" and "make an honest confession," Kirk published "A Stalinist's Confessions" in *Land og Folk*. After denouncing the editor in chief for his pro-Nazi editorial work during the occupation, Kirk argued that Stalin had been a symbol of the Soviet people and its strength. Although the Soviet Union had become strong and open enough to declare that much that had been done under Stalin was not good, Kirk insisted that "in his time Stalin was our hope. . . . One would have had to have been a fool not to support Stalin."[14]

As a child accompanying his father, a northern Jutland rural physician, on house calls, Kirk had already learned that many patients suffered from "the disease they call hunger."[15] Though

---

[13]Thing, *Hans Kirks mange ansigter* at 264, 297, 329-31; Hans Kirk, "Svar til Politiken," *Land og Folk*, June 3, 1956, at 10, col. 1 (quote).

[14]Hans Kirk, "En stalinists bekendelser," *Land og Folk*, May 27, 1956, at 10, col. 1. For Kirk's fulsome paean to "Our Stalin" in the newspaper of the Soviet writers' organization entirely devoted to such offerings in the days after Stalin's death, see Hans Kirk, "Bez kolebanii, vperëd c vernymi coratnikami stalina! [Unwaveringly, Forward with Stalin's True Comrades-in-Arms!]" *Literaturnaia gazeta*, Mar. 17, 1953, at 4, col. 3-4.

[15]Hans Kirk, *Skyggespil* 71 (Copenhagen: Gyldendal, 1998 [1953]).

## Introduction

not yet a party member at the time he wrote *The Fishermen* in the mid-1920s, he had adopted the perspective of psychoanalytically enriched Marxism.[16] As he once told a Danish weekly, if he could take only two books to a deserted island, one of them would be Karl Marx's *Das Kapital*.[17] To be sure, Kirk stressed that "Marxism is a scientific instrument, a purely scientific working hypothesis; but the good Marxist cannot approach matters completely coldly and intellectually—he must nourish a love for the people he's fighting for...."[18]

His communist reputation had been sufficiently widespread that when, having tired of too much reading after his university law exams in 1922, he applied for a job as a rural postman, the general director of the postal service refused to hire him lest he make the red-coated letter carriers red in their souls as well.[19] Later that year, after Kirk had served as a volunteer in the Danish embassy in Paris, the ambassador put an end to Kirk's diplomatic career by reporting to the foreign ministry that he had acknowledged having communist or bolshevik ideas.[20] In 1923, one of Denmark's leading lyric poets, Otto Gelsted, dedicated his influential poem, "Reklameskibet" to the young Kirk. At the close of

---

[16] J[ørgen]. S[andvad]., "Søndags-Samtale med Manden i Fyrrerne: 'Skriv om Millionærer,'" *Politiken*, Mar. 12, 1939, at 5, col. 3, at col. 5.

[17] Julius Bomholt, *Moderne Skribenter* (1933), reprinted in *Omkring Fiskerne* at 175.

[18] Cai Clausen, "Den gode marxist kan ikke gå koldt og intellektuelt til sagen," *Frit Danmark*, Mar. 1954, reprinted in *Undertrykkere og undertrykte: Et Hans Kirk-udvalg* 199-207 at 201 (Ole Ravn ed.; Copenhagen: Gyldendal, 1977).

[19] Elias Bredsdorff, "Marx, Freud og Adler i Hans Kirks roman 'Fiskerne,'" in Elias Bredsdorff, *Fra Andersen til Scherfig* 168-90 at 170-71 (Copenhagen: Gyldendal, 1978 [1975]). Bredsdorff provides no source for the direct quotation he attributes to the postal director. In an interview in 1939 Kirk himself merely said that the general director was doubtless afraid of "communist foolishness." J[ørgen]. S[andvad]., "Søndags-Samtale med Manden i Fyrrerne: 'Skriv om Millionærer,'" at 5, col. 5.

[20] Thing, *Hans Kirks mange ansigter* at 55.

*Introduction*

the poem, which dissects capitalism's social and cultural contradictions, "an ordinary blond Danish student" (presumably Kirk) symbolically blows up capitalism's "Show Boat."[21]

After two boring years as a civil servant in the building department of Copenhagen city hall, Kirk left to become a book reviewer for the provincial paper, *Lolland-Falsters Folketidende*.[22] Explaining why he had abandoned his legal career, Kirk told an interviewer in 1939 that law was the choice of all who were unfit for anything else: it was a very easy degree involving only some memorization.[23] Kirk nourished a critical and at times contemptuous attitude toward a legal system and profession he viewed as devoted to construing as the highest form of justice the plundering of the poor by the rich.[24]

*The Fishermen*, which Kirk rewrote eight times before its first publication while continuing to be fully engaged in his journalistic career,[25] takes place in northern Jutland over several years in the 1920s, more or less contemporaneously with its composition.[26]

---

[21]Otto Gelsted, "Reklameskibet," in Otto Gelsted, *Jomfru Gloriant* 40-42 (N.p. [Copenhagen]: Gyldendal, 1968 [1923]). For an English translation of the poem, which could also be translated "The Advertising Ship," see Otto Gelsted, "The Show Boat," 53 (117) *Life and Letters* 147-49 (May 1947). On the connection to Kirk, see 7 *Dansk litteraturhistorie: Demokrati og kulturkamp 1901-45*, at 269 (Gunhild Agger et al. eds; Copenhagen: Gyldendal, 1984); Ib Bondebjerg, "Hans Kirk," in 2 *Danske digtere i det 20. århundrede: Fra Tom Kristensen til H.C. Branner* 198-230 at 203 (Torben Brostrøm and Mette Winge eds.; Copenhagen: Gads, 1981).

[22]Bondebjerg, "Hans Kirk" at 203.

[23]J[ørgen]. S[andvad]., "Søndags-Samtale med Manden i Fyrrerne: 'Skriv om Millionærer'" at 5, col. 5.

[24]Hans Kirk, "Eventyret om den første sagfører," reprinted in *Undertrykkere og undertrykte* at 47-52 at 52 (first published in 1940).

[25]Carl Bergstrøm-Nielsen, *Analfabeternes forlægger og den glade magister: Forlæggerprofiler, digterportrætter* 67 (Copenhagen: Gyldendal, 1974); Ole Ravn, "Hans Kirk og hans forfatterskab," in *Undertrykkere og undertrykte* at 277-326 at 287-94.

[26]Inger Højlund, *En udviklingslinie i Hans Kirks forfatterskab: Udviklingen i historicitet og historiekonception eksemplificeret ved analyse af Fiskerne*,

## *Introduction*

It tells the story of a solidary group of fishermen and their families who move inland from the desolate and impoverished West Coast of Jutland, where they had fished in the North Sea. They are impelled to uproot themselves by the life-threatening conditions of deep-sea fishing, which also yields them only a scant living, and by the floods and sand-drifts to which their village is exposed.[27] In contrast, their new home to the east, the Limfjord (Lime Fjord), is a much more prosperous region for fishermen and farmers. (Though still called a fjord, it has been a sound since the North Sea broke through the western sand barrier in 1825; about 180 kilometers long, the Limfjord cuts through Jutland, about two-thirds of the way up the peninsula, connecting the North Sea and the Kattegat to the east.)[28] West Coast fishermen, who had

---

*Daglejerne, De ny tider, Djævelens penge og Klitgaard og sønner* 18 (Copenhagen: Samleren, 1978), also dates the action to the 1920s, but erroneously asserts that Kirk fails to provide any direct chronological historical data. In fact, the references to the return of North Slesvig to Denmark and the beginnings of commercial radio receivers clearly date the book to the 1920s. See below *The Fishermen* pp. 174, 271-72. Mads Liland, "Arbeid, erotikk og ideologi," *Norsk litterær årbok 1977*, 106-24 at 107, incorrectly asserts that the book takes place right before or after the turn of the century.

[27]On the fishermen's working and living conditions in Harboøre, the presumed residential origin of the novel's fishermen, see Karen Thuborg, *Det gamle Harboøre: Optegnelser* 38-61 (Henrik Ussing ed.; Copenhagen: Det Schønbergske Forlag, 1928). On the floods and sand-drifts in Harboøre, see J. P. Trap, *Kongeriget Danmark* 5: 502 (3rd ed.; Copenhagen: Gad, 1904). Alone on November 21, 1893, a storm killed forty-nine fishermen on the West Coast; twenty-seven fishermen from Harboøre, including nineteen fathers, drowned. Florian Martensen-Larsen, *Ulykken på Havet den 21. November 1893*, at 46, 48 (Thisted: Sparekassen Thy, 1973). Fishermen's incomes throughout Denmark were below average in the 1920s, and Limfjord fishermen's incomes were among the lowest. Danmarks Statistik, Det Statistiske Departement, *Folketællingen i Kongeriget Danmark d. 1. Februar 1921*, tab. 17 at 107 (Copenhagen: Thiele, 1925); Tage Sørensen, "Fiskernes indtægtsforhold og fiskeriets samfundsøkonomiske betydning," in *Fiskeriet i Danmark* 2:543-55 (H. Blegvad ed.; Copenhagen: Selskabet til Udgivelse af Kulturskrifter, n.d. [1947]).

[28]For a broad account of the Limfjord, see Det Danske Selskab, *The Limfjord: Its Towns and People* (Else Gress Wright and Percy Wait, trans.; Copen-

## Introduction

been fishing every year since about 1900 off Gjøl—the scene of the novel's action— introduced more advanced fishing techniques along the fjord's coasts.[29]

Unlike the West Coast villages, the Limfjord was also the secure seat of the Evangelical Lutheran Church, the Danish state church (to which virtually the entire Danish population belonged) under the strong influence of Grundtvigianism,[30] a movement named after Nikolai Frederik Severin Grundtvig (1783-1872). Grundtvig was a theologian, clergyman, poet, creator of a new Danish hymnbook, and founder of residential folk high schools for young adults.[31] Reacting against pietistic and rationalistic currents in Lutheranism, engaging worldly problems and pleasures, and propagating a common rural folk culture, Grundtvigianism became an optimistic ideology for Denmark's growth-oriented, prosperous farmers after they had extricated themselves from the control of the large landed proprietors.[32]

Though also Lutherans, the North Sea fishermen were members of the Church Association for the Inner Mission in Denmark, a puritanical, pietistic, revivalist movement, which was founded

---

hagen: Det Danske Selskab, 1964). For an account of the Danish fishing industry with special reference to the Limfjord, see F. V. Mortensen and A. C. Strubberg, *Die dänische Seefischerei* 49-55 (Stuttgart: Schweizerbart'sche Verlagsbuchhandlung, 1931). See also Great Britain, Naval Intelligence Department, *Denmark* 264-77 (N.p.: n.p., Jan. 1944).

[29]Hans Jeppesen, "Fiskeri fra Gjøl," *Bygd*, 6 ( 2): 6-15 at 9 (1975).

[30]In 1921, 98 percent of the entire population of Denmark and 99 percent of the rural population belonged to the established church (Folkekirke). Calculated according to Danmarks Statistik, *Statistisk Aarbog 1924*, tab. 11 at 19 (Copenhagen: Thieles Bogtrykkeri, 1924).

[31]See Kaj Thaning, *N.F.S. Grundtvig* (David Hohnen trans.; Copenhagen: Det Danske Selskab, 1972).

[32]See Martin Zerlang, *Bøndernes klassekamp i Danmark: Agrarsmåborgerskabets sociale og ideologiske udvikling fra landboreformernes tid til systemskiftet* (Copenhagen: Medusa, 1976); Andrew Buckser, "Tradition, Power, and Allegory: Constructions of the Past in Two Danish Religious Movements," *Ethnology* 34(4):257-72 (Fall 1995).

*Introduction*

in 1861.³³ Calling themselves "de hellige" ("the Pious," "the Holy," or "the Saintly"), they focused on confession, repentance, conversion, and salvation, and rigidly proscribed amusements such as dancing, card playing, and alcohol, which, as in *The Fishermen*, they often tried to suppress in their communities.³⁴ The Inner Mission revival in Harboøre, the West Coast fishing village residence from which the fictional fishermen emigrated, was nationally known as especially fanatic.³⁵ The Inner Mission (because it was formed as a domestic counterpart to foreign missionary activity, it is also sometimes translated as Home Mission) fielded an increasing number of proselytizing tract-hawkers or "Innermissionaries"³⁶ like the novel's Peder Hygum. It became particularly successful in recruiting adherents among the impoverished working class in rural Jutland, who were excluded from the agrarian economic growth that underwrote the spread of Grundtvigianism. Whereas the continuity between this world and the next that Grundtvigianism proclaimed was plausible to thriving farmers, the gulf that the Inner Mission preached resonated with pauperized laborers, who wished their period of trials and tribulations to end definitively with death. This inner-Lutheran conflict was reproduced in North America between groups popularly knows as the "Happy Danes" and the "Holy Danes."³⁷

---

³³Paul Holt, *Kirkelig Forening for den Indre Mission i Danmark gennem 100 år* 93-229 (Copenhagen: Lohses Forlag, 1961).

³⁴See Margaretha Balle-Petersen, "The Holy Danes: Some Aspects of the Study of Religious Groups," *Ethnologia Scandinavica* 79-112 (1981); Andrew Buckser, *Communities of Faith: Sectarianism, Identity, and Social Change on a Danish Island* 99-101, 156-62, 168-73 (Providence: Berghahn, 1996).

³⁵P. G. Lindhardt, *Den Danske kirkes historie: Tiden 1849-1901*, 7:330 (Hal Koch and Bjørn Kornerup eds.; Copenhagen: Gyldendal, 1958).

³⁶Filip Beck, "Indremissionærer og kolportører," in A. Fibiger, *Kirkelig Forening for den Indre Mission i Danmark gennem 60 aar* 26-30 (Copenhagen: Lohse, 1921).

³⁷For a brief account, see Eugene Fevold, "Coming of Age: 1875-1900," in *The Lutherans in North America* 253-328 at 267-72 (E. Clifford Nelson ed.; Philadelphia: Fortress Press, 1975).

*Introduction*

Kirk laid out his view of the quasi-natural geographic distribution of religions in a newspaper sketch three years before publishing *The Fishermen*: "On the West Coast people become Mission members just as rich fields yield Grundtvigians. In the poor parishes the living conditions are harsh, and the outlook on life is austere. When the struggle for daily bread is so difficult, what wouldn't one give in payment for eternity."[38]

*The Fishermen* probes the many-layered and intertwined sexual, social, economic, class, religious, moral, gender, generational, legal, and property conflicts that arise out of the settlement of a small Inner Mission colony in the Limfjord area. Indeed, an anthropologist recently observed that the novel's treatment of the clash between two cultural groups and their value-universes could have been taken from a late-twentieth-century anthropological monograph.[39] The group's members consist of four married couples (Lars and Malene Bundgaard, Thomas and Alma Jensen, Jens and Tea Røn, and Povl and Mariane Vrist) and their numerous children, a widower and his stepdaughter (Laust Sand and Adolfine), and a bachelor (Anton Knopper), all of whom have bought fishing rights from estate owners along the fjord. They experience these conflicts: individually (for example, Laust Sand's and Anton Knopper's sexual temptations, or Thomas Jensen's betrayal of Christianity when his material interest in his fishing grounds induces him to join the others in a brutal physical assault on rival fishermen at least one of whom is also Pious); within the group (as when Jens and Tea Røn struggle with their daughter Tabita over her embrace of the city's secular life and morals, or Povl Vrist becomes alienated from the Inner Mission); and between the group and the outside world (for example, with

---

[38]Hans Kirk, "Brev fra Limfjorden," *Ekstra Bladet*, Jan. 20, 1926, reprinted in *Omkring Fiskerne* at 50, 51. For an application of this geographic class analysis to Gjøl itself, see Christiane Morisset Andersen, "L'Homme et son environnement dans "Fiskerne" ("Les Pêcheurs") de Hans Kirk," 32 (4) *Études germaniques* 380-85 at 382 (Oct.-Dec. 1977).

[39]Lisanne Wilken, "Fiskerne," *Kritik*, No. 93, at 22-33 (1990).

*Introduction*

the Grundtvigian Pastor Brink over the control of the village church, with local fjord fishermen over fishing rights, or with the innkeepers Mogensen and Kock over dancing).[40]

The only figure who seems to stand above these conflicts is a woman, Mariane Vrist, who comes from a different socioeconomic and religious milieu. Of her the *Columbia Dictionary of Modern European Literature* said there are "few more vivid and memorable figures in modern literature. . . ."[41] Mariane, whose moral and emotional consciousness is far removed from that of the book's other characters, may at times speak for Kirk, whose terse and objective style precludes editorializing.[42] Though hardly the same kind of ideal-harmonious figure, another woman, Tabita Røn, symbolizes the liberation from the dysfunctional group morality that the city and its rising industrial working class promise.

Kirk, who was born in 1898 and grew up in northern Jutland, was intimately familiar with the conditions prevailing in the localities he describes. On his father's side, many of his relatives were West Coast Inner Mission farmers and fishermen from Harboøre, while his mother's family owned a large farm in the Thy district north of the Limfjord. At an early age he learned that "[m]y father and mother belong to two clans with different gods. Up in rich Thy reigns Our Lord, who is everyone's father, an old farmers' god, and in Harboør rules Jesus, who is strict and de-

---

[40] Local groups of fishermen resentful of the invasion of their precincts by fishermen from others areas of the Limfjord and the West Coast had engaged in bloody sea battles for centuries. Hugo Matthiessen, *Limfjorden: Fortoninger og strejflys* 189-90 (Copenhagen: Gyldendal, 1936).

[41]*Columbia Dictionary of Modern European Literature* 446 (Horatio Smith ed.; New York: Columbia U.P., 1947). For the argument that Mariane runs the risk of becoming an empty shell because the reader gains little access to her consciousness, see Ulrik Lehrmann, "Da 1800-tallet gik på hæld: Hans Kirk *Fiskerne*," in 3 *Læsninger i dansk litteratur: 1900-1940*, at 165-81 at 177-78 (Povl Schmidt et al. eds.; Odense: Odense Universitetsforlag, 1997).

[42]A reviewer of the French translation felt a malaise as a result of Kirk's failure to take a position as between the Inner Mission and the Grundtvigians. J. Charnoz, review of Hans Kirk, *Les Pêcheurs*, 258 *Études* 286 (Sept. 1948).

*Introduction*

mands prayer and repentance and submission."[43] His paternal uncle was a West Coast fisherman who moved to Gjøl shortly before Kirk in the mid-1920s.

In 1925 Kirk took up residence in Gjøl—a small village, home to twenty-six commercial fishermen in 1921—in the eastern part of the Limfjord fifteen kilometers west of the industrial city of Aalborg, and immersed himself in the people and conditions he would depict in the novel.[44] Some of his relatives in Gjøl were so convinced that *The Fishermen* was a roman à clef that his aunt Marie Kirk even ripped out and burned the pages of her family's copy because she was offended by their portrayal of a character (Tabita) she believed inspired by her daughter as giving birth without being married.[45]

The political analysis and, in Kirk's words, "solid theoretical foundation" that underlie *The Fishermen* can be read straightforwardly from several essays that Kirk published in radical cultural journals at the time he was writing the novel.[46] After all, as he himself stated programmatically, despite the misgivings of many who feared Marxism as a chaff-cutting machine, "literature cannot be understood" without clarifying its economic and social back-

---

[43]Kirk, *Skyggespil* at 67. Kirk's mother's family practiced an old-fashioned pre-Grundtvigian Lutheranism. Clausen, "Den gode marxist kan ikke gå koldt og intellektuelt til sagen" at 200.

[44]*Fiskeri-Beretning for Aaret 1921*, tab. 3h at 70-71 (F. V. Mortensen ed.; Copenhagen: Gad, 1922). In 1921 Gjøl's population was 920. Danmarks Statistik, Det Statistiske Departement, *Folkemængden 1. Februar 1921 i Kongeriget Danmark efter de vigtigste administrative inddelinger* 94-95 (Copenhagen: Bianco Lunos, 1921). Gjøl (or Gøl, as it is spelled today) had been an island until World War I, when damming and dike work connected it to the northern part of Jutland (Vendsyssel). See J.P. Trap, *Kongeriget Danmark* 4:162 (3rd ed.; Copenhagen: Gad, 191).

[45]Maren Kirk, *Fra Harboøre til Gjøl: "Tabithas Barndomserindringer"* 45-46 (Herning: Thuesen, 1978); Maren Kirk, *Teas baggrund og eftermæle: Kommentarudgave til Hans Kirks "Fiskerne"* 112 (Køng: n.p. 1973).

[46]J[ørgen]. S[andvad]., "Søndags-Samtale med Manden i Fyrrerne: 'Skriv om Millionærer'" at 5, col. 5.

*Introduction*

ground.⁴⁷ Despite the well-developed socioeconomic and political views that prompted Kirk to take as the subject matter of his novel the influence of the Inner Mission on rural workers and the impact of changing economic conditions on their religion, his treatment of the pietistic fishermen is in no way formulaic.⁴⁸ To the contrary, his novelistic skill is underscored by remarkably subtle, sympathetic, ironic, and often comic characterizations. Indeed, Kirk wrote the novel, as he insisted to an interviewer a quarter-century later, as a "protest against the then prevailing view of the Inner Mission. I wanted to show that they were serious, honest, and worthwhile people."⁴⁹ What an anthropologist found fascinating was Kirk's ability to look both over and under his Marxist-Freudian glasses and "let himself be seduced by . . . reality."⁵⁰ Even anti-Marxist reviewers paid tribute to Kirk's search for the truth, which led him to refrain from propagandizing.⁵¹ Indeed, the Inner Mission itself viewed *The Fishermen* as having depicted its members in a "relatively friendly" light.⁵²

In a newspaper interview published several weeks before the book's appearance, Kirk himself gave its gist as simply the story

---

⁴⁷Hans Kirk, "Om Proletarkunst," *Kritisk Revy*, No. 2: 14-16, at 14 (1927).

⁴⁸Unlike two later novels, which dealt with capitalist profiteering collaborators with the Nazi occupying forces and were serialized in the Danish Communist Party's newspaper, *Land og Folk*, and published by its press. *Djævelens penge* (Copenhagen: Tiden, 1952); *Klitgaard & Sønner* (Copenhagen: Tiden, 1952). To be sure, Kirk wrote this thinly fictionalized account as a direct political response to the sentencing of another party member to three months imprisonment for libel in presenting these charges in *Land og Folk*. Kirk himself characterized them as more political satire than literary works. Clausen, "Den gode marxist kan ikke gå koldt og intellektuelt til sagen" at 204.

⁴⁹Letter from Hans Kirk to Samuel Aaagaard, in *Omkring Fiskerne* at 48, 49 (Mar. 10, 1957).

⁵⁰Wilken, "Fiskerne" at 29.

⁵¹See, for example, Helge Rode, "Fiskerne," *Berlingske Tidende*, Jan. 24, 1933, reprinted in *Omkring Fiskerne* at 167-73. See generally, Bredsdorff, "Marx, Freud og Adler i Hans Kirks roman 'Fiskerne'" at 168-69.

⁵²Holt, *Kirkelig Forening for den Indre Mission* at 808.

## *Introduction*

of a "troop of Mission North Sea fishermen who settle in a Limfjord district with a somewhat old-fashioned population. As time goes by, they reshape the parish while their own religion becomes less strict under the milder conditions of the new place. It was my intention to portray religious life with its prerequisites and the humanity which unfolds in it. People who don't know the Mission regard it as a dark and life-inimical doctrine—which of course it is to a certain degree—but one must not forget that living conditions created it."[53] In the wake of her daughter Tabita's having given birth out of wedlock, Tea Røn's staunch advocacy of compassion against the stern censoriousness of the new Inner Mission Pastor Terndrup symbolizes this softening of religious dogma amidst greater prosperity.

Kirk viewed fishermen as sharing industrial workers' insecurity in the sense that a relatively insignificant event could destroy their livelihoods. Unlike factory workers, however, the rural proletariat—which included farm laborers and small farmers—had little opportunity to improve their conditions by organizing against their exploiters. Indeed, Kirk's novel does not even portray the fishermen's poverty as resulting from exploitation by another class.[54] In 1921, large-scale capitalist fishing operations were al-

---

[53]"Fiskernes liv og tro," *Klokken 5*, Oct. 19, 1928, reprinted in *Omkring Fiskerne* at 45.

[54]For this reason alone, the contemporaneous claim by one of Denmark's leading radical poets and critics that the novel is "true, artistic Marxism" is suspect. Tom Kristensen, "Dansk Prosa," *Tilskueren*, Mar. 1929, reprinted in *Omkring Fiskerne* at 134-37 at 135. For a later example of a literary critic who exaggerates and romanticizes Kirk's proletarian class analysis, see Jens Peter Lund Nielsen, "Hans Kirk und die literarische Gestaltung von Proletariern," 9 *Nordeuropa Studien* 25-39 (1976). At the other extreme, Inger-Lise Hjordt-Vetlesen, "Klasse og køn: Forskydning og fortrængning in *Fiskerne*," in *Omkring Fiskerne* at 291-307, especially at 293-94, criticizes Kirk's "deficient class analysis," which fails to follow the fishermen beyond the local fish buyer; she attributes Kirk's failure to elaborate the process of class differentiation within the group of fishermen to the collective novel genre itself, which focuses on the autonomous group rather than on individuals. Yet even she has to recognize that Kirk subtly adumbrated the incipient intragroup differentiation by

## Introduction

most unknown in Denmark: the industry was carried on by 10,059 self-employed fishermen and their 3,642 "helpers."[55] Instead, he describes their conditions as determined by their individual fortunes in struggling against nature. (Kirk did not weave into his narrative any references to the state's heavy subsidies to and close regulation of commercial fishing, especially in the Limfjord, or to the existence of a nationwide fishermen's association, which advocated on behalf of state intervention.)[56]

---

showing Vrist and Bundgaard as owning more and better means of production than the others and even employing a worker. That Kirk was well aware of where the fish were sold is clear from his accounts of the Limfjord in Hans Kirk, "Rejse gennem Limfjorden," *Land og Folk*, Dec. 13, 1954, at 7, col. 3; and Hans Kirk, *Danmarks rejsen* 46 (Copenhagen: Erichsen, 1966 [1957]). Nevertheless, even in a travelogue in the communist party newspaper in the 1950s, Kirk's description of fishermen's working conditions focused on the skipper's characterization of fishing as a lottery and the crew members' being their own masters. Hans Kirk, "Mayday—Mayday—Mayday," *Land og Folk*, Oct. 24, 1954, at 11, col. 1-5.

[55]The occupation was overwhelmingly male: only 182 women were returned as fishing and 43 as helpers. The helpers included fishermen's male children over the age of fourteen. Danmarks Statistik, Det Statistiske Departement, *Folketællingen i Kongeriget Danmark den 1. Februar 1921*, tab. 15 at 74-75, tab. 17 at 106-107 (Copenhagen: Thiele, 1925). By a somewhat different calculation, 1,674 of Denmark's 13,504 commercial fishermen operated in the Limfjord in 1921. *Fiskeri-Beretning for Aaret 1921*, tab. 2 at 25.

[56]Fishing was Denmark's second most heavily subsidized industry (after shipping). The state gave loans to buy motorboats, did experiments to locate new fishing grounds, provided rescue boats, and subsidized compulsory accident insurance for fishermen. James Hornell, "The Fisheries of Norway and Denmark," in *Madras Fisheries Bulletin*, 14:1-40, especially at 36-39 (1921); Jens Warming, *Danmarks erhvervs- og samfundsliv: En lærebog i Danmarks statistik* 231 (Copenhagen: Gads, 1930); Mortensen and Strubberg, *Die dänische Seefischerei* at 89-91. In 1921, state loans for purchasing fishing boats exceeded half a million crowns. *Fiskeri-Beretning for Aaret 1921* at VIII. These subsidies were in part the result of active lobbying by the Danish Fishing Association (Dansk Fiskeriforening), which dated back to 1884 and whose membership numbered in the thousands. M. C. Jensen, "Dansk Fiskeriforening," in *Fiskeriet i Danmark* 2:559-70. On the state's program for transplanting young fish into the Limfjord, see C. G. Joh. Petersen, "The Yield of the

## Introduction

In this seemingly free-floating existence many therefore turned to religion—and not just any religion, but the Inner Mission. For this underclass the world was not full of Grundtvigian growth and luxuriance, but a place where people had to take great pains to extract their food from the poor soil and sea, and fate could smash everything to bits at any moment. To find meaning in such a world permeated by "cold contingency," the rural poor, in Kirk's view, had to assume that justice prevailed somewhere in the world. That place was heaven: "For a man of this type the world is not a paradise, which is to be continued in the next, but a path of suffering, which has to be gone down before the real life begins. He is a pessimist, and it is the mystic darkness in Christianity he feels attracted to: Christ on the cross and renunciation. . . . That is the Inner Mission."[57]

Despite the rejection of the "proletariat's methods of fighting," the Inner Mission's teaching of submission and humility had to be viewed as a "religious proletarian movement"[58] that "literally

---

Limfjord Fisheries in Recent Years and the Transplantation of Plaice in 1908," in *Report of the Danish Biological Station to the Board of Agriculture*, Vol. 18, at 3-14 (Copenhagen: Centraltrykkeriet, 1909). Limfjord fishing alone had also been subject to close state regulation for centuries. Mortensen and Strubberg, *Die dänische Seefischerei* at 50-51. See also *Betænkning angående afløsning af retten til fiskeri med ålegårde og andre særlige rettigheder til fiskeri på søterritoriet afgivet af den af fiskeriministeriet under 24. Januar 1952 nedsatte kommission* 14-22 (Copenhagen: Lützhøft, 1955); Holger Rasmussen, *Limfjordsfiskeriet før 1825: Sædvane og centraldirigering* 366-440 (Copenhagen: Nationalmuseet, 1968); E. Thiel, "Fiskerilovgivningen og fiskeritilsynet," in *Fiskeriet i Danmark* 2:573-606. The Law on Salt Water Fishing of 1917 prescribed in detail when, where, and how seine nets, eel-traps, and other equipment could be used. Special provisions in the statute regarding fishing in the Limfjord even prescribed the size of the mesh in the nets. A special fishery police enforced the law. Lov om Saltvandfiskeri, June 2, 1917, in *Lovtidende for Kongeriget Danmark for Aaret 1917*, at 825-50 (Copenhagen: Schultz, 1918).

[57]Hans Kirk, "Religion og Hartkorn," *Clarté*, No. 4-5: 135-39, at 137 (Apr.-May 1926).

[58]Kirk, "Religion og Hartkorn" at 138.

*Introduction*

made a virtue of a necessity."[59] It could attract adherents because it was an effort—albeit an irrational one—to create a life-view containing the rational kernel of refusing to accept the existing order in any way. "But it is dangerous, from a Marxist point of view, because it projects its protest against the social disorder into eternity."[60]

The enormous political importance that Kirk attributed to religion's role in rural life in largely agricultural Denmark—as late as the mid-1920s, agriculture still accounted for 36 percent of the labor force[61]—can be gauged by a short essay he published the same year that *The Fishermen* appeared, titled "Can Denmark Be Dechristianized?" The piece opens by observing that the endearing thing about the towering Danish literary and social critic, Georg Morris Cohen Brandes, was that he had hated Christianity from his earliest youth to old age and had accepted the unpopularity that haunts a heathen in a Christian country. Unfortunately, however, Brandes "took care of the matter with a kick, the way one treats a fool without ever investigating where the foolishness came from." By contrast, Kirk concluded that if one wants to eradicate rats, one has to become familiar with their biology: "It's not enough to assert that it's an ugly and harmful animal. Our time's struggle against Christianity must be conducted differently. We must see the popular, religious culture in its context with and dependence on the material living conditions. . . ."[62]

Because Kirk was also persuaded that the Inner Mission's most nefarious impact on rural workers was sexual, he argued that the rural proletariat could be liberated from religion only by means of sexual liberation: "The strict sexual morality is reli-

---

[59]Hans Kirk, "Om den sociale Ønskedrøm," *Kritisk Revy*, No. 3: 26-27, at 27 (1927).

[60]Kirk, "Religion og Hartkorn" at 138.

[61]Svend Aage Hansen, 2 *Økonomisk vækst i Danmark: 1914-1970*, tab. 1 at 203 (Copenhagen: Akademisk forlag, 1974).

[62]Hans Kirk, "Kan Danmark afkristenes?" *Kritisk Revy*, No. 3: 47-50, at 47 (1928).

gion's essential condition, and religion is inextricably connected to political reaction. ... The Mission is the consequence of a sexual moral system that can only be changed by means of enlightenment and birth control technique." Despite the Inner Mission's imposition of a rigid moral code that had become dysfunctional, Kirk made much of the fact that the sect had also relaxed rural relations by enabling the Pious to talk freely about anything that moved them even if it would otherwise be regarded as scandalous: "Previously it was whiskey, now it's the Mission. Everything can be said if it happens in the name of Jesus."[63]

Even after publication of *The Fishermen*, the need to earn a living forced Kirk to lead a "literary double life," writing serious novels during the day and "trivial literature" (often pseudonymously) for weekly papers at night.[64] Among Kirk's other novels, two (of a projected trilogy) deserve special mention because they are also collective social novels set in Jutland. *The Day Laborers* and *The New Times* depict the rise of industrial capitalism and the transformation of a traditional rural proletariat into an organized social-democratic working class. They also proved critical and popular successes and were translated into several languages.[65] Though outstanding models of their genre, they lack the subtlety of *The Fishermen*. For example, as appropriate and even humorous as it is in the context of *The Day Laborers*, this blunt response by the novel's central capitalist figure to a request by an Inner Mission pastor for a donation to build a mission house would be unimaginable in *The Fishermen*: "If we're going to have a religion, then it at least has to deal with the problems of the times. Found a new religion, Pastor Gamst, or modernize the old one. Let's get the Eleventh Commandment: Thou Shalt Not Strike."[66]

---

[63]Kirk, "Kan Danmark afkristenes?" at 50, 48. This last sentence reappears almost verbatim in *The Fishermen* p. 75.

[64]Bondebjerg, "Hans Kirk" at 221.

[65]*Daglejerne* (Copenhagen: Gyldendal, 1936); *De ny tider* (Copenhagen: Gyldendal, 1939).

[66]Hans Kirk, *Daglejerne* 186 (Copenhagen: Gyldendal, 1975).

*Introduction*

Kirk wrote the third volume of this trilogy in an internment camp where Danish authorities held him and other enemies of Nazi Germany, which had occupied Denmark in 1940, to accommodate the Gestapo's demands. Kirk had been among the first group of Communists arrested on June 22, 1941, as Germany was invading the Soviet Union.[67] Earlier that year, copies of *The Fishermen* had been publicly burned. Although Kirk escaped from the camp on August 29, 1943, the Germans destroyed the manuscript of the third volume, which he worked on after the war, but never reconstructed. Kirk, whose ceaseless, defiant protests of his treatment to the Justice Minister and other Danish officials had earned him six months' solitary confinement, joined the underground resistance movement.[68]

Kirk wrote another novel during his internment, which the Germans were also "naturally so unfriendly as to burn" in the aftermath of his escape,[69] but he succeeded in rewriting and publishing it after the war. *The Slave*, "the occupation period's weightiest literary work,"[70] is a philosophical allegory about power (and the capitulation to the Nazis) set on a ship carrying gold and passengers representing various classes and strata from Veracruz to Spain in 1679. The novel, which Kirk considered his best book, is driven by the contest of wills between a slave and his owner, an immensely rich female capitalist.[71]

---

[67]The Danish authorities arrested many more communists than the Nazis had requested. Werner Thierry, *Hans Kirk* 69 (Copenhagen: Gyldendal, 1977).

[68]Thing, *Hans Kirks mange ansigter* at 230-31; Eric, "Mennesket må selv gribe ind i sin tilværelse," *Land og Folk*, Sept. 26, 1948, at 9, col. 1; Hans Kirk, *Breve fra Horserød* (Børge Houmann ed.; Risskov: Sirius, 1967); Hans Scherfig, "Minde om Hans Kirk," in Hans Scherfig, *Tre Digtere* 47-65 at 50 (N.p.: Sirius, 1963). For speculation that Kirk did not complete the novel because his literary strengths did not extend to realistically describing the urban industrial proletariat, see Bondebjerg, "Hans Kirk" at 211-12, 220.

[69]Tom Kristensen, "Hans Kirks nye roman," *Politiken*, Nov. 10, 1948, at 8, col. 1.

[70]Scherfig, "Minde om Hans Kirk" at 55.

[71]Hans Kirk, *Slaven* (Copenhagen: Gyldendal, 1998 [1948]). See also Bo

## *Introduction*

*Note on the Text*: Kirk's simple style has been praised for "let[ting] the readers forget that they are reading; it seems to one that one is experiencing and participating."[72] The translation retains three important elements of Kirk's impressionistic style that contribute to this effect: the use of long dashes to indicate changes in time and place introducing new episodes in the narrative mosaic; the marking off of chapters solely by a few extra lines of spacing; and the strict nonuse of quotation marks, even in direct dialogue, which is designed to facilitate transitions between characters' thoughts and speech and to increase the distance between author and reader by creating a type of objectivity in which the narrator disappears behind the characters and their collective group.[73]

*Marc Linder*

---

Elbrønd-Bek, "At sejle er nødvendigt: Ikke at leve—et essay om Hans Kirks roman *Slaven*," in *Bag ved bøgernes bjerg: En hilsen til Mogens Iversen* 191-213 (Copenhagen: Danmarks Biblioteksskole, 1978); Bo Elbrønd-Bek, "Breve fra Hans Kirk vedrørende "Slaven," 1983 *Danske studier* 111-24.

[72]Scherfig, "Minde om Hans Kirk" at 58.

[73]On this technique of *oratio tecta*, see Thing, *Hans Kirks mange ansigter* at 58-59, 96; Borup Jensen, "Fra roman til drejbog" at 335.

# Further Reading

Not surprisingly, the English-language literature on Kirk is sparse. Perhaps the lengthiest account is Elias Bredsdorff, "Hans Kirk," in *Twentieth-Century Danish Writers* 245-53 (Marianne Stecher-Hansen ed.; Detroit: Gale Research, 1999). For brief sketches, see: *Columbia Dictionary of Modern European Literature* 446 (Horatio Smith ed.; New York: Columbia University Press, 1947); P. Mitchell, *History of Danish Literature* 246-47 (2d ed.; New York: Kraus-Thompson, 1971 [1957]); *Dictionary of Scandinavian Literature* 332-34 (Virpi Zuck ed.; New York: Greenwood, 1990); Niels Ingwersen, "Critical Realism," in *A History of Danish Literature* 366-68 (Sven Rossel ed., Lincoln: University of Nebraska Press, 1992). For readers with some knowledge of Danish, a selection of the most useful works about Kirk and *Fiskerne* follows. The best biography is Morten Thing, *Hans Kirks mange ansigter: En biografi* (Copenhagen: Gyldendal, 1997). More compressed sketches of his life and works are Ole Ravn, "Hans Kirk og hans forfatterskab," in *Undertrykkere og undertrykte: Et Hans Kirk-udvalg* 277-326 (Ole Ravn ed.; Copenhagen: Gyldendal, 1977); Ib Bondebjerg, "Hans Kirk," in *2 Danske digtere i det 20. århundrede: Fra Tom Kristensen til H.C. Branner* 198-230 (Torben Brostrøm and Mette Winge eds.; Copenhagen: Gads, 1981). A comprehensive reader is *Omkring Fiskerne* (Bo Elbrønd-Bek and Ole Ravn eds.; Copenhagen: Reitzel, 1977). The most complete bibliography is Frank Büchmann-Møller, *Hans Kirk: En bibliografi* (Copenhagen: Gyldendal, 1974); a shorter one is *Dansk skønlitterært forfatterleksikon 1900-1950*, 2:110-11 (Svend Dahl ed.; Copenhagen: Pedersen, 1960). Insightful criticism includes: Jørgen Holmgaard and Ralf Pittelkow, "Samfundskritik eller sjælepleje?—Aage Henriksen og 'Fiskerne,'" *Poetik* 4(4):1-39 (1971); Jens Kr. Andersen and Leif Emerek, *Hans Kirks forfatterskab: Et forsøg på en litteratur-*

*historisk revision* (Copenhagen: Vinten, 1972); Finn Klysner, *Den danske kollektivroman: 1928-1944*, at 25-50 (Copenhagen: Vinten, 1976); Ralf Pittelkow, "Religionen, arbejdet og naturen: En analyse af Hans Kirk: Fiskerne," in *Analyser af danske romaner* 2:102-233 (Jørgen Holmgaard ed.; Copenhagen: Borgen, 1977); Carsten Jensen, *Folkelighed og utopi: Brydninger i Hans Kirks forfatterskab* (Copenhagen: Gyldendal, 1981).

# Acknowledgments

The extraordinary generosity of many people made this translation possible. Gracia Grindal, Professor of Rhetoric at Luther Seminary in St. Paul, Minnesota, and a leading translator of hymns, translated the folk ballad and all the hymns not previously published in English. Bente Villadsen, a Jutlander from Viborg and professor at the University of Iowa, endured scores of picky questions about Danish idioms, grammar, and syntax, and the Jutland dialect with endless good cheer, while Else D'Angelo from the Limfjord town of Struer put up with almost as many. Morten Thing, Kirk's foremost biographer and librarian at Roskilde University Centre in Denmark, provided much important background information about Kirk and *Fiskerne*. Frank Hugus, Professor of Germanic Languages and Literature at the University of Massachusetts and a translator of Danish novels, kept his promise to criticize a draft brutally. Poul Houe, Professor of Danish at the University of Minnesota, illuminated several ambiguous passages. Four other Danes—Asger Aaboe, Else Friis Sherson, Palle Jørgensen, and Susanne Branson—explained textual puzzles. Eric Andersen answered theological questions and commented on a draft. Niels Ingwersen, Professor of Scandinavian Studies at the University of Wisconsin, Tiina Nunnally, the leading English-language translator of Danish literature, and Marianne Stecher-Hansen, Associate Professor of Scandinavian Studies at the University of Washington, all offered useful advice and encouragement. Larry Zacharias recorded the typos in the first edition. Rebecca Schleifer emended the King James translation of a passage in Deuteronomy and suggested many colloquialisms. Poet Jan Weissmiller read the entire manuscript, pointing out the need for many changes. Judy Polumbaum, editor of all trades, despite having gone over the whole manuscript with the finest of fine-tooth combs, shares no responsibility for any remaining infelicities.

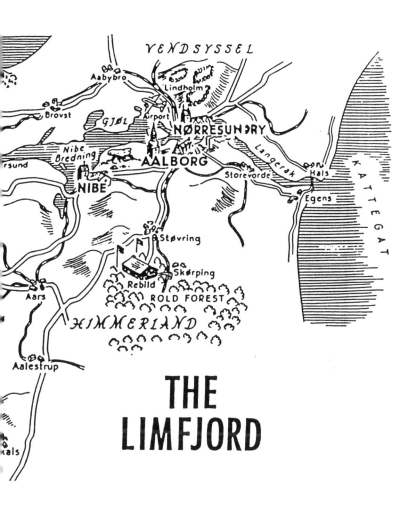

# THE LIMFJORD

# Cast of Characters

Aaby—teacher
Adolfine—Laust Sand's stepdaughter/Mads Langer's wife
Brink, Henrik—Grundtvigian pastor
Brink, Sofie—Pastor Brink's wife
Bundgaard, Lars—West Coast fisherman
Bundgaard, Malene—Lars's wife
Bundgaard, Karl—Lars and Alma's son
Bundgaard, Teodor—Lars and Alma's son
Dorre—Laust Sand's sister
Esben—Katrine's father
Fabian, P. L.—dry-goods merchant
Fabian, Maria—Fabian's wife
Hygum, Peder—hawker
Hygum, Laura—Peder's wife
Hygum, Kirstine—Peder and Laura's daughter
Jensen, Thomas—West Coast fisherman
Jensen, Alma—Thomas's wife
Jensen, Maren—Thomas and Alma's daughter
Katrine—hotel maid/Esben's daughter/Kock's wife
Kjeld—Tea Røn's brother
Kjøng, Anders—Lars Bundgaard's laborer
Knopper, Anton—West Coast fisherman
Knopper, Andrea—Martinus Povlsen's daughter/Anton's wife
Knopper, Little-Martinus—Anton and Andrea's son
Knud—carpenter
Kock—customs official/shoemaker/innkeeper
Kolby, Jens—fjord fisherman
Koldkjær, Mogens—Thora's father
Langer, Mads—stoker/Laust Sand's nephew/Adolfine's husband
Mogensen—innkeeper/laundry owner

Mogensen, Mrs.
Povlsen, Karl—fjord fisherman
Povlsen, Mrs.—Karl's wife
Povlsen, Martinus—Andrea's father
Røn, Jens—West Coast fisherman
Røn, Tea—Jens's wife
Røn, Little-Niels—Jens and Tea's son
Røn, Martin—Jens and Tea's son
Røn, Tabita—Jens and Tea's daughter
Sand, Laust—West Coast fisherman
Spliid, Jørgen—fjord fisherman
Terndrup—Inner Mission pastor
Thomsen, Kresten—West Coast Inner Mission pastor
Thora—Mogens Koldkjær's daughter/Kjeld's wife
Toft, Lars—fjord fisherman
Toft, Laurids—Povl Vrist's laborer
Væver, Niels—fjord fisherman
Vrist, Povl—West Coast fisherman
Vrist, Mariane—Povl's wife

Baker
Consumer coop manager
County magistrate
County sheriff
Farmer
Police chief

A small troop was standing at the far end of the wharf peering out across the fjord into the warm summer evening. They were wearing fine, blue suits with shiny boots and dark hats. They were the fishermen from the West Coast, waiting for the ship bringing their wives and children.

It had been decided they would settle here and remain for all their days. They had bought fishing rights—old landed estates' rights to eel grounds and seine net fishing. Povl Vrist had already lived here for several years and was satisfied and earned good money. The others had fished here for a time, traveling over every spring when the herring fishing was to begin, and leaving for home in the fall when the eel-traps were taken in. But only now were they moving here. As long as their families were in the North Sea parish, their home had been there of course. But now it was going to be different.

They were all solemn. That was easy with good clothing on, which was used only for church-going and funerals. There was a distinct gravity to the smell. But Anton Knopper had said it was fitting to put on their best clothing so the women would understand they were welcome. That's how thoughtful Anton Knopper was, and he was right—it was a grand occasion.

Whenever Anton Knopper tried out a joke, they smiled slightly from pure politeness. Anton was a bachelor with no responsibilities to ponder. Now all of a sudden the undertaking seemed so daring. At home in the North Sea parish it was hard to get food. If fishing failed one year, there was distress and misery, but there was comfort in the memory of the salty sea runs and stormy days. And what fate awaited them on foreign shores now lay in God's hand.

Lars Bundgaard had readied his pram so they could row out to the schooner as soon as it dropped anchor. His face was discolored by tar and sunburn in his dark beard. He was tall like a giant with large bony hands. Lars Bundgaard was silent and restless. There were reasons for it. Malene was pregnant and expecting shortly. She'd had second thoughts on whether she dare risk the trip, but had come along.

The sun hadn't set yet. A mild fragrance of hay rose from the meadows. Out in the fjord some fellows were bathing from a boat. As they swam, their bodies glistened silver-white like mother of pearl. The evening was full of warm salvation. Jens Røn and Laust Sand stood next to each other. They had been fishing together in the boat almost as long as they could remember. Both were a little stooped, but otherwise there no was resemblance. Jens Røn was broad and large-limbed, his face with its pale-red beard at times tinged with roguery, although life had dealt hard with him. Poverty and bad years and adversity in all directions—that had been his lot. Now he was standing with a cautious smile and looking forward to Tea's arrival. He had rented a house; it was old and not without defects, but there was certainly a prospect some day of their being able to get their own. And the children—Jens Røn felt he hadn't seen them for many years, although it was only five months.

Laust Sand was tall and lanky with a peculiar intimidated face behind his dark dishevelled beard. His eyes filled easily with water. Laust Sand was a widower and was waiting for his stepdaughter, Adolfine, who was to take care of his house.

None of them was entirely young, but neither were they old. Laust Sand was the oldest and had just turned forty-five. The youngest was Povl Vrist at thirty-four. Lars Bundgaard, Anton Knopper, Jens Røn, and Thomas Jensen were about forty. No, they were far from biblical age, and surely none of them would come to suffer want. God certainly had a way out for them, and without him there was no earthly progress—that they knew full well.

Povl Vrist had good eyes and saw the schooner first as a little dot to the west in the fjord.

Now I'd almost believe it's coming, he said. And soon the crackling of the motor was audible far off, echoing in the hills toward the south.

The women were standing in the bow and staring toward the unfamiliar country. To the south the hills were checkered with green and yellow fields, and to the north lay the village with broad farms. At home the land was waste, the sea fog went in over the sandy fields, and the wind scorched the grain black. Here the farms lay between high, green trees, and on the fields the grain stood golden and dense.

Malene stood shapeless among her flock of children. She had wrapped her shawl around her head against the evening cold. Her large, powerful face caught the scent of land. It looked good and wonderfully fertile—you had to admit it. Tea and Alma, Thomas Jensen's wife, stood next to her. How pretty it is here, Tea observed, and Alma nodded. There was no west wind here to tear at the houses. And now the church bell rang the sun down. It was a good omen, Tea said, but what were the people like they'd be placed among? That was worth knowing. Tea was worried: what was all the world's glory if you didn't have Jesus in your heart?

Adolfine was standing a little way apart from them and staring toward land. The sunset gave her cheeks a warm tinge, but her gaunt figure was thoroughly worn out. She'd been seasick and near death and had wished she lay on the fjord's cold bottom. On deck children were playing and running. The old tub was like a sparrow's nest. They were everywhere—in the cargo hold, up in the mast—and the skipper had his troubles. Of every age there were: girls who soon would be preparing for confirmation, half-grown lads, and small grimy kids stomping along the deck planks. In the afternoon something terrible had almost happened. One of Jens Røn's toddlers crawled out onto the bowsprit and was in danger. The sailor had to go out and get him, and in the meantime Tea stood and groaned with her heart in her throat.

There was no room for the baggage in the cargo hold, and the furniture was stacked on the deck. It looked singularly strange, though familiar—the old sofas, yellow-painted beds and brown fir-tree tables, shiny from wear and tear. A mirror had shattered, and the shards lay strewn over the deck and shone red in the sunset, the frame gaping destitute.

Now the children, too, had to go to the railing and look in toward the unfamiliar country. Tea got busy putting hers in order. They weren't to make her ashamed now. The schooner had barely dropped anchor before Lars Bundgaard and Jens Røn were there. First Malene was helped down into the pram, and after she had shaken the men's hands loosely, she sat down ponderously in the stern and folded her hands over her extended belly.

Laust Sand called in from the wharf in his thin, nervous voice:

Adolfine has come, hasn't she?

He hadn't seen her, as she stood a little behind the others. Now she went up to the railing, but didn't have the courage to answer while so many people were standing and listening. She took her handkerchief and waved to her stepfather. Laust Sand brightened up—everything was the way it was supposed to be.

It took time to get the children off the boat. The smallest ones cried and were afraid of being forgotten, and the pram had to go out three times before they were all on dry land. The wives tallied the flock, each had her own. Finally they stood in a cluster on the wharf among the old trunks, boxes, and bundles of feather-beds and clothes. The men walked around and said hello. They were all somewhat embarrassed; even Alma, who always knew what to say, was silent and reserved. Around them the natives were standing and staring so they hardly dared turn around.

Anton Knopper had tied up the pram and came up on the wharf with the boat hook. He didn't have anyone to welcome, but he got hold of a couple of boys and questioned them as to whether the seasickness had been bad. Seasickness! The lads were insulted—he could be seasick in the fjord himself. Yes, of course, Anton didn't want to offend anyone—far be it from him—but they looked pale. That's how what Adolfine had gone through came to light, but after all she was a female. Adolfine cast her eyes down and was about to sink into the ground. It was like becoming the talk of the town.

Anton Knopper thought something was lacking. They couldn't stand and look at one another like strangers. Suddenly he made a playful sally with the boat hook. He poked a little at Tea, and was himself doubtful about it, but cracked with gaiety. Tea warded off the blow and screamed and then blushed because she had screamed. Anton was a fool—what must these strangers be thinking? But Anton Knopper became irrepressibly frolicsome: each of the women had to have a shove; he rushed around with the pole like a savage. Those were some pranks, but still it wasn't so bad, because all around the people smiled at the peculiar game and surely noticed that these were folks who stood their ground.

As they walked through the village street, the women looked about with cautious glances. These houses were solid and pretty, with well-maintained gardens. Tea became very confident in view of all that prosperity, but the people didn't behave properly. They stood at the windows and doorways and stared. One of the little girls stumbled and fell, and Tea scolded her gently and was herself on the verge of crying. Now was that a way to attract public attention?

Povl Vrist led the way. They were all to eat at his house. He was big and powerful, with broad shoulders. His face was sharp-featured with keen eyes and brown, bristling mustache. Thomas Jensen had taken the two smallest ones in his arms and was telling Alma about the spring fishing. It had been so tolerable, and now he was about to erect ten new eel-traps. Thomas Jensen was a small, temperate man with a gentle, serious face, mild in speech and strong in spirit. Every word came gently from his mouth, yet it would still hold firm.

Povl Vrist had rented himself an old house with a garden in front, and they had to walk one by one in order not to step in the flower beds. Mariane stood at the door and welcomed people. Yes, Povl Vrist said, now they had to make do and not expect anything great. Mariane was large and vigorous with beautiful, cheerful features and heavy brown hair. She was a farmer's daughter from the interior and far different than the gloomy North

Sea women. She cooed a welcome in her peculiar, unfamiliar idiom. Both Tea and Alma got a feeling of a dangerous frivolity from Mariane and cast down their eyes when they said hello.

Now by all means you must come into the parlor, she said laughing. And make do with the little bit we can offer. Take off your coat, Thomas Jensen's wife! Go ahead into the parlor, Lars Bundgaard's wife! You must be exhausted after the long trip. The men have been in low spirits all day; I believe Jens Røn was just on the verge of being afraid the old tub was shipwrecked.

Inside in the parlor space was tight, but the wives got seats with the smallest ones on their laps, and it felt good to get some rest. Adolfine collapsed in the chair, still with a sense as if the world was rocking under her. The men had gone to get featherbeds and bedding. Mariane was working busily. In the scullery she had set up a table for the children. The little ones were to have theirs first. They were plenty tired and could barely keep their eyes open. The wives thawed a bit. Mariane wanted to make things good for them—that was clear. It was pretty in the parlor—white-scoured floors, flowers in the windows, and many pictures. The wives looked at the pictures thoroughly—because they weren't of the edifying kind. "Sunday Afternoon in a Parsonage" was written under one of them, but the priest with his long pipe most resembled a Grundtvigian. And ships on the sea, but not a single scriptural sentence or word of grace. The Savior wasn't having good days here.

When the men came back, the adults sat down at the table. From the kitchen three towheaded boys peered in, but whenever someone looked their way, they scampered behind the door like scared mice. Mariane brought the food, and there was a short silence. It was custom among God's children to read something before a meal. But Povl Vrist calmly said to Thomas Jensen:

Perhaps you'll say a verse before we eat!

Thomas Jensen read the prayer from the hymnbook:

Lord Jesus, in Thy name we now
With grateful hearts before Thee bow:
Bless Thou these gifts and grant that we

May always thank and honor Thee.

Afterwards it was hard to part company. It was reassuring to sit a while among friends before you gave yourself over completely to unfamiliar surroundings. Anton Knopper rocked back and forth a little and asked:

How are things at home? You must have something new to tell.

Yes, the women knew many things and most of all Tea, who was well-spoken. The priest's wife had been sick, and the fishing had failed for most of them in the spring. There were many who had a hard time getting food. Tea's round face became serious . . . she certainly knew what *that* meant. But then she had to tell about a new shop, which was fitted up, a shop with postcards and amber things for the tourists. Those were just nonsense, but one big thing had occurred. Tea sat for a bit and saved it so the tension could mount: Anders the smith had been converted and had confessed his sin to the Lord.

Lars Bundgaard nodded: well, Anders the smith had found the way. Yes, after all, there was no use kicking against the pricks.

Tea peered obliquely at Mariane, who came in with coffee . . . to see if this word didn't hit home. But Mariane was unmoved, and Tea sighed and told of meetings and beautiful get-togethers. The men sat silently and listened. Yes, home was home. They'd probably never become so familiar with things here that they'd really feel part of what was going on. The roar of the sea, the fog that rushed in over the sandy fields, storms, death, and poverty were old acquaintances. But you certainly wouldn't think of ever putting down roots here.

But what about the people in these parts, asked Malene, and took a deep breath.

All the women looked at Thomas Jensen. The gentle man was a leader of God's children. Thomas Jensen hesitated a bit before he answered.

Things aren't the way they should be, he said. There are probably those who have found salvation, but most are far from it. When you go by the inn on a Saturday evening, they're dancing inside. And the priest . . . well we should be reluctant to speak harshly, but that's not God's word he's preaching. He folded his hands and bowed his head. Now that we've moved from our home, we must surely remember we've taken the Savior and his grace along in our sinful hearts.

One by one the children had stolen into the parlor. The smallest ones had lain down on the floor and were sleeping. You couldn't get up without stepping on them. At times one would wake up with a start and look around bewildered. But they were used to hymn-singing and hard floorboards. The grown-ups remained sitting for a time yet and sang hymns under the hanging lamp's yellow light.

— Thomas Jensen got up at the cold break of day. He had lain awake for a long time and couldn't calm down. He dressed carefully and stole by the beds with the sleeping children. A damp fog lay over the meadows, and the grazing cattle looked like black spots in the whiteness. But all around there was a chirping of thin voices.

He walked through town. Dew drops hung in the roof thatch, and delicate cobwebs glistened in the grass in the ditch. The day was new, and the air cold to the lungs. In the middle of town he turned down a path to the church. It stood on a hill, and for awhile he stood by the wall and looked about. The fjord was placid with bright, sparkling streaks. Close to the wharf lay heavy prams, blue and green boats, black-tarred traps and fish-chests. To the north the flat land was intersected by gleaming ditches. Thomas Jensen felt bitter rancor in his heart. Out in the poor parishes towards the west the people were in need of grace. But here in the rich, beautiful parish people thought only of the world and its follies. He went to the church and looked in the window. Between the caulked walls the pulpit beamed with sparkling carvings. Would God one day take possession of his kingdom?

He knelt in front of the church door and prayed. The words formed themselves ponderously in his mouth. That Jesus now would give his blessing to the little troop, which had moved from house and home to foreign parts. While he prayed he felt the power growing in him. When he stood up, the sun was high in the sky. Peat-smoke was rising from the chimneys . . . it stung his nose like pungent spice. Now Thomas Jensen knew what the Lord wanted. Never had he felt the bliss of grace as on this clear morning.

On his way home he nodded good-naturedly to people he met. The Lord can act leniently, but in the end he will prevail. When he reached his house, he sat down in the shed and mended fish traps. He worked all day long. God would surely show the way—that was certain.

Tea, too, had awakened early and couldn't stay in her bed. She stood up and wandered about in the house, tending to everything. There was no splendor. The roof was leaky and it had rained in. The walls were green and moldy from dampness. Everywhere the paint was peeling, and the floors were black like earth. Tea went through both rooms and out into the kitchen and pantry. In a small room lay all kinds of junk, musty footwear, and stinking rags. They were the previous residents' effects. A skinny cat stole in and rubbed itself plaintively up against her leg. It had probably been left behind. What kind of people were they, Tea thought, not even to spare a thought for the dumb animals. She found a drop of milk in a bottle and poured it out for the cat.

Tea went into the parlor and sat down on the low window frame—there weren't any chairs. She felt unhappy and mistreated and began to cry; was this a change for the better? No, the old house back home was far prettier, even if it was plain enough. The tears ran down her cheeks. It was a cross God had laid upon her, always to fight with poverty and misery. Better she had died in the spring of her youth, though that was a sinful thought.

Jens Røn came in drowsy and stared at her bewildered.

But little Tea! he said.

Tea couldn't help being annoyed by her husband though she knew it was wrong. He was standing friendly and kind in his stocking feet and wished to console her with good words. But

Tea had now become mad. Was it really Our Lord's intention that a man should be so peaceful?

Are you longing to go back? Jens Røn asked anxiously.

I long only for my grave, any time God wills, Tea wailed.

The children were about to get up. Little-Niels opened the door a crack and saw what was brewing. Then all five of them were in the parlor. The smallest ones darted into their mother's petticoats, where she sat, and began weeping. They cried in high shrill voices, and suddenly Tea stopped and said, frightened: Shhh—look how you're behaving! If the neighbors hear this, what are they going to think!

She dried their eyes with her apron and went out to make coffee.

After they had eaten breakfast at the dirty kitchen table, it occurred to Tea that there was no use wailing. It was better to take your misfortune from Our Lord's hand without complaint. Jens had borrowed a horse and wagon from a neighbor to bring the furniture home. The children were already out on strange expeditions. But Tabita and Martin, the two oldest, had to help.

Tea got down on her knees and began to scour the house clean. She used the brush in all corners, and the sweat dripped from her. What kind of people had lived here before? They hadn't been fastidious, but she'd show people now. First, it had to be cleaned up and afterwards the place would be painted, because she was tidy—she was aware of that. And little Tabita was washing doors with soap as if her life were at stake.

Jens Røn came home with their belongings; Anton Knopper had come along to give a helping hand. They got coffee in the kitchen, which had the fragrance of soap, and heard about how filthy the house was. Anton Knopper had to go into the parlor and see that the dirt lay an inch thick in the corners. But they agreed that Tea was a regular crackerjack who would certainly get it to shine.

You were surely born in a thunderstorm, that's why you're so partial to water, Jens Røn joked, and Tea batted at him affectionately. The work had taken her sorrows from her. But Anton Knopper was full of honest admiration.

The way you can do things, he said. Your hands, by the way, they really know how to move.

Those were refreshing words. Now it was indeed somewhat clean in the small rooms, and Tea thought everything had become brighter. She regretted having become hot-headed, and was moved. It was her strict disposition. She'd gladly admit that there wasn't much good in her, and she'd been a bad wife to Jens Røn. People weren't wrong about that. Many an hour she had left him and the children without tending to them, while she herself drank coffee at the neighbors'. But she had sought God's kingdom honestly and uprightly in humility, though she had her faults and was a sinner. But now she made the promise and took heaven as her witness that everything was going to be better. She would refrain from bad habits and was very touched by the thought of how good she would be to her husband and children. Faithful in things big and small. That was what Tea intended the future to be.

She hung up curtains and dragged furniture into place. Jens Røn had to come in from his traps and help with the heaviest things, the chest, beds, and bureau. The pieces of furniture looked really curious in their new places. It was as if the furniture didn't really feel at home. Tea stroked the old brown-painted bench in a friendly way. She had sat there many a time with good friends. But when the framed scriptural passages were hung up—"May God bless your entry and your departure," over the parlor door, "Let your communication be, Yea, yea; Nay, nay," over the bench, and "Jesus" and "Mercy" in the bedroom—Tea was gripped by a feeling of cosiness and had to thank God, who guided everything for the best. The chocolate pot with its gilt ornamentations looked so pretty on the bureau! And the pictures on the wall in the shiny frames!

She found time to cast a glance out into the little garden in front of the house. She wanted to take care of it one of these days. Now it was full of weeds and grass. But people valued the good gifts so little. As a child, she could recall, she had a yellow pansy in the garden and every evening she put a flower pot over it to protect it from sea fog and night cold. But it died anyway.

Here it could grow if you just stuck a stick in the ground—that was easy to see.

The children came home and got food and were put to bed. First they had to go round and touch the furniture and sniff the clean aroma. After the children had been bundled up in the small room, she sent Tabita out into the shed to ask Jens Røn whether they should get Anton Knopper for evening coffee. After all, he had helped them.

Now you've made it pretty, Tea, Jens said, when he came back with Anton Knopper.

You mean that seriously? Tea asked flattered.

Indeed, Jens Røn meant it. He was always filled with astonishment over how industrious other people were. And Tea with her depth of soul had quick hands. His own abilities were quite slight.

Tea sighed satisfied and thought to herself: it was pretty here. But what about the people—that was a question worth probing. How many believers were here?

Yes, there weren't many, Anton Knopper declared.

And the pastor?

Anton Knopper's unsuspecting face darkened. It was best not to talk about the pastor. He was far from the right path. But otherwise there were many good people here. Anton Knopper brightened up. Some day there could be a fine harvest when God found that the time had come. Viewed rightly it was a fine place.

But now Tea became playful: hadn't Anton found himself a sweetheart?

Anton Knopper shook his head, there was really no one who would have him. There was supposed to be Tabita, whom he was waiting for. Tabita turned up her nose at him—she wouldn't have any of that. Indeed, when he couldn't even get a redhead, Anton Knopper said, then he'd surely remain a bachelor the rest of his days.

Tabita was on the verge of crying over being scoffed at for her red hair. Anton Knopper got busy making up for it. Red hair was among the most beautiful, he knew, and in the big cities there were women who dyed their hair red to be fashionable.

You never needed to do that, Jens said to Tea.

You shouldn't compare me to that kind of woman, Tea answered offended.

But Jens became cheerful. After all, they were sitting cosily and drinking coffee. Now Anton Knopper was to hear how Tea had run after him before they were engaged. She was collecting for the Oriental mission, and she wouldn't let him go in peace. She always popped up with her collection list in her hand, and finally he had to propose to her—otherwise he would have gone bankrupt.

How can you say something like that, Tea blushed. Anton Knopper could easily believe it was serious.

Jens Røn assured him it was serious, and tickled Tea carefully with his finger. She wriggled affectionately, but began to think it was nonsense.

Now you mustn't be silly, she said with dignity,

There was a knock at the door—Lars Bundgaard and Malene had come to visit.

We just wanted to look inside, Malene said. It's nice here, but if it might be said all the same, our husbands rented some old hovels for us.

Yes, Tea sighed. But we just have to take things the way they come. And there's also something more important.

It was odd, it seemed to Malene, to be in an unfamiliar house. You'd have to get used to that. Lars Bundgaard had struggled with chests of drawers and beds all day and hung up curtains in elegant pleats. Malene was full of praise. He was so ingenious with his fingers, and she hadn't had anything to do but sit and watch.

Tea made a new round of coffee, and the talk came round to Povl Vrist.

He's a fine man, said Jens Røn. So willing to serve that it's almost too much. And he's an industrious fisherman. He's one of that kind everyone likes, and, believe you me, before many years he'll have become a big man—maybe both in the parish council and the consumer cooperative.

But in the vineyard, Lars Bundgaard said darkly.

No, Tea replied in a low voice. But I'll say this to you—I believe Mariane is holding him back.

They sat a little silently. Outside on the road you could hear laughter and frolicsome girls' voices. Lars Bundgaard said:

There are many things here that should be otherwise. The young people have nothing to think about but tomfoolery. Every evening they stand and gawk on the road and smoke cigarettes and act foolishly with the girls. Indeed, we probably shouldn't judge, but it's the pastor who's of no use. He has formed a youth association, which holds meetings in the assembly house. Afterwards they often dance.

They dance! Tea said, scandalized.

It was half-dark in the parlor, and the evening cold pushed in through the open window. There was a torrid scent from the jasmine bush, and Tea had to close the window. Malene sat big and shapeless in the armchair and merged with the darkness. Only her heavy breathing was audible.

It wasn't good when your own children got into something like this, said Tea.

Thomas will surely be the one who'll make a change in that, Lars Bundgaard observed.

They recovered their breath. Yes, Thomas Jensen knew a way out. He went about everything quietly, but the Lord led his steps. Never had anyone heard that Thomas did a bad job. He was meek, but a flame burned in him.

— Thomas Jensen was finished with his work and had eaten. Alma wanted to go to bed early, and Thomas took a walk up to Laust Sand's. Laust was sitting in the kitchen and eating when Thomas came.

Perhaps I've come at an inconvenient time?

No, no, Laust answered with his doleful smile. You're so heartily welcome. Take a chair and get a cup of coffee.

Yes, we're here with all that we have, Laust Sand, Thomas Jensen said after Adolfine had poured the coffee.

Laust tarried a bit. We've taken the good along, and the bad surely follows on our heels, he answered in a low voice.

Thomas Jensen didn't know what to say. Laust often suffered from temptations. He took to talking about fishing: now you had to have the traps finished in time. Thomas Jensen had to laugh. One of the fjord fishermen had come to him and seen his new, big traps. The man had become very frightened. After all, they were used to small, miserable equipment here in this place.

Laust Sand became reanimated and lively. Yes, the fjord fishermen! When there was a little wind, they were afraid to go out! They should try the sea when there was high water.

The sky was bright with stars when Thomas Jensen went home. There was light on the farmsteads, and in the doorways and behind the hedges people whispered and laughed.

The harvest began with hot summer days, warm haze, and thundershowers.

Swinging cartloads of grain were driven through the village. The year was so rich the barns could barely hold the grain. But the heat was almost too violent, the air heavy and glimmering, the foliage on the trees yellow and scorched, and the flowers dried up in the gardens.

For the fishermen they were days of peace. From morning till evening they patched old traps and put up new ones. Everything was to be ready for the first autumn darkness. A time of peace. You sat in the shed, where it was half-dark and cool, and could ponder many things, God and the world, fish and human conditions. Often you looked in on your neighbor and talked about what you had thought through in solitude.

Thomas Jensen had it easy—his two oldest boys had a facility for the work. They had quick fingers and helped out a lot. Thomas Jensen was a fortunate man—he realized it and couldn't be thankful enough for it. Alma was an efficient wife, though she was from another social class and city lineage. She was slender in stature with a freckled, thin face and reddish-blond hair, but she had a child every year, and could you demand more of a wife in the country or town? Thomas Jensen didn't think so, though it would never occur to him to pride himself on what was his.

The sun fell in streaks between the wall boards, and the tarred netting glistened bright and black. In the corners it was dark, but where Thomas Jensen was sitting, the light from the door streamed in broadly over him.

One afternoon Lars Bundgaard came to visit. They chatted a bit about the weather and the heat.

What do you think about this area here, Thomas? Lars Bundgaard asked.

Oh, Thomas Jensen had no reason to complain. If the fishing is good, it'll be a good place to live.

Lars Bundgaard was silent for a moment.

But God's kingdom—he said.

Thomas Jensen looked down at the ground.

I've thought a lot about this thing, he answered. You know very well, Lars Bundgaard, it means just as much to me as to you. But I have the conviction that Jesus himself will surely give us a sign.

You're certainly right about that, Lars Bundgaard conceded. But it seems to me there's something we should take care of. Sundays the children come home with ice cream cones they've purchased at the baker's. It's bad enough he doesn't keep his store closed on holidays. I think it would be right for us to go together and have a word with him.

Thomas Jensen nodded and got up. They went to the baker and got him out into the back room.

We'd like to talk to you about this Sunday trade of yours, Lars Bundgaard said. It's wrong of you to keep open.

But the baker didn't want to listen.

But it's lawful, he said and feigned naivete.

I'm not saying you're doing something that isn't lawful in the eyes of the world, Lars Bundgaard responded meekly. But Our Lord has made the day of rest so we would keep it holy, and we've come to ask you whether you couldn't keep your store closed.

With dignity the small broad baker put his hands on his back: I pay my taxes, he said, and that means I have my rights. It may well be that you don't like the way I run my business, but you'll have to keep that to yourselves. I don't come to you and criticize how you go about catching fish. Because that's none of my business.

You should think a bit more thoroughly about this matter, Thomas Jensen said seriously. Surely you know there's a word in the Scripture about him who gives offense. And the time will come when you'll regret that you did it.

I'm not in the Inner Mission, the baker answered. And if there were something wrong with selling bread on Sunday, it would surely be prohibited. But what I'd like to hear is: what about the farmers. Aren't they permitted to milk their cows on Sunday either?

Yes, they're permitted, Thomas Jensen said. That can't be otherwise. But if they're God's children, they don't drive the milk to the dairy.

And the fish that go into your traps on Sundays?

We don't empty the traps on holidays, and we're not the ones who determine the fishes' migration, Thomas Jensen explained. But we'd like to ask you amicably whether you can't keep closed. You're leading others to temptation who hardly have the strength to resist. It's just a small matter for you.

Now I'm going to tell you two something, the baker answered angrily. If you have something to complain about regarding the bread, you can come about that. But I myself determine when the store is open. I can definitely understand that you two are busybodies who meddle in everything and can't let others take care of their affairs in peace. But you can just keep your noses out of my store.

We can understand you don't want to, Thomas Jensen said almost meekly. But you yourself must accept the responsibility now that you've been warned. It will be plenty hard for you someday when you'll have to account for yourself.

No, the baker was hemmed in by the cunning of evil and couldn't be moved. It was hard on Lars Bundgaard to see the little ones on Sunday fight against temptation. Lars Bundgaard had gathered the whole troop and impressed upon them the law's commandments, but their thoughts centered on the bakery shop's cool splendors. It got to the point that Lars Bundgaard went to town, even though a day was wasted, and bought a freezing-machine for a lot of money, which could make ice cream cones according to a book that was part of the deal. And the next Sunday he sat all afternoon and turned the crank-handle and froze ice cream for his children.

Such a machine was an invention and a phenomenon, and Tea and Jens Røn had to see it. Lars Bundgaard and Malene had rented a house far down near the fjord. Access was along a narrow passage and past a cowshed, and Tea conceded there was no better place to live. They had to taste the ice cream—it wasn't cold, but it was sweet and good. Malene had gone to bed; she was tired and heavy and awaited her imminent delivery.

If only there were a capable midwife here, Tea said anxiously. You never know ahead of time if she's any good.

But Malene was of good cheer. She was used to having children. She had so many she was almost an able-bodied seaman. That was a joke, but Tea doubted whether it was appropriate for a serious soul on a Sunday to boot. Malene now looked at life brightly. She had been afraid of giving birth on the fjord, but in a bed there was no fear of it—she knew that. It was fine in the rooms, and Lars Bundgaard brewed himself coffee. Sara, the oldest daughter, was about to put the little ones to bed.

How can Malene manage all that? Tea asked.

Lars Bundgaard explained they had a lot of help from Mariane. She was a capable woman and had a good heart. She came every day and helped out. The only thing was—if it might be said all the same—she sang all the time while working, and they weren't spiritual songs, but dance melodies.

The information made Tea somber. But maybe it wasn't so bad. The words could be pretty even if the melodies were enticing tones. However, in her heart of hearts Tea did have her doubts. One usually went with the other.

Late one evening Lars Bundgaard had to go for the midwife.

With the years he had become used to the trip, but still he wasn't himself every time it happened. But Malene was a good soldier, the whole thing was over with by the time he came back, and Mariane was already brewing coffee. It was a big, healthy boy, and Mariane beamed with admiration. The next day Lars Bundgaard cranked the ice machine until he sweated. The children were supposed to take notice there was a festive occasion in the house.

It was the tenth one Lars Bundgaard had been granted. Ten children, healthy and well-formed, may the Lord be praised therefor! Food he could surely provide so long as he was healthy and the fjord had fish, but shelter was tight in the two small rooms. In the evening children were lying in every corner, on sofas, and in bureau drawers and boxes, which could be piled up during the day.

And when Tea and Alma came to visit during Malene's confinement, what Lars Bundgaard had been secretly pondering was revealed. It was Malene who betrayed it, although it was actually too early to talk about it yet. Lars Bundgaard was thinking of buying land and building their own house.

The news took the women's breath away. It was good that people could see they weren't paupers, but people who had come from the West Coast with means and could become free-holders. It happened that one day Lars Bundgaard had cast a glance at a piece of land east of town, not far from the wharf. He had money—the place back home had sold well. Mariane was fire and flame. Now Malene had to take care that a cellar was fitted up so everything could be kept fresh. And the garden, oh mercy; Mariane had herbs and flowers in surplus, which could easily be transplanted if Malene just wanted them.

Though the matter was disclosed in an untimely manner, Lars Bundgaard was not the man to blame a woman lying in. He went over and bought the piece of land, getting it for a reasonable price, and the next day he reached an agreement with the mason and carpenter. It was supposed to be ready for the fall.

And every day Mariane poured coffee strong as fire by Malene's childbed. Here the other women really got to know

Mariane. She laughed and chatted and was always in good spirits, but things were not so well in her heart. Wasn't she a whited sepulcher? The others came in good, dark clothes and were decorously solemn, but Mariane was clothed in light dresses of an all too noticeable cut, and her mouth never stopped while she passed around the coffee.

Oh, here's yours, she laughed. Now take another cup! Here's yours, Alma! But surely you think your own is better when you get home!

And when there was talk of serious things, Mariane laughed and said things that could never be right. If they talked about the inn and the wild life, she openly was of the opinion it wasn't so bad. But now Tea also took on a fine voice like a crested lark and said:

I think dance is a sinful lust and I'll really object if my own girls should go dancing when they get bigger.

Believe you me—they certainly will, Mariane teased.

I wouldn't like to experience that, Tea said. Now it's not so much the dance as what happens afterward. Believe you me—I know all about it.

Mariane assumed an innocent look and asked mildly: How in the world could you possibly know about that, dear Tea?

But Tea wasn't afraid to confess her shame and let them understand that she too had been on the dangerous path. She answered sorrowfully:

I surely know it because I went to a dance twice when I was a young girl. That was before I met Jesus.

And then what happened? Mariane asked. What was Tea supposed to answer? Nothing had happened that could fill the others with horror. At most she could have recounted that someone wanted to kiss her. But Tea couldn't speak untruth.

Surely there was no harm to you, was there? Mariane asked with a smile.

Yes, yes, you can easily talk, Tea said, and had tears in her eyes. But I hate unchastity. And dancing never leads to anything but unchastity. Believe you me— there are many who get into a scrape at a dance.

I danced a lot in my day, Mariane said dreamily.

At this point it really wasn't possible to say anything. But each one was entitled to think what she wanted, and Tea and Alma looked at each other. It would surely have been better if Mariane had used her time in another way. You understood more and more why Povl Vrist was not one of God's children.

Week after week went by in boiling heat with an unchanging low sky and blinding sun. It was roasting. The children romped in the fjord, a naked, splashing throng. There were merry days in the shed where Anton Knopper toiled. Anton sat in the doorway with his netting and talked to all who came by. Anton was saved in his whole heart, but a social butterfly and a chatterbox. He already knew the whole parish, knew who was married to whom, and whether a fellow had money or was an alleged father. Soon there wasn't a boy in town who wasn't friends with Anton Knopper. He was full of fun and noise, a boy at heart of forty summers. But with women he was shy and reserved and didn't know what to say. There were many secrets regarding the female sex. Now, for example, the hotel serving girl, who went to the baker for bread every day and nodded to him while passing by. Was she a flighty hussy? Or did she have a friendly disposition? She was a big, strong wench, rough-haired and broad-bosomed—there was nothing wrong with her appearance. Anton shuddered at the audacious thought.

The work with the traps wasn't easy for Jens Røn. His equipment was old and worn out—it was almost like darning a stocking full of holes. Nevertheless he was in good spirits. Next year he wanted to buy new traps if luck came his way. God never forsook his children. It was tiring to sit bent all too long and he had picked up a little rheumatism on the cold sea. But he then came to think about the hard times when fishing had failed, and he had had to take work at the dam. It went at a furious pace— the workers were mostly young fellows who incited one another. Contented, Jens Røn sighed. The Lord had shown his goodness by removing him to better parts. In the fjord fishing was mere play.

One day the pastor visited Laust Sand, and Adolfine fetched

her stepfather from the out-building. The pastor was young and friendly, with a cheerful face and a deep, euphonious voice. He sat down on the bench and chatted about fishing and showed he knew it thoroughly. Laust Sand barely dared to raise his tortured eyes from the floor, and Adolfine stood pale in a corner. Pastor Brink observed that they were pitiful poor people, and grew even more dignified and fatherly.

And that's your daughter, he said.

No, no, Laust Sand said. Not *my* daughter, but my wife's. She died, and her first husband died at sea.

That's truly good fortune you have an assistant. It's not easy with strangers in the house.

Laust Sand mumbled an answer and looked down at the ground.

Yes, yes, the pastor concluded and rose. I've come here because I'm your pastor and must support you if I can. Dear Laust Sand, should anything ever oppress you, come to me without any qualms. Perhaps I can help you.

Tea had seen the pastor coming and just managed to don a clean apron. Red and embarrassed, she received him, for a pastor was a pastor even if he was almost a heathen. Pastor Brink took a seat and looked around.

It's so nice here, he said. You can see that good people live here, unlike those who used to live here.

That was delightful talk and Tea couldn't restrain herself, but explained how filthy, to put it bluntly, it had been when they moved in. Didn't pastor want a cup of coffee? Pastor Brink had just drunk some before he left home, but he earnestly asked for a glass of milk.

And your husband, where did he go?

Yes, it was so unfortunate he was on the fjord emptying a cod trap.

You are indeed such good Christians, you people from the West Coast, the pastor said. And such active churchgoers.

Here Tea should have opened her mouth and offered her opinion. That would have been her true Christian duty. She could have uttered a word about rogues and eye-servants and ungodly Pharisees. That would have been bearing witness! But afterwards Tea had to admit to herself remorsefully that she had forsaken her savior the way Simon Peter had while the cock crowed. She took the pastor's hand in bidding him farewell and even thanked him for coming. She could just as well have thanked the Antichrist, and she would have to expiate it ever after.

Pastor Brink walked on in the sunshine and felt calm and quite well. In the gardens the apple trees were laden with fruit, and the hens bathed in the warm sand. The world was good and full of good will to men. It was beautiful to wander here doing the Supreme Being's work.

The pastor found his own way out to the shed, where Thomas Jensen sat at work. When he entered, Anton Knopper was standing with his hands in his pockets and watching.

Thomas Jensen got up.

It's the pastor, I see, he said.

I was just looking in while passing by, the pastor explained. You have a nice place to sit and work. And Anton Knopper keeps you company. Splendid weather today—if it just keeps up.

Yes, Thomas Jensen said absentmindedly. It's beautiful weather.

If it just keeps up, the pastor repeated and felt truly unwell. The air in the shed was heavy and had the acrid smell of tar and old rope. The two men's faces were half hidden by dark shadows. Through the door the sunshine broke in with blinding brutality.

I'll tell you, now that you have come, Pastor Brink, Thomas Jensen said in a low voice. It's *not* God's word you preach!

That startled Anton Knopper. That was strong language even if it was true. The pastor stood silently. Anton almost felt sorry for him when Thomas Jensen continued: What's your relationship with Jesus, Pastor Brink?

I'm a pastor, am I not, the pastor answered. You can surely understand that I meditated on the matter a long time ago. Everyone has his private closet where he's alone with God. You can rest assured I trust fully and firmly in our savior. But we two belong to different church movements.

A bit nervously he dried the sweat from his forehead.

There's no such thing as movements, the fisherman said. There are only those who love Jesus and have found mercy, and those who are against him. There's no evading mercy and conversion—I know that personally.

We must not be quarrelsome, the pastor answered. Many paths leads to God. But we must talk together another time. Now we must say farewell, dear Thomas Jensen. I have others I have to visit today. Farewell, Anton Knopper.

He gave the fishermen his hand and left the shed. Thomas Jensen got going again with his work with shuttle and thread. His fingers were swift—he had mended netting since he was a boy. Anton Knopper broke his silence.

You managed to drive him into a corner, he said a bit dubiously.

I would rather he had stayed, Thomas Jensen replied. A pastor can be a good servant to Jesus.

What Thomas Jensen had said to the pastor didn't remain a secret. Nearly every evening a little troop of believers gathered for their edification. Scripture was read aloud and the praying and hymn singing was so loud it could be heard in the neighborhood. And they weren't only little people. The old teacher Aaby came who was as learned as any bishop. Those who had been in his parlor could testify it was full of books, and he firmly controlled the children in school. The consumer cooperative manager, he, too, was saved and did what he could on behalf of God's kingdom. He outright refused to trade in playing cards and dress shoes. He was a big heavy man, a bit spongy and with flabby features. When he sold soap or baking powder he placed a slip with scripture text in the package. He had had that printed at his own expense. It was a fine thing.

But in church there was no edification to be gotten. In the front rows the Grundtvigian farmers sat and listened to the mild words from the pastor's lips. Children were baptized and people laid in their graves. The large room was white and cool. Christ hung in his torment on the altar piece, but an ungodly pastor stood in the pulpit and poured wormwood for thirsting souls.

The first fall darkness came before anyone thought about it, even though there was a cross placed next to it in the almanac. Now it was time to get the traps out, and as soon as it was barely light, heavily laden wagons were driven up into the sand pits where the tar pot stood. Two by two, black and shiny from tar and smoke, the men stood by the cement cart and hoisted the traps down into the bubbling deep. Afterwards the nets were spread to dry and lay shining in the green grass.

Everywhere people were bustling. Netting and stakes were loaded on to the big prams and dragged out to the fishing spots. From miles away you heard the dull boom of mallets when the stakes were hammered into the bottom. Also the fishermen from the southern side of the fjord were out. The air was filled with the noise of motors, and a glistening, rainbow-colored oil film lay on the water. Boats with red, patched sails swept south and north. The fjord was alive.

In the evening the fishermen came home, bowed from toil. Black and sunburnt with tar-shiny arms they walked up toward the village. Early in the morning they went out on to the fjord again. Povl Vrist and Lars Bundgaard had engaged laborers for the fall months and had good motorboats. For them it was easy. The others had to join together in pairs. Anton Knopper and Thomas Jensen had an old, broad-bellied sea-going boat, built to take the breakers. They needed an hour every morning to coax the motor into starting. It coughed and spat, but once it got going, there wasn't a better boat in the world. Jens Røn and Laust Sand dragged the prams out with a sail boat and rowed when the wind died down. It wasn't the speed of lightning, but they made progress.

The small farmers fished the fjord with wretched, old-fashioned traps. The eel had to twist themselves to find their way into the traps, Anton Knopper teased. North and south, east and west, the rows of stakes grew up from the water. It was heavy work to hammer the poles into the bottom. You stood in the pram, which rocked with every blow, and it had to be done solidly—otherwise the netting was overturned in the first storm. Thomas Jensen was the ablest of them. He planted the stake and gave it a couple of blows with the mallet, and it stood firmly as if for eternity.

One day when the wind was blowing too strongly for the netting to be placed, the fishermen gathered in clusters on the wharf. They sat on the tarred beams and fish-chests and smoked and chatted. At home they couldn't settle down. Fishing was supposed to bring blessing and good gifts to God's children and the sinners according to the Lord's wisdom. The fjord could give wealth and poverty, penury or daily bread. But the world and its pains must not be permitted completely to take your mind and thoughts. That was the view of the North Sea fishermen and the others who were saved. Some were slaves of this world and chatted only about good fishing years, when the eel went into the traps, and no one had seen the likes of it. Here Anton Knopper could not restrain himself, but said the best thing would be for us all to go into one net, and that was Our Lord's. Lars Bundgaard added there was another net we humans wouldn't elude, and that was the black grave.

To be sure, a lot could be said about the thing if you had rhetorical gifts, said Niels Væver, a lean, cunning fjord fisherman. But how that worked, surely no one knew. The eel was supposed to go into the pan—that was its destiny. The West Coast folk nodded and their look turned gloomy. Maybe there were many who had to be put over the fire. And Anton Knopper said straight out: hell was precisely that kind of pan.

There was no more talk about it. The West Coast fishermen knew what they knew. God had lashed them with the west wind, destruction, and poverty. Fishing had failed year after year, sand drift and sea fog had ravaged the parish, and brothers and friends had drowned before their eyes. Only one thing was certain: God's word. Only one thing gave strength: God's mercy. If you didn't lay your burden on Jesus's shoulder, earthly existence was insufferable.

Down at the shore sand pipers preened themselves, and gulls flew shrieking after fish. The children splashed at the water's edge and caught blenny and sticklebacks in little traps, and the cows grazed patiently in the meadows. A little ways out in the water red and violet seaweed were growing, and in the sun the tarred prams were shining black. A rain shower moved across the fjord, and the fishermen went into a shelter behind a shed.

In the meantime Kock came sauntering over—he was a customs official and shoemaker and a well-read man, who owned books and liked discussion. He was smart and knew about science and theosophy. So talk came round to subjects where you had to hold your thoughts together and not get all fired up.

But Anton Knopper had a hard time remaining calm when Kock asserted the Bible had to be reformed and rewritten according to true scientific principles. Much had become incomprehensible in the course of the years.

Anton was of the opinion this was presumptuous talk and God would never tolerate that his sacred word be touched.

Well, Kock declared, adjusting his glasses. Should one as a reasonable man and matter-of-fact person believe in the story about Jesus, who drove the evil spirits into two thousand swine at the lake of Gennesaret sea? Stuttering and stammering, Anton Knopper managed to say that when it's in the Bible it's true down to the commas and periods. Why otherwise should it be written down there? There were indeed spirits, of both light and dark. Hell's hosts are talked about there more than enough.

Kock smiled and dropped the matter. Such ignorance couldn't be dealt with. But Jonah in the whale's belly! It was a scientific fact that a whale of that shape couldn't swallow so much as a kitten. And was one supposed to think it had taken Jonah with his skin and hair and vomited him out again? And one more thing: How could Jonah breathe in the whale's belly?

But Anton Knopper couldn't be moved. What was written was settled and fixed. There could be other whales in Judea, and it was in God's power to make miracles. Anton Knopper's eyes lit up; now he had one proof. If things had happened completely naturally, it wouldn't have been a miracle, but the Lord's power surpasses all comprehension.

No scientific discussion could be conducted in such a way, and Kock shook his head. Luckily he wasn't obliged to discuss the problems with ignorant people. No, he went to the parsonage and talked about theosophy and religion with the pastor and his wife, came there for afternoon coffee, and ate pastry and exchanged viewpoints like a well-bred man.

The traps went out and now the eel were to begin to migrate. From lakes and sloughs they go out into the deep sea. It's not hard work to go out in a boat every other day, untie the ropes on the main stake and take the steel-gray and bronze-brown eel, sparkling in delicate, soft colors. You can get a lot done on the side, maintain the boat, patch the herring nets from the spring, and prepare new traps. Lars Bundgaard had the most work with his house. He himself lent a hand. The carpenter Knud was a middle-aged grouser with a dangerous big mouth. Such a fellow got around and was up to date on people in distant parishes. But the way he cursed was ugly, and it singed Lars Bundgaard's soul to hear the devil conjured up here on his own land. One morning Knud had been especially bad, and the fisherman asked cautiously:

Does that make it easier?

Does what make what easier? the carpenter asked.

All the curses—you must be using them for something.

Knud became sulky, and put a lock on his mouth. Lars Bundgaard no longer was kept informed of other people's habits and fates of a curious sort.

There were many difficulties and cares with the house. To begin with, there was the name. It had become the custom to name a house just like a ship or a dog. You could understand it was practical both for mail and people, who had to know the way. Lars Bundgaard had at first been of the opinion it was arrogant to paint a name on the gable, but to Malene it seemed to belong there. She wanted it to be called "Bethlehem." It was nice to think of the additional lives that would be born there as the years went by. But Lars Bundgaard said no immediately. It was much too big a name for an earthly abode. He himself had thought about "Capernaum." But first he consulted with Thomas Jensen.

Thomas Jensen nodded, the name was pretty, but it wasn't fitting for God's children to put biblical names in stone and brick. Lars Bundgaard conceded that and thought about "Malene's Delight." But Malene didn't like it—it was a name people would find odd. Finally "Gleam of Sunshine" was settled on. It was a pretty name he had once noticed on a house in town, and it was painted on wood with black letters with flourishes.

In the beginning, when the traps are out, the eel are small. There wasn't much to do, and therefore it was opportune for visitors to come. Laust Sand's sister's son, Mads Langer was his name, one day came promenading the two miles from the closest town with a railway station with a travel bag in his hand. Handsome he wasn't, tattooed blue on his hands and arms and his face wind-furrowed, but he could talk your ear off. He hadn't sent any notice he was coming, and Adolfine blushed like dripping blood when she saw him standing in the parlor in clothes of an unfamiliar and elegant cut and asking whether Laust Sand was at home.

Would the gentleman sit down until Laust comes?

The nephew took a seat on the sofa, and Adolfine fetched her stepfather at the wharf, where he was about to tar a boat. He could scarcely remember Mads Langer, who had gone out to sea early and had become a stoker. Laust's melancholy face didn't brighten—the visit offered no comfort.

But the seaman felt well and was full of strange stories. He had been in all the world's ports, and his pronunciation had something English about it. As a boy he had fallen down from a hay loft and hit his head, but the blow truly had not made him weak-brained. Rather, he surely had become smarter from the concussion. He knew all about everything—ships and foreign cities. Laust Sand wanted to be friendly toward him since he was, after all, kin. But it was hard for him to answer with anything other than no or aha or yes indeed. More and more Laust came to resemble someone being crucified—narrow cheeks and wax-yellow skin and a gnawing pain in his eyes. At the table he fell into prayer and prayed until the food became cold, while Adolfine bowed her head. For Mads Langer it was hard to keep silent for so long.

But for Anton Knopper the stoker was an experience. You got to know about the earth's lands and places. For hours on end Mads Langer sat in Anton Knopper's parlor with the brass spittoon between his feet and chewed tobacco, as if that meant something, but nevertheless chatted just as well. Anton shook his big, wooden head and shuddered when the stoker dipped into the depth of his knowledge: how full the world was of afflictions and dangers!

And these women here who sold their bodies—didn't anyone ever notice any repentance among them?

Mads Langer didn't know anything from his own experience about that. Because he was converted and was well-mannered and had been so all his days. But as far as you heard from your comrades, they surely didn't repent. So long as they got the seaman's money, they couldn't care less, but they did get hideous diseases often—both they and their fornicators.

It was God's punishment, Anton said with satisfaction. You understood that—it was righteousness.

But there are also just too many temptations for the young people in the big cities, he said. I can remember, when I was a soldier in Copenhagen, in these museums and many times in the gardens and on the streets there were statues of naked women without so much as a skirt. They say it's art, and the learned people can easily, I dare say, tolerate looking at that kind of stuff. For the rest of us simple people—I don't really like it.

Indeed, pshaw, Mads Langer spat. It was nothing. There were pictures that agents went around and sold in harbor taverns—they were something else. They showed both this and that, and it wasn't nakedness alone, you know.

Anton Knopper didn't feel well hearing that information. His temples got a little red. With an oblique glance at him, Mads

Langer took his elegant leather pocket book out of his pocket and found in one of its compartments a little notebook. Seeing is believing. Did Anton want to take a little look at it?

Anton Knopper turned white and red—the words were a foreign language, which he didn't understand, but the pictures were plain enough. Alas, it was a dreadful world. He flung the shameless pictures away and for a moment felt almost dizzy with disgust and horror.

How did you come by this? he said hoarsely. I thought you were a decent man.

But the stoker had an explanation ready at hand. It had been bought in Argentina—a seaman's missionary had asked him to take it home with him. He wanted to have it to use as a warning. Mads Langer was truly not of the kind to carry lewd pictures around for his own enjoyment. Anton Knopper was in a dark mood for several days; the hideous pictures tormented him in his dreams and disturbed his tranquility. Two nights in a row he had to get up and put on the light and read strong words in the Scriptures. Finally he got a grip on the old Adam again.

He enjoyed Mads Langer's company as often as he could. Many hours went by chatting about skyscrapers and ocean steamers that held more people than a whole parish. And about life in seamen's gin-shops where there was drinking, reveling, and knifings so bad the blood squirted over the tables and benches. But personally Mads Langer abided by his word and his savior and was on the safe side. Here, too, he had curious things to announce. In a few years the world would be destroyed, and sinners and whoremongers thrown into the fire. Mads Langer's eyes became wild as he explained about the furnace it was his job to tend to. He threw a shovel full of coal in the flaming opening. That's what hell was like!

In the guest's honor coffee klatches were held round about among the West Coast fishermen—that was the custom, and he was listened to in devout silence as a man from the great seas. His tattoos made the children open their eyes wide, and he had a gold watch and a chain of gold coins riveted together—several hundred crowns worth in hard cash. It didn't escape anyone's attention that he kept close to Adolfine. She was quiet and withdrawn, as is proper—no one could complain about her deportment. But it would be good if she could get married to such a stable man. He could provide for her, and she was a believer and of good family. Yes, it was fine if Adolfine could get a ring.

When the men were out on the fjord, the women had their work to do. Mariane did a big cleaning every other day and scoured and scrubbed and made coffee and went visiting. There was always a fragrance of clean linen and warm soapy water about her. And when anyone stood in need of encouragement, she was always at the ready. She was always busy and always had a marvelous time. It was otherwise with Tea, who only had sorrows in this earthly life. She no longer got visits from the pastor and didn't know who was pregnant and who was about to sink under great sins. No, Tea was ignorant of everything in that area and didn't feel at home. That's why she found her way to Mariane and did what she could to convert that unbelieving soul. But Mariane resisted and took it as a joke and couldn't be caught hold of. There was life and warmth in her; she alone was like a whole parish.

And yet from her own life Tea could prove that peace was found only in Jesus's bosom. In her youth, she had been tempted almost beyond measure. Wherever she set foot, she had fellows at her heels, and it was by the skin of her teeth and only with the help of providence that Tea had escaped that danger. She had experienced great grief. A fellow she had taken a fancy to had shown his ugly side, and Tea had almost thrown herself into the sea.

Mariane was moved by her story. With her whole heart she understood the sorrows of love, and she felt it almost as a lack that she herself had never experienced the bitter pain. Mariane laughed at Tea and looked down at her a bit, but she couldn't stop admiring her delicate soul. The story was told over and over again in sorrowful devotion.

At last Mads Langer departed. The last day he was there he confided his love to Adolfine. Adolfine began to cry and said only:

I can't marry you.

The seaman blushed, and a scar on his forehead shone faintly. Without saying anything he seized her hand, forced it up and put the ring on her finger. It was of gold with two hands, which squeezed each other, and better merchandise couldn't be found. But Adolfine scarcely saw it. She was white as a corpse, and her face tightened as if in a spasm. She accompanied Mads Langer to the mail coach. The other West Coasters came to say good-bye, and the stoker chatted with a smile on his odd, ravaged face, while Adolfine stood silently at his side. Everyone had seen the ring on her finger, but it was not proper to hint at anything. At the last minute Anton Knopper shouted:

Well, so are we now permitted to congratulate you?

The stoker waved and swung his cap so his tousled black hair fluttered in the wind, but Adolfine stuck her hand under her apron. When she came home, she pulled the ring off and hid it in her dresser drawer. It aroused astonishment that she no longer wore it.

— The man who had gotten Mariane as his mainstay—the least of his arts would be catching fish, and Povl Vrist came home every day with scores of eel. For the others, too, the getting was good on the waters they had bought from the landed estates, The Black Horse, The Block, The Flat Sea, Blue Bank, and whatever the fishing grounds were called. The only one for whom things were tight was Jens Røn. He rowed laboriously out to his traps—never was there much in them. But there was still time before the eel fishing was over, and there was no question of Tea's becoming bitter or rebelling against the almighty. A human eye could barely discern why Povl Vrist, who was almost a heathen, had luck, while others, who submitted to the word, got so sorry a lot. But Tea would rather bite her tongue off than use it to complain.

Later on in September Lars Bundgaard's house was fixed up. It was a fine house with red bricks and a slate roof and paint and flowered wallpaper. But Lars Bundgaard shook his head: what it had cost! Every time he came from the fjord, Malene had thought up improvements, more shelves in the kitchen or brass racks in the entrance hall. When everything was finished and in good order, company was invited—Malene wanted to show off the house. The wives viewed the drawing room, where the fine nickel coffee things beamed from the sideboard, while the green plush furniture looked unapproachable. But Malene took most pleasure in the bedroom, which was roomy and shining white, and here, she reflected, other little lives would indeed open up their eyes in the world.

In the out-building a room was fitted up for the fishing helper Anders Kjøng so he no longer needed to take lodgings with strangers. It was a pretty little room with table and chair, and Lars Bundgaard had hung up a few small pictures on the wall. One represented Jesus looking after the lost lamb. The helper was supposed to look at and draw lessons from it. And if that didn't help, there was a second one above the bed. It depicted Sodom's destruction in the sea of flames. Perhaps it could awaken useful thoughts.

People were surprised that Lars Bundgaard wanted to have Anders Kjøng eating his bread. Because to put it bluntly, he was a scoffer. He didn't believe in anything, and was by nature sullen and unapproachable. But Lars Bundgaard was indulgent toward him and sought to win him for the Lord. Had Saul not become Paul? Sundays Anders Kjøng didn't go to church; instead he took a boat and put out into the fjord. There he lay on the bottom of the yawl with his coat bundled up under his head and looked up into the clear fall sky. The current carried the boat along quite slowly. Anders Kjøng had no intention to go hymn singing with the Pious. But he dreamt of many things. What if he saved up his wages and took the school teaching exam? That way people would surely learn to respect him, and the girls wouldn't avoid him. Anders Kjøng thought about the parish's young women, the broad-hipped, strong wives and the slim girls. No, they'd certainly learn to take note of him.

That fall Jens Røn had to own up that an empty boat is heavy to row. Almost every day he emptied his traps. When he unfastened the line from the head post and lifted the front of the net into the boat, he instinctively mumbled a prayer, just a few lines. But it was of no use, the eel didn't come into his netting, and winter was at the door like a frozen ghost. The winter, when fuel and groceries had to be provided, and when you couldn't live on small fry and bread. Laust Sand didn't catch much either, but it wasn't noticeable with him. When Jens Røn gently said:

It's not working for us two, Laust! he hung his head and answered ponderously:

Let's hope that's the worst thing that ever happens to us.

There was something wrong with Laust Sand. His eyes were hidden under his forehead. What was gnawing at him? Laust Sand was a lonely man all his days like the leafless tree or the corpse in the grave.

The days became short, dark, and full of sleet, and blowing clouds moved heavily across the fjord. The rain lashed the fishermen's faces when the traps had to be emptied, and the waves splashed in over the boat. One night the storm overturned all of Anton Knopper's stakes. He had to ask Lars Bundgaard to lend him Anders Kjøng for a while. For a week the two men toiled at erecting the stakes again; wet and exhausted they returned home in the evening. And at nightfall, when the blue cutter fought its way in from the broad waters, the fjord was full of terror and eeriness. The waves foamed white in the twilight, and the birds flew screeching home. The old people in the village knew about those who had drowned, who hadn't found peace in death. And further west, Anders Kjøng related, was a head, which glided over the ice on winter nights and shouted: Oh, my liver! Oh, my lung! Probably a sinner, who'd gone through an opening in the ice while he was spearing eel one Christmas eve.

Every Saturday evening there was a dance at the temperance inn. It was a low, white building with jagged gables. From a distance it looked quite churchly. But it was only a phantasm. There was nothing good to say about the place. The owner, Mogensen, was a small loquacious man, who had gone into innkeeping. He always had new plans. Here in the parish you could easily operate a hotel for bathers. The building was situated near the fjord. But for the time being people would just have to dance.

He had managed to track down a nickelodeon in the market town, which cost three hundred crowns and was worth the money. You placed a 10-øre coin in a slot and got music. It filled a whole cabinet and played waltzes with drums and flutes and screeching violins. One day he journeyed in and bought the machine for cash and brought it home in a motorboat. Someone tried it out already on the wharf. Niels Væver offered up a 10-øre coin, and half the town stood and watched. Tea had come down there with the children. A clown jumped out of a trap-door in the cabinet and stuck out his tongue, bowed, and sparred with its arms. The children had never seen the likes of it, but on the way home Tea explained the truth to them. It was the disgusting dancing devil, which came forward and did its tricks to lure honest people into perdition.

But the young people amused themselves evenings at the inn. The men waltzed around with the girls squeezed tight, while they sang:

And listen, Susanne, if thou wouldst marry me,
I'll buy a snail shell and live in it with thee.

When the machine stopped, a new 10-øre coin was offered up immediately. Mogensen sat behind the bar with a sheet of paper and in long rows of figures accounted for how things stood with the return on the music box. Between dances the fellows gave rounds of coffee or beer. Space was tight at the tables and the girls had to sit on the fellows' laps. Their cheeks were red and hot, their hair was in disorder. But as soon as the music boomed they were on their feet and danced so hard the windowpanes jangled.

Tea had to go over and see how bad things were. With a shawl over her head she ventured up to the hall windows and looked in. She became hot and cold and got heart palpitations. As she turned, she ran right into Anton Knopper in the dark.

Is that you, Tea? he said. Yes, it's an ugly sight.

His voice was inflamed, and Tea said he was right.

Did you see the fellows sitting with the hussies on their laps, she answered. That kind of thing should be forbidden.

Yes, it's totally terrible, totally terrible, Anton Knopper mumbled. How are these wretched people supposed to get on.

But the girls—that they can let themselves do it, Tea said, and her voice trembled. They just have no shame. I'll say this now—if it had been at home, where *we* come from, I wouldn't have believed my own eyes.

She grabbed Anton Knopper by the arm and pointed toward a dark figure standing near another window and looking in. That's Anders Kjøng, she whispered. They say of him that he prowls for girls in the evening.

Tea didn't have the power, as she had the purpose, and couldn't prevent people from going the broad way of sin, as distressing as that was. The innkeeper let the machine play and pondered new things that could bring him customers. This time it was a theater performance. He got a small company of actors to go round the parish, but here his calculation didn't work out. The rural postman, who was to distribute the posters, was a believing man. He delivered them only to respectable people.

I know you people don't go to that kind of tomfoolery, he said, and put the placard on the kitchen table. They want to perform a piece they call *Jeppe of the Hill*. The placard here mustn't fall into the wrong hands. When the actors came, the hall was half empty.

Consolation was also found for the pious heart. Thomas Jensen had begun a Sunday school. Teacher Aaby let out one of the school rooms; he himself felt too old for the work. Thomas Jensen didn't do it to behave arrogantly, but young people's needs were not uppermost in the pastor's mind.

So Thomas Jensen, fisherman and God's child, had to edify the little ones every Sunday. The children sat devoutly on the brown benches and listened. If one fell asleep with his head against the back of the bench, he was gently wakened. Thomas Jensen's troop filled a whole row. It was a little kingdom of God.

The dark nights lay heavy over the land. During the sleety

days teacher Aaby promenaded on his walks along the shore. He walked with his bible in his pocket and sat down and read where there was a bit of shelter. He was gaunt like an old bird, and his clothes hung on him. The fall has its admonishing voice.

They had become accustomed to the new region, but they didn't feel at home. Much was so different from what they were familiar with. There wasn't the same feeling here of belonging together in life and death and belief as in the parish they came from. After all, there almost all people were poor, but here the well-to-do farmers sat in their good, inherited places with Bavarian beer and whiskey on the table and fed and drank themselves into perdition. In the parish here big things hadn't happened as long as people could remember. The farmers tilled their land, the fishermen fished the fjord, and in church they had their consolation if something befell them. Our Lord attended to his affairs and humans to theirs, but in a pinch you could always ask him for a hand. If you honored God and obeyed the authorities, things would never go completely wrong. The young people worked and danced, some were wild, but most of them were well-behaved. It was an old-fashioned district. It lay separated from the land by the mile-wide stretch of meadowlands, and the big movements had gone around it. Hither and yon there was a temperance man, a Baptist or one of the Pious, but it meant nothing.

To be sure, meetings had been held throughout the summer, now at the house of one, and now of another of the North Sea residents. A few had found the way to repentance, mostly common people from the bog or craftsmen from the village. But little notice was taken of it. Thomas Jensen was smart. He saw where things were headed—he had learned from life. Back home it had happened that people had moved to other districts and at the beginning strongly held on to their faith, but as time went by, they had become alienated from Jesus. When they became better off, they forgot their native customs. When they came among nonbelievers, their own faith cooled. Indeed, Thomas Jensen knew you surely had to seek God in your private closet, but you also had to cultivate him in society. He had thought much about how he ought to be of use to the cause of Jesus in this foreign place, and now he was of the opinion that the Lord had sent him a warning. It was an odd thing, and Thomas Jensen didn't mention it in front of others. He had dreamed that he cast a glance into hell. He saw people there he knew in fire and torment. Among them was his own father. But most clearly he saw the pastor and some of the farmers from the district, people who stood far above him in wealth and prestige. They stretched their hands, their fingers, which were bent in suffering, supplicating to him. Thomas Jensen was gripped by fear and wanted to flee, but his legs would not carry him from the spot. He awoke bewildered and bathed in sweat and thought about the dream for many days. God admonished him to take up his revival work to save the souls that would otherwise be damned. One thing he didn't understand: why he had seen his father in that place—after all, he had died a pious person. But God surely wanted to remind him that he should nourish the same love for needy souls as for his own father.

Now it was time for God to make his haul. They were no longer the people from the West Coast, who came in the spring and left again in the fall, but settled people whose word and deed were significant for the parish. But that was the way! It had to be considered, and he talked to Lars Bundgaard about whether he wanted to take over the leadership and stand against the pastor. Because without struggle against the pastor and unbelievers there'd be no progress. Lars Bundgaard shook his head—such a big deed was not for him. But otherwise Lars Bundgaard enthusiastically supported the thought. There was the inn: things would never be good until the dancing was stopped. And in the meeting hall revelries were held that ended with dancing. They could just as well take down the cross from the gable and jump around on it. And first and foremost their hearts had to be ignited in flame. Without it there would be no progress. Meetings had to be held where good, safe speakers were present. Lars Bundgaard became unusually lively—he saw the whole thing in his mind.

And there was one thing especially, Thomas Jensen added. It had to be arranged in such a way that the believers got their own house.

Lars Bundgaard cast down his eyes:

Now you're probably thinking I've just built a house and haven't given a thought to Jesus's abode.

No, truly, no, Lars, Thomas Jensen answered. I have no right at all to that kind of thought. You must take care of those who are entrusted to you, and if Jesus had wished anything else, he would surely have let you understand that.

He surely would have, Lars Bundgaard sighed, reassured.

— They talked to the other believers. They had to go forward cautiously, with shrewd deliberation but intrepidly when the struggle came. That set off a light in Tea's mind. There was consolation in the fact that the Lord's cause was making progress even if things were going rather badly for Jens Røn's fishing. Tea saw the stiff necks bent and the bewildered souls pacified in chastity's harbor. Perhaps she could still come to feel joyful on earth. Anton Knopper was fire and flame. The sinfulness of the surrounding area made him feel oppressed too. Povl Vrist and Mariane stood apart. When talk turned to God's cause, their looks became rigid and they held their tongues. They were unreachable. Mariane's mouth took on hard features—no, she'd surely never become one of the Pious.

It was decided to send for Pastor Thomsen from the old parish so he could preach in the church. He was a revivalist preacher, whose words tore into people's souls. But it wasn't prudent for it to happen before Christmas was over. Before Christmastime hearts were occupied with the upcoming festivities; it was better to wait until January or February, in the middle of the harsh, dreary winter when it seemed it would be an eternity before spring came. Thomas Jensen went to the pastor. It was a bitter, sleety November day with clouds drifting in the cold sky. It had to be arranged so Pastor Thomsen could speak in the church one Sunday. Thomas Jensen had put on his good clothes and felt as if the boots hurt him a bit. This journey could bring about both the one result and the other.

Thomas stood for a long time and dried his boots on the mat in the hall before knocking on the door to the study. The pastor himself came out and answered the door. He looked surprised, as if reluctantly, at the fisherman, but invited him inside in a friendly way. Stammering a bit, Thomas Jensen said there was a matter he'd like to talk to the pastor about. But he'd hate to come at an inconvenient time.

But you're not inconveniencing me at all, the pastor said. We were just sitting and drinking our afternoon coffee. Come in and drink a cup with us, Thomas Jensen.

The lady of the house and customs official Kock were sitting in the parlor at the elegantly covered coffee table. It was a snug and light room with carpeting on the floor and mahogany furniture with red damask covers. In front of all the doors were portieres and on the walls pictures in wide gilt frames. There was a cozy glow in the big, white porcelain stove, and the table cloth for coffee service was embroidered with flowers and embellishments. Thomas Jensen felt oddly coarse and inferior in the fine room. He happened to think about the fact that the soles of his boots were studded with iron cleats, and he lifted his legs high so as not to damage the carpet. But Kock, feeling at home, sat with his legs crossed and leaned back in the chair.

Please, sit down, dear Thomas Jensen, the pastor said, and his voice sounded uncertain, which did not escape the fisherman's attention. And enjoy my wife's coffee cake. Maybe you'll like it better than my sermons.

Yes, we do indeed think there is much sugar—the words slipped out of his mouth. As soon as he said it, he regretted it. You ought not insult a man grossly in his own parlor, which he had hospitably invited you into. But it didn't sound as though the pastor had heard it. He didn't move a muscle. His wife poured the coffee into the fine, thin cup. She was a small nervous woman with frightened brown eyes.

When the conversation came round to fishing, Thomas

Jensen gave an account of how it was going. He could say precisely what each individual had caught. When he came to Jens Røn, the parson didn't think it was much.

Oh, that's a pity for the good, frugal-living people, the wife said with sympathy. People say things are so tight for them. Can't anything be done to help them?

Yes, yes, the pastor said. It can't get that bad. You'll see, there will yet be a way out. Jens Røn has friends. That kind of Christian doesn't abandon people in distress.

He drummed on the table top with his fingers, and Thomas Jensen got the feeling there was something suspicious in the air. There was, as it were, a hidden challenge in the pastor's words. He was actually satisfied; with the task he had, it was best not to become all too friendly beforehand.

No, we'll certainly help him, as best we can, he said frankly.

Oh, I know myself what it is to be in need, the pastor's wife said and smiled to Thomas Jensen. My husband's first post was so small that many times I just plain hid when the butcher came into the yard. The bill had become all too big.

Thomas Jensen cast a glance round at the shiny mahogany furniture. The pastor caught it.

It wasn't actually need—he added with irritation.

No, but one can *imagine* how it is, his wife said. But don't you want to take another piece of pastry? I truly baked them myself.

Thomas Jensen looked at the wife's hands—they were white and well-groomed. This sort of people had, so to speak, different flesh on their bones. He glanced over at the pastor, who sat broad and prosperous, still young with a hint of a stomach and a fresh, almost rosy-red face. No, these people were different creatures. He happened to think about the parsonage back home. Truly there was neither fine furniture nor carpets on the floor, but children and hubbub, and pecuniary distress. Pastor Thomsen was no better off than a simple fisherman. He was one of the friends and a brother in life's struggle for salvation. And he wouldn't invite a freethinker like Kock as a guest. Thomas Jensen felt strong and was itching to provoke the pastor a bit.

Now I certainly hope I didn't interrupt the conversation, he said with a little smile. Because I know that pastor values talking to Kock about learned matters.

No, not at all, the pastor said peevishly.

Absolutely not, the customs official seconded seriously. It was only the latest results of psychic research we were discussing. The most recent curious phenomena— —

Kock preened himself like a turkey-cock. He straightened himself out in the chair and spoke with luminous eyes. Now it had been revealed and would be rumored all around the parish that he had sat all afternoon in the pastor's parlor and discussed learned things. It was the triumph of science and enlightenment. Now it was time—Kock would show how broad his intellect's embrace was.

I don't know anything at all about such matters, Thomas Jensen said. I don't have much of a head for understanding it. But the pastor and you —

Thomas Jensen was humble, but pastor Brink noticed the teasing. He got up and nodded to his wife.

So let the two of us go in and talk together, he said. You'll look in again another time, Mr. Kock.

Confused, the customs official got up. Was he now being banished from paradise and shown the door? His round eyes looked from one to the other. What was the matter? But the riddle was without a solution. He collected the fragments of his dignity and took leave with polite bows. Thomas Jensen followed the pastor into the study, which was filled with books from ceiling to floor. Pastor Brink was a bit insecure. It annoyed him that the fisherman had lumped him together with Kock, who was a half-educated person. Thomas Jensen sat and collected his thoughts for the fight. After all, it was hard to ignore that the man was a clergyman and, despite everything, held a sacred office. That mustn't be forgotten. The truth should be said, but in decorous words.

So what do you have on your heart? Pastor Brink asked.

I wanted to ask you whether anything would prevent Pastor Thomsen from back home from holding a meeting in the church,

Thomas Jensen said. We who come from the West Coast are accustomed to his preaching, and we'd so much like to hear him again.

Pastor Brink walked up and down a couple of times. Here in his own parlor he felt well and could take up the struggle. And the little fisherman looked almost a bit ridiculous in his fine city clothes and with the oversized shirt collar. Now the customs official was out the door, and his wife couldn't say stupid things. Pastor Brink prepared himself for the spiritual battle.

I neither can nor want to forbid you to do it, he said and stopped his pacing. But let's be honest with each other, Thomas Jensen. I dare say I understand where this is leading. You people fetch the sharpest revivalist preacher you can find. If you people had the power, as you have the intention, you'd chase me from my pulpit.

That's not absolutely wrong, the fisherman conceded calmly.

But is it right of you people to sow discord in a parish where people until now have lived in peace and toleration? the pastor said. After all, we know what goes along with envy and rancor and malice on both sides. If you people want a fight, you'll get a fight, and I'll stand with the whole parish and parish council behind me. You people are sowing wind and you'll come to harvest adverse wind. But listen now: when we talked together in the summer, I cautioned you about a spirit of intolerance, and I want to repeat my words. I don't reproach you people for fighting for what to you is a matter of salvation. It pains me to see you people sitting in church and disapproving, so to speak, of every word I say. You people may have your view, but the rest of us must construe the gospel our way. But here's what I want to suggest: isn't it best if you people look for a church somewhere else? South of the fjord they've gotten a Mission pastor. If you people dissolved your obligation to use the services of your parish pastor here, it would, after all, be very easy for you to slip over there every Sunday in a motorboat.

Thomas Jensen shook his head. We Pious shall remain where God has put us, he said. Dissolving obligations to your parish pastor isn't a good thing. We shall remain in the parish and be its salt. I don't want to hide this from you: I believe many souls can be won for the Lord here in the parish.

You don't know the area. The old way of doing things has taken deep root in people's minds.

Then we'll have to fight to get it pulled up.

The clergyman was now standing with his back to the window and was looking at the fisherman. No, truly, the man was not ridiculous. He was lean and sinewy, limber like an animal and with that singularly gentle yet severe face. He was serious about this. He was a leader, unconquerable in gentleness, unbending in severity, smart and bright and refractory. Pastor Brink suddenly felt soft in his bones.

Sit down, Thomas Jensen, he said and he himself took a seat at the writing table. Let's talk like two Christian men. Where does your courage come from? How dare you damn those who think differently?

I damn no one, the fisherman said. I don't even know whether I myself will be damned. I have only one thing to stick to, and that's Jesus's voice in me. I *believe* your teachings lead to damnation. I *know* only one thing: I've experienced mercy and meeting with Jesus. And that's what I'd like all people to attain.

Yes, experience, Pastor Brink said pensively. Naturally I understand you well, but don't you believe I've had my spiritual experiences? You mustn't misunderstand me—I'm not talking about bookish knowledge, which means so little, and what do I know when push comes to shove. I stick my nose a bit in one barrel and a bit in another and sniff the contents, but as a rule one must, after all, rely wholly on others' judgment and guidance. Christianity, the purely personal relationship to God, is the only thing one can't take other peoples' word for. I understand completely the consistency of your view, but you look at it too narrowly. We have our experiences and you have yours. Perhaps we experience God each in a different form.

But I can't know anything about your experiences, I know only my own, and then you forget one thing, repentance, which must also be part and parcel of it. We have to give ourselves up totally to Jesus with life and goods and everything we have. I said before, I don't think what you preach is Christianity, and I stick to that. We have to give up the world.

Christ didn't abandon the world—he took it into his gentle hand. He wasn't some dark man hostile to life. Do you remember the wedding in Canaan where he transformed water into wine.

But on his cross—there he got only a hyssop sponge to drink.

The clergyman got up again and began to pace. He had an awkward feeling that he hadn't completely clinched his point. From childhood he was accustomed to encountering friendliness and understanding. He had been cultivated by his parents, by his wife, by his parish. Yes, the pastor was a sunny person, who thrived in warm weather and obtained his strength from others' confidence. He stopped in front of the fisherman and placed one hand on his shoulder.

So tell me, Thomas Jensen, how did you experience your salvation?

That's a long story, the fisherman answered. There's really not much for others to hear. But for myself it's the most beautiful thing I know. My father strongly opposed the new revival and kept us children away from meetings of the Pious. Yes, I can say that without sorrow because he was saved before he died. I know what it means—I've seen my own brother drift dead onto land, and he was not saved. I was already 25 or 26 years old, and I was a rather capable fellow at getting things done—if I must say so myself. But there were many terrible instincts in me. It was not so much what I did—I was an honest fellow living among decent people—as the terrible things I felt like doing. It kept lying in wait in me; I surely knew it was wrong, but whom should I have talked to about it? Then one evening I'm walking by a brick manufactory, located in the vicinity where I was working at the time. There were crackling fires in the furnace, and I stood a bit and looked into it. First I thought: it must be horrible to be burned to death, and I began shaking. Just suddenly it occurred to me: hell's fire is a thousand times worse, and it burns eternally. It was as if I could see the sinners' torment before me. The sweat burst out of my skin, and I thought: if you die now, you're going there. And suddenly I threw myself on the ground and prayed to Jesus to stand by me. I cried and prayed in the dark with the gleam of the fire before me, and all at once I felt that now Jesus had taken the burden of sin from me. Every time evil came again, I went to the Savior, and he helped me with his wonderful mercy. A short time after I met Alma, who is now my wife, she was also saved. — Yes, since that day, I truly say, I've had only peace and joy in my soul, and I can never be thankful enough for that. You should also walk that way, Pastor Brink! Come to Jesus, Pastor Brink!

Thomas Jensen had talked himself hoarse, and his eyes were filled with a dry and hot luster. The pastor felt at once attracted and repelled by the fanatic glow radiating from the man.

Pastor Brink, Thomas Jensen said. Will you pray together with me?

The clergyman was startled. The man was smart—now he was setting a trap. But he was just as smart and didn't let himself be tricked. No, truly he wouldn't forsake the pious people who relied on *his* preaching and shared his joy of an innocent life and the gospel's joyous message.

When you pray, go into your private closet—he said.

But I want to pray for you, the fisherman answered firmly and gave him a handshake as a farewell.

In the little circle of the Pious there was indeed talk of the meeting with the clergyman. Thomas Jensen gave an account of the whole matter. Now days of struggle were at hand. A letter was sent to Pastor Thomsen, and they waited impatiently for an answer. Finally it came. At the end of January he'd be able to speak. That was a joyful message. Anton Knopper sang hymns lustily. In every house hung a picture of the church back home. It had a frame like a life buoy and was pretty to look at in melancholy times. But now it was as if the church itself was going to come to them.

Winter didn't want to arrive, and it kept raining; frost didn't come, but just black slush and gray crows, which roamed over the fields.

Jens Røn had scraped money together for the house rent—the others helped him as they could, but they had substantial expenditures. The boats had to be repaired and new nets bought for the spring fishing. Money was tight. Jens Røn caught a little with his eel-prong, but it would have been better if there had been ice on the fjord.

Groceries were the worst problem. Jens Røn had to go to the coop manager to ask whether he couldn't be given a little credit until better times came. He entered the store, a bit stooped—it was a distressing errand. The manager was standing behind the counter weighing groats in bags.

What can I do for you, Jens Røn, he said. Come in.

They went into the office, and the manager sat down on his desk chair. On the wall hung a framed sign with the inscription: "Seek ye first the kingdom of God, and his righteousness; and all these things shall be added unto you!" And over the old safe was printed: "Gold and silver belong to the Lord!" It gave Jens Røn more courage and confidence—they were fine words at a difficult time.

The manager leafed through his book and pushed his glasses back on his forehead. You've already got a great deal on your account to begin with, Jens Røn, he said.

Yes, the fisherman admitted. Things had just been terrible with the eel-traps in the fall. But I'll pay all the same if the Lord will give me the least bit of success.

The manager nodded seriously: as such it's a problem to keep giving credit. Before you know it, it has added up, and you know of course that we're not at all *permitted* to do that. No, we truly must not.

No, Jens Røn said dispirited.

And I also don't always believe that you people save the way you should. For example, the other day the children wanted syrup. You people could actually eat your porridge without syrup now that you don't have money, and frugality is a fine virtue.

Jens Røn didn't know what to answer. It was wrong to gorge

themselves on syrup—that was for sure. But it was so easy to offend without giving it a thought.

But the manager was not an unreasonable man. His voice remained friendly and conceded that misfortune could indeed befall anyone. If sureties could just be procured, two good and solid men, he would gladly give Jens Røn credit and trust him. The manager closed the ledger with a snap: naturally there also had to be sureties for the sum that was already owed.

So Jens Røn again had to go to good friends: Lars Bundgaard and Thomas Jensen. They gladly wanted to help, but it was a heavy burden. It became harsher just before Christmas. Some money was raised for a couple of loads of peat, but they had to be economized on, and Tea heated with old fishing nets. The tarred remains of the nets burned up with a puff in a second—it was a lot of toil to maintain the fire. Sometimes the West Coasters came with a little meat, a hen, or two dozen eggs. And they also got coffee. It was Mariane who put a half-pound on the kitchen shelf each time she visited. Yes, Mariane, the gentle heart, she was a consolation in need. She came with salted bacon and clothes for the children and potatoes, and appeared as if nothing were the matter, and always had something new to tell.

Tea reciprocated as best she could. She sought to save Mariane's lost soul and spared no efforts. But Mariane was obstinate. One single time Tea got her to go to a friends' meeting, but during the hymn singing she fell asleep. She had gotten up early and couldn't keep awake no matter how much Tea poked her.

In the meadows the water stood in cold puddles and small lakes. The houses in town stood squeezed together under the heavy sky. From the chimneys peat smoke settled down heavily on the road. Nothing happened—one day went by like the next. The last traps were taken in, and nets were mended again. The nets were green and slimy from algae and grass.

So the men sat bent over the nets, but in the winter it was no fun. The damp weather was oppressive, and it was hard to have the dirty nets in the parlor. But the worst was when you were gnawed by anxieties. And Jens Røn had his cares. He had borrowed and was in debt—he owed both money and thanks; it wasn't easy to see how things would work out. There was no prospect of joyous Christmas festivities. Not that Tea demanded luxuries. But the way the manager treated them was harsh. When Tabita went to the coop for goods, he took the slip of paper she brought along and went through it rigorously. Coffee was out of the question, and so was the fine American flour or a bit of sweets for the children. The manager looked disapprovingly at the slip of paper: "raisins" was written there! Decent people didn't eat raisins with other people's money.

But there were other things they could get. When some flour had become moldy, Tabita got to take it home in her basket. God's gifts should not be wasted, the manager said, and a price reduction was given. It was very distressing, and Tea cried. Other people were standing in the store and heard how they were treated, and it gave them no esteem. A couple of weeks before Christmas Tea became sick and had to lie down.

So Tabita had to take care of the house and prepare the food. The little ones got to know what authority was. Tabita was a sharp homemaker: she scrubbed them before they went to school till they were red with cleanliness; there was no mercy. The littlest ones were full of complaints: she's combing me so hard my head is bleeding, Little-Niels cried, and Tea raised her tired face from the pillow and comforted him.

Tabita was very energetic for fifteen—lean and hardhanded, but upright. She took care of her father with the pride of a housewife when he came home from the fjord in the evening. Almost every day he lay out there in a flat-bottomed sloop and speared eel. He was tired and wet when he came home; the catch wasn't large, but everything had to be taken along. Tabita gave him warm potatoes and salted herring. When the bread she baked wasn't so good, it wasn't Tabita's fault. She couldn't do anything about the fact that the flour was moldy.

Every afternoon Mariane came, and it was as if Tea got a little better. She drank a drop of coffee and listened to Mariane's sharp tongue. Several of the young fellows from town fished with nets out in the islets and lived in a shed, which they had built from planks and peat. But loneliness had made them crazy; they had gotten hold of a bottle of whiskey, and one of them was beaten severely. And there was more: at the inn, two fellows had courted the same girl, and had come to blows. But the girl had fallen down foaming at the mouth in convulsions. Now she was lying in the hospital and was wild. Laurine was her name and she was from the eastern fens.

Tea also had her piece to say: it was unchastity that avenged itself—you'd see. But Mariane didn't think it was so wrong—sickness could befall anyone. Mariane laughed and couldn't restrain herself: now you're lying there yourself! Tea's eyes became dull—that was something else. She realized she couldn't be charged with that kind of thing. And sickness of course could also come in a natural way. Mariane groused: Yes, yes, that goes without saying. But surely convulsions can also be natural enough when the fellows stand and quarrel over you! Tea couldn't discuss that and said briefly: Sin and unchastity—you can't call them natural: they're just evil nature.

Anton Knopper also came to visit and brought along gifts. He blushed when he saw Tea lying prettily in her blond-laced night-gown. After all, he was a bachelor and in a state of innocence. Tea noticed it, and that tickled her a bit, but naturally it wasn't right to have those kinds of thoughts. Anton Knopper had bought coffee cake and was embarrassed about being a benefactor. He took Niels in his arms and wrestled with him. The boy was jubilant when Anton swung him.

But the evenings, when Malene and Alma had time to come in, were the best times. The air in the little bedroom was heavy and sultry, but they sat there a few hours and sang hymns by Tea's bed. Alma's voice was beautiful to hear, and she spoke the words so cautiously—she had city diction. And together they talked about how things would be when Pastor Thomsen came. Would the district listen to his admonishing voice? It gave Tea relief to think about the great time that was to dawn. In the parlor the children sat under the hanging lamp and read lessons until it buzzed—verse, tables by rote, and dates. Little-Niels lay in his bed and didn't want to sleep with all that conviviality—he chirped the hymns in his feeble bird's voice.

Christmas eve it rained like on a day in November. In the church the saved and the nonbelievers sat side by side on the yellow benches. It smelled damp and musty from wet clothes. Old people had crept out of the nooks once again to hear the Christmas gospel in the full, illuminated church, and the children sat with astonishment in their eyes and looked at the many lights, which flickered consecutively.

Povl Vrist and Mariane had come to church and sung to their hearts' content, and now it was apparent that Mariane sure enough could sing hymns when it mattered. But the Pious kept to the back rows of benches and looked with dark glances at the farmers and their wives in substantial festive attire. It wasn't good that the old-fashioned difference in social status was preserved in God's house. The clergyman's sermon was like everything else—it refreshed no one.

Tea had gotten up from her couch a few days before Christmas. She wasn't well, but she couldn't keep lying and not care about anything when baking had to be done and things had to be prepared for the festivities. In any case it had to be clean, and now she knew it was done thoroughly.

Outside the church people were standing and wishing one another a blessed Christmas before they tramped home in small clusters. Warmth and peace radiated from all the windows; no young people were making noise in the road—they were sitting round the table in snug parlors. At Jens Røn's they were able to afford the stump of a spruce, and Tabita had made baskets out of coffee bags—they looked fine and were filled with spice-nuts. Mariane had come with a basket with all manner of magnificent things, and even the coop manager had softened Christmas. With gentle gestures he had put a bag of bonbons in a basket for Tabita, but Tabita wasn't the kind to mince her words; she put the cornet back on the counter again. What, the manager said, are you perhaps too high and mighty to eat candy? No, Tabita whined in her young girl's voice, but we don't want any gifts here! Tea had the joy in her misery that her children knew how to appear with dignity in the right places.

While the food was sitting and purring on the kitchen range, Tea got a chance to run up to Laust Sand's. It was dark in the parlor, and Laust was sitting by the window and staring out. You're sitting alone, Tea said, don't you want to turn the light on? No, Laust Sand answered. After all, you can see enough to think.

Tea went out into the kitchen. It was apparent that Laust Sand had fallen into melancholy. Adolfine was standing over the fire in the range and her cheeks had gotten a bit red.

You two weren't in church, were you? Tea asked. I couldn't catch sight of you.

No, Adolfine answered. We just didn't really seem to feel like it.

I didn't think generally you had to feel like hearing God's word, Tea sighed and looked humbly at the floor.

You know, it can just take hold of you, Adolfine said calmly.

Just as long as there's nothing wrong with you two, Tea said.

Adolfine turned quickly from the range and looked Tea in the eyes.

What might that be? she asked.

Well, at home you two wouldn't not have gone to church Christmas eve. Even if he's an unbelieving clergyman, we must still seek God's house. It's as if you two are about to separate yourselves off from the rest of us.

But Adolfine was busy again, occupied with stirring the pot.

Yes, yes, Adolfine, Tea said. Well, otherwise I just wanted to hear if one of you had become sick or there was something else wrong.

Jens Røn was all cleaned up and had gotten his beard clipped: he looked dignified in his nice black clothing. In his cautious voice he read the gospel aloud before they sat down at the table, and the prayer this evening was especially long and heartfelt. But then they sat around the table. The children were solemn—Tabita had washed them until they were red-streaked with cleanliness.

The tree was lit; it wasn't big—the whole display could be in a flower pot. There was of course no way for there to be gifts, but Tea and the children still had a surprise in reserve. A pipe for Jens Røn, a little cutty, but with room for much tobacco. She and the children had saved up for it, setting aside øre after øre of the scarce money that had come into the house. Jens Røn was glad and moved and made a din, and sucked persistently to test whether there was a draft. Indeed, there was a terrific draft—he had never had the likes of this pipe.

Tea got out the hymnbooks, and they sat down to sing while the lights slowly burned down. They heard Christmas hymns from all the houses. The whole town sang. Yes, of course, Tea thought bitterly, the one time of year people turned toward heaven, but otherwise they had a hard time finding the way of the cross. There wasn't much strength in this religion—it lulled the conscience to sleep: Tea knew that for certain.

When the lamp had to be relit, it turned out all the petroleum was used up—there wasn't a drop in the house. Tea clasped her hands and burst into complaints—were they now supposed to sit in the dark this holy evening? They could of course go and borrow from one of the neighbors, Jens Røn suggested, but no, Tea said, she wouldn't do it for everything in this world—such shame would be unbearable.

Yes, Jens Røn observed, what about borrowing a bottle of petroleum.

No, Tea complained. Then they'd have that to talk about—that I'm so slovenly I can't even have that in my head. After all, she still had a bit of pride.

One Christmas light remained in the box, and it was carefully lit and placed on the table. Everything in the parlor cast deep, dark shadows, and the faces were illuminated in an oddly unreal game. The children were busy with spice-nuts, and Martin put out his hand: Even or odd. Little-Niels pondered, but finally said even. Then you lose, Martin said, because it's five.

Frightened, Jens Røn turned toward them: What are you doing? he said. That will never do—to be playing games on the eve of a holy day. Stop it.

A bit embarrassed, Martin pocketed the spice-nuts, and Tea added:

No, you must promise me, Martin, that you'll stay away from games no matter how innocent it looks.

And Tea recalled from what she had learned as a child the story about the girl who spun one Christmas day and saw a bloody hand outside the window, while a ferocious voice sang:

There you see what I won,
because Christmas day I spun.

Little-Niels looked anxiously toward the window and crept close to his mother. But if we just stick to God's grace, then nothing can happen, Tea consoled them.

When the light had gone out in a smoldering wick, Tea drew the curtain back from the windows. It had stopped raining, and the sky was clear with luminous stars. Jens Røn took Niels on his lap and explained to him about the child Jesus, who had been placed in a manger out in a country far away. And the three kings and the shepherds from the field had come to the place, guided by the star Our Lord had placed in heaven. The boy pointed toward the blue night sky and asked: Where's it now, father? It's not there anymore, Jens Røn answered. Because now our savior has gone to heaven again.

But Tea spoke and explained that the star of Bethlehem still shone for sinful souls. Tea's voice became tender when she talked about sacred matters, and she wasn't far from tears. But the children were to have good words on festive occasions so they wouldn't become heathen. The little ones sat snugly on Jens Røn's knee, and the big ones, Martin and Tabita, listened on the bench. In the oven the peat embers glowed, and Tea's heart became gentle and good: if you were so poor that life was wretched, there was still a wealth that was not of this world.

There was a cautious knock at the door. Tea opened and it

was Anton Knopper. He had been at Lars Bundgaard's, but wanted to look in and wish them merry Christmas.

But why are you all sitting in the dark? he asked. I almost thought you had gone to bed.

We're sitting and looking for the star of Bethlehem, Niels jabbered. Can you find it, Anton Knopper?

Anton Knopper became pensive. Yes, that star—it's easy to recognize it, he said. And astonished he jabbed Tea in the side. That boy had real talents, and thus spoke God through the voice of the innocent.

Embarrassed, Tea explained that they lacked petroleum and were reluctant to borrow any, but if she put peat on the fire, they could have coffee.

Coffee was made, and Anton Knopper sat quietly and looked at the weak light from the oven. The children chatted very softly, outside lay the night, and there was a special holiday occasion in the dark parlor.

Yes, the world is beautiful, he said suddenly.

— Christmas was rainy and foggy, there was slush for days when it was best to be indoors. Furthermore, they were, after all, holidays, and when you'd been in church, it was surely not appropriate to go visiting. In dark clothes you sat around the table and had nothing to do. Only Anton Knopper, who didn't own a home, wandered out. And he brought along variety. Although you ought to be serious on solemn occasions, he had a hard time restraining himself, tumbled with the children, and was full of fun. Tabita shook her head and imitated Tea; he was just too superficial, that Anton Knopper.

But Jens Røn had time to borrow newspapers and sat with his glasses in front of his nose reading. He also looked through the children's school books—it was good to recall the knowledge of his youth. Much was forgotten and passed away during expeditions on land and sea. But the biggest reader was Povl Vrist. He had many books and sat and absorbed wisdom about everything in the world. When old teacher Aaby came to visit, he was fire and flame—for example the inquisition: that was shameful the way they treated people—broke them on the wheel and burned them alive. Was that really true?

Indeed, teacher Aaby nodded. That's the way people were back then; in the meantime, the world had progressed.

I just about go crazy when I read that kind of thing, Povl Vrist said. Beating people to death—I can understand that; but torturing people alive. —

You shouldn't read so much, Aaby said. Nothing good comes of it.

Those are odd words for a school teacher, Povl Vrist said and laughed. You yourself have read all books imaginable.

Aaby shook his head sadly. But I've had to seek the truth elsewhere, he said.

Povl Vrist didn't reply, but after a pause he raised a different question. He didn't want to talk about religion. He had his views and others had theirs, but they could nevertheless be good friends and keep the peace. But as soon as the Christmas holidays were over, Vrist breathed free and went to work again. He had a lot to do—fishing would start up in the spring! Povl Vrist loved the work and the navigating, and he was lucky. From morning until evening he toiled with the netting for the spring fishing and fastened stones and cork to the big seine nets. Often Mariane helped out. Things were so easy when she sat with him in the shed. She had gotten a petroleum oven out there to warm it up. Mariane was thoughtful.

Anton Knopper was also industrious, but he made time to talk to people. He did what he could to make people familiar with the big event that was imminent. It was a meeting where everyone was to come and get profit for the soul. Anton Knopper was not himself a man of the word and couldn't win souls for the Lord. But what he was able to do he did. For example, there was that Katrine, the servant girl from the hotel. Anton Knopper began stammering when she was at the baker's for bread, and they chatted. She had a silver cross on a necklace around her neck, and that was a good sign. But Anton Knopper couldn't help looking a lot at the cross, which rested securely on her full breasts. He became breathless and red when her breast heaved and sank. Didn't Katrine think it was nice that brighter days were coming? Yes, the girl gladly admitted it. Then Anton Knopper broached more serious matters: Wasn't that dancing at the inn completely terrible? After Christmas they were again dancing Saturdays. But Katrine turned up her nose and her voice became a bit harsh: there's nothing wrong with it.

Yes, yes, Anton Knopper said. Maybe some day you'll change your mind. I believe you're a decent girl.

Katrine went off after a brief good-bye and was insulted. There was no hiding her firm round legs under the short skirt. Anton Knopper threw himself headlong into the worst work he could find so he wouldn't go astray. Oh, the world was full of dangers and the night of odd dreams.

But finally Pastor Thomsen came. The last days had gone by in excitement and with breathless preparations. He was to live in Lars Bundgaard's new house, where there was a guestroom, but everyone wanted to have him for a meal or at least a cup of coffee. Thomas Jensen arranged everything so no one felt offended or slighted. Pastor Brink had announced after the service on Sunday that the meeting would be held. Tea listened carefully to his voice, but there was nothing special to notice about him. He knew how to control himself. Small placards were posted on the telephone poles all over the parish. The coop manager had written them in an elegant hand. Everyone did his part. Thomas Jensen and Lars Bundgaard went door to door among all the common people and day laborers during the final weeks. They talked about the wind and weather, about parish politics and wages and finally broached the subject of the meeting, which was about to be held. Didn't the people want to come? It didn't cost anything, and Thomsen was a fine preacher, who knew how to find the way to people's souls. The little people in the parish weren't used to being straight out invited. Many promised to come.

All the West Coasters were assembled on the wharf. Thomas Jensen fetched the visitor in a motorboat in one of the fjord towns—it was a couple of hours' sailing, but easier than a land trip. They were solemn and anxious—after all, he was the first person from back home who had come to visit here in the new place. Finally the motorboat came into sight. The pastor sat in the stern next to Thomas Jensen. When he caught sight of the men on the wharf, he waved his hat.

Kresten Thomsen was a broad-shouldered, square-built man. He had a vigorous dark mustache and intelligent, sharp eyes in a weather-beaten, round face. His voice was deep and resounding—with a smack like that of a sergeant commanding his people. His hands were large and hairy, and hair grew out of his nose and ears. His clothes were coarse and of a simple cut, and he had awkward heavy boots. He resembled more a cutter commander or fish merchant than a pastor. The people shook hands with him and didn't say much. But an odd sense of security came over them.

Up at Lars Bundgaard's the rooms were full of women and children. When Pastor Thomsen tramped in it was like a trumpet fanfare. He greeted every single person and hadn't forgotten anyone; even the children he still recognized by name. Indeed, that's the way he was! There was nothing too slight for him to be interested in. How had the fishing been? How was the district and were they well? Then he too had to tell how things stood back home. His oldest son had gone to Latin school and was well-behaved. In the parish everything was as it had been—after all, they knew from letters what had happened. They felt like one big family! Intellectually, Kresten Thomsen was their superior; he was their pastor and spiritual guide, but he was one of their own. Together with them he lived their lives and let them participate in his; he was just as poor with all the children the Lord had bestowed on him, and just as rich in faith. It was as if a dear relative was visiting them. He looked in to see Lars Bundgaard's smallest boy, who lay asleep in the old wicker cradle. He liked children and smiled at the little red face. In the parlor he had two of the smallest ones on his lap. Tea's heart swelled with joy—one of them was Niels. The pastor talked and asked many questions. Thomas Jensen said Pastor Brink had hinted that it was surely proper for the guest to stay at his house. But Thomas Jensen had thought — Yes, the pastor interrupted. To be blunt about it, I didn't really come so much to visit him.

He used the familiar form of address with the men, and they spoke to him with a peculiarly submissive cordiality. His intimacy was not to be misused.

But where's Povl Vrist? the pastor asked and looked around. He lives here too—is he perhaps sick?

There was a small silence, and they looked down at the floor.

Yes, he isn't among God's children, Thomas Jensen finally said. He's probably decided he doesn't want to be present at such an occasion.

The pastor's face suddenly became serious. He nodded and didn't discuss the matter further.

They drank coffee, and the pastor inquired into the state of the spirit here in the parish. There was enough to tell. It was mostly Thomas Jensen and Lars Bundgaard who were the spokesmen, and the women were reserved. It wasn't appropriate for them to be outspoken here at such a serious moment. But Tea couldn't restrain herself. In her finest voice she called attention to the fact that the inn and dancing were the worst things. Pastor Thomsen listened carefully. His face was dark and thoughtful. He caught every word that was said to draw a picture of the place he had come to. Were there many large farmers? No, they didn't exactly have so much land, but many of them owned old prosperous farms. But there were a good many little people out in the fens, and in town itself there were fishermen, craftsmen, day laborers, and small agriculturists. The pastor cleared his throat like a horse neighing. In his estimation there were good prospects for the Lord's cause.

But you people must be the leavening, he said. The point is there has to be someone who goes ahead and stops again. You have to keep trying and keep trying and remember that it's the drop that hollows out the stone. He gave them good, prudent advice, while they listened devotedly and breathlessly. It was the Lord's time. Outside it was about to get dark, but no one thought about putting on the lights.

Malene was busy in the kitchen, and the women were out giving her a helping hand. But now and then they had to go in to hear the men's words. Now Malene came and asked everyone to the table. Pastor Thomsen folded his hands and said grace with a resounding voice. He ate heartily. They didn't talk much at the table, but there was a tranquil, warm exaltation of the spirit. It was just like communion in the old church back home. Not only was the pastor a fine person, so good-tempered and straightforward, but you perceived that God's spirit had taken up residence in him.

They accompanied the pastor to the church in the dark, muddy evening. Thomas Jensen was anxious. What if people didn't come—what if they had done their work badly? So much depended on this evening; so much was at stake for saving souls. But on the way to the church they met people in clusters, and when they entered the illuminated room, it was already half full. The Pious sat in the front pews, where the best seats were. It was as if the local people felt uncertain and preferred to distance themselves a bit. Joyously Tea felt the time had now come. Now it was God's friends who sat with humble spirits under the pulpit, while the unbelievers hid in the corners.

Little by little the church was filled to the last seat. Many had to stand up all the way in the back near the door. Thomas Jensen turned around and looked out over the assembly while the introit was being sung. They were altogether people he knew. First, the little troop of the Pious with bright, expectant expressions. Then all the people he and Lars Bundgaard had visited. They were sitting a bit subdued and didn't really know what to think. There weren't many farmers—no, that was to be expected. Only few of their wives. And you didn't see much of the young people either. But in the last row he caught a glimpse of Pastor Brink. Indeed, he too could truly benefit from a word that spoke to the soul.

When the hymn singing stopped, the church became quiet. The light in the ceiling chandeliers cast flickering shadows on the white calked walls, and the high vaults over the choir lay in darkness. During the singing the pastor had knelt before the altar; now he stood in the pulpit, charged with strength and dangerous in his black robe. For a moment he stared down in the church without moving. His eyes glided from one person to the next. In a special way it intensified the mood. People lowered their heads under his sharp gaze. The stillness lasted and lasted; no one dared move—it felt as if a crash of thunder had to come now and tear everything down.

But when he finally began to speak, it was in a very soft, almost gentle voice. It relaxed the tense mood in an all too violent way. His words penetrated into the furthest corner, and people felt painfully uncertain. He talked about peace in Jesus; the West Coasters sat with open, ecstatic eyes and followed along. Indeed, that was the truth—that's what grace was: an infinite peace, a brotherhood between God and humans. Tea felt the tears running down her cheeks; she hadn't felt so happy and warm in her heart since she had come from home on the West Coast.

Imperceptibly the pastor's voice rose. Now he spoke of human nature's deceit and evil. It was schnapps with a bite. The women sat with downcast eyes and felt a horror when he got hold of unchastity. The pastor knew all about every secret instinct, every hidden and shameless longing in the depths of the soul. He placed a mirror in front of honest people where they saw themselves in a hideously distorted form, and the devil stood behind them and laughed. In a thunderous voice he went through the litany: drinking, dance, card playing, atheism, adultery—he raised his clenched fists as if to smash the pulpit to pieces, but instead of a roar he whispered: *Hell*. The word took on a strange sinisterness. A woman gave a choked shriek. And now he began inveighing in a voice that resounded and echoed from the vaults. He whipped the people with storms of brimstone and fire. His roaring eloquence struck the people in the head as if with axes. With cunning craftiness he bored an awl in where it hurt most. He drove them together into a collective feeling like frightened sheep in a storm. The women wailed quietly or cried. The men sat with fixed stares and rocked restlessly back and forth. He had them in his power. He conjured with them like a sorcerer until they no longer had any will or understanding and had completely forgotten who they were. The Pious were totally transported into excitation. Tea's face was red, her eyes half closed, and her mouth open. Anton Knopper sweated so much the water poured down onto his face. Adolfine squeezed her thin hands; her mouth was distorted as if she wanted to scream. Each of them felt the horror and elevation as a shaking in his soul. Never had the pastor spoken as he did this evening. Never had the Almighty's spirit thundered with such force from his lips. With a roaring incantation, which made the air quiver, the pastor abruptly stopped. You heard the women's sobbing and the men's dry clearing of their throats. Deep groans rose from distressed hearts. The white room with the flickering stearine candles floated off in the fog. Shaken and breathless, but with a certain sharp joy in their spirits, the people waited to see what would happen.

But now the pastor stood tranquil and mild in speech and spoke of mercy and peace in Jesus. Repent and come to Jesus! He spoke in plain, almost simple-hearted words and called on each of the listeners as an equal and brother. After the collective horror came the feeling of collective happiness and peace.

When the closing hymn resounded through the church there was an elevation in the sound. The familiar words had become new and gotten a special meaning.

Little by little the church emptied out. People didn't look at one another—it was as if they were a bit ashamed. But here and there one or two remained sitting with heads bowed. They were people who had now decided to seek God. The pastor talked to them one after the other. His face had taken on its usual tranquil expression; he gave them a bold handshake and some good advice. Thomas Jensen sat in his seat and carefully noticed who it was. It was surely prudent to talk to them in the next few days.

The sexton was already putting out the lights, and the pastor had put his overcoat on. The other West Coasters had gone ahead. Only Thomas Jensen was waiting.

Well, Thomas, the pastor said and tapped him on the shoulder.

That was a beautiful experience, the fisherman said. I believe it will have great importance here in the area. And for myself I want to say thank you, Thomsen. That was the most edifying sermon I reckon I've heard.

They walked out through the door to the porch. Pastor Brink sat on the bench and waited. He got up, a bit embarrassed, and said who he was.

I thought I'd say hello to you, he said. I don't know whether you feel like coming along to the parsonage. My wife is prepared.

Thanks, Pastor Thomsen replied. But I'm always in the habit of living with friends. Surely you understand—they're my old parish children, and we have a lot to talk about.

There was a little pause. Pastor Brink stood as if he had more to say, but just couldn't figure out how to begin. It was half dark in the porch. Outside you saw the clouds drifting and a glimpse of a yellow, floating moon. The Mission pastor waited without saying a word.

I'll walk on ahead, Thomas Jensen said, who felt the tension.

Inner protest was about to make Pastor Brink burst. He had a dream about mastering his listeners and leading them according to his will. Elevate them to salvation and sling them into the deep. Possess the power of the spirit. But what was he compared to the fire-brand standing before him and resembling the common man worn down by toil. No, he didn't have the ability to seize the purely primitive element in people. But, on the other hand, a certain integrity, intellectual and religious, a human and Christian cautiousness also had to be required. This stuff here had simply been violence.

Pastor Thomsen had quickly taken the man's measure. *He* was not created to be a force in the Lord's hand. And purely instinctively he felt an intense aversion toward him. Vague and weak, pretty clothes and white hands and an educated tongue in his mouth. Automatically Pastor Thomsen made his manner still gruffer, his language more coarse and boorish.

Yes, excuse me, it's perhaps somewhat intrusive, Pastor Brink said. But I think I wanted to thank you for your testimony. As you know, I'm part of a broader movement, but your words also gave me something—in any case, you taught me to understand the valuable religious power in your preaching. But—

But? Pastor Thomsen asked when he fell silent.

I'm a bit afraid of the violent suggestive pressure you put on your listeners, Pastor Brink explained a bit insecurely. The consequences can easily become dangerous, it seems to me.

Suggestive pressure, Kresten Thomsen said snappishly. You must remember, Pastor Brink, I'm a simple man. I call God God and the devil by his name. That's what I know.

Pastor Brink cleared his throat nervously and didn't know what to reply. But without saying a word, Pastor Thomsen took him by the shoulder and pulled him to the church door. He pointed up toward the altar where the candles were still lit.

Look, he said sternly. Jesus is hanging there on his cross. You're his priest! That's what I have to say to you.

Pastor Brink stood for a moment and stared into the half-dark church. He wanted to say something, but Thomsen turned his back to him with a brief good night and found Thomas Jensen out near the churchyard wicket.

They walked through town without talking. The pastor was tired, and Thomas Jensen dared not disturb him. Even though there were many things he would gladly have heard his counsel on.


Pastor Thomsen was a morning man. He liked the first hours of the day, when the world lay in all its fresh magnificence. He was standing half naked and shaving himself in the narrow guest-room. Off to the side he heard Malene setting the table. He did his morning gymnastics, saw the floor planks rock, and splashed cold water over his muscular, hairy body. Often he had a burning need to throw himself into hard, manual labor. But that wasn't possible—a pastor was a man of the spirit and could neither thresh grain nor play leapfrog; Pastor Thomsen sincerely felt the seriousness and responsibility of his calling and made do with morning gymnastics.

He talked for a few hours in the morning with Thomas

Jensen and gave good advice; he was a smart man—Thomas Jensen had to attest to that heartily. After they had discussed conditions in the area, and no one had been forgotten, the pastor asked about the children. He wanted to see them before he left. The biggest ones were in school, but the three little ones came in, and the pastor remembered them as well. Alma was proud and beaming.

Then he went to visit Laust Sand. Laust was pale and grief-worn as never before, and Adolfine, frightened, kept in the background. But she had always been shy. The pastor looked searchingly at the fisherman and knitted his brows.

There's something wrong with you, Laust, he said.

Laust Sand sighed, but couldn't get a word past his lips.

You should lighten your heart to Jesus, the pastor admonished.

I've gone so far I scarcely believe it would be of any use, Laust Sand whispered.

The pastor rose from the chair and went over to him.

Those are almost blasphemous words, he said seriously. You've surely forgotten about the thief on the cross. You can't have such grave temptations that Jesus can't take them from you. His mercy is infinite. If Jesus can carry all the world's sins, he can also take yours.

Laust Sand lifted his desperate face toward the pastor. It's the devil who's gotten into me! he said hoarsely.

Surprised, the pastor stepped back a step, but didn't get time to answer. Adolfine sank on to the floor without a sound.

But in Jesus's name, he burst out terrified. Laust Sand, you mustn't say such things—you're going to take your daughter's life. Hurry up and get hold of one of the neighbor women.

Laust Sand ran, and the pastor lifted the lifeless form up onto the sofa. After he had struggled with her a bit and loosened her bodice, she opened her eyes.

Oh, can't you help, can't you help? she moaned.

Little child, the pastor answered uneasily, Jesus can help. Show Laust the way! Pray for him! Stick to Jesus until he helps...

Laust came with a few women, who got the girl into bed. The pastor left, and Laust followed him to the door.

I want to give you some advice, Laust, he said. Whatever doubts and temptations you may have to endure, you must not shut yourself off. Talk to God's other children about it. Otherwise it will gnaw deeper and deeper, and one day it will undermine your whole soul. And pray! pray! pray! as long as you have a word in your mouth.

The pastor walked on into the damp, misty day. Laust Sand had a gloomy and difficult disposition. But there was no way other than prayer, no hope other than mercy. At Lars Bundgaard's he got lunch and visited Tea and Jens Røn. Tea had been festively dressed since morning, and when Jens wanted to go out and work on the nets, she was opposed. Wasn't he ashamed? Didn't he have any feelings? Wasn't it a holiday when their old pastor came to visit? Jens Røn washed himself and sat in white shirt-sleeves at the long table and waited. All the children had been kept home from school. There was one thing they were not to do without: to see a real man of God with their own eyes. And Aaby would surely bear with it. They sat with their books and playthings and made the time pass. Tea had the coffee pot boiling. The pastor should surely get to eat something in the house of good friends. And ahead of time she had baked the pastry she knew he cared for.

Tabita kept watch outside on the road and had turned blue from the cold in her thin cloak.

He's there now, she said and came running in.

Tea got busy smoothing her hair and cast a quick glance around in the parlor. Indeed, everything was in order.

Hurry up and get your jacket on, Jens! she said. And be polite, children, so the pastor can see you're well-behaved.

When the pastor knocked on the door, Tea's face was sheer joy and bliss. Her voice had an affectionate little undertone when she showed him the rooms and explained how they were doing. Jens Røn didn't say much. He walked behind them and was surprised by Tea's oratorical talents; he was truly not so talented. While they drank coffee the pastor made detailed inquiries into their conditions. Tea said how things were, that their conditions were humble, but she also managed to declare that when Jesus was just in people's hearts, life was nothing but joy. Indeed, Pastor Thomsen said smiling. But on the other hand there was also no harm in having food. Then the conversation naturally turned to God's kingdom and its progress.

Now don't be too zealous, the pastor said gently. That wasn't a word Tea liked. It almost seems to me I must say you can hardly be zealous enough in this matter. Yes, yes, the pastor nodded; it wasn't to be understood in that way, but you had to be hard on yourself. It wouldn't do to frighten the doubters with harshness. Gentleness and unyieldingness have to go hand in hand, and everything in its time.

Tea bowed her head and felt a little uncertain. If the pastor meant that she exaggerated and judged, then she was an unhappy woman. Because Tea was conscious that she never bore malice toward anyone except for Jesus's sake. But the pastor reassured her.

I know you are believers, he said. I don't mean anything bad when I say that. But if our belief is to prevail, there is first and foremost one person who can be an instrument, and that's Thomas Jensen. I said that to Lars Bundgaard, and I say to you that you mustn't do anything without hearing his advice. There can very easily arise dissension and unrest if one person doesn't hold the reins. So long as you don't have a believing pastor in the parish, you must regard Thomas Jensen as the Lord's servant, and just rely on him. You see, we Pious can do that because we're like brothers and sisters and don't strive to rule over one another.

Yes, Tea said meekly, and bowed her head. Thomas Jensen is by far the smartest one among us, and he has Alma at his side, and she is also a capable and sensible woman.

That's the way Tea was: she could see others' virtues; in no way did she slander anyone. But there was one thing she urgently wanted to ask of him. It was perhaps all too much and couldn't be done, but the matter rested heavily on her heart. Whether the pastor couldn't speak just a single little word to

Mariane. And Tea explained straight out the way Mariane was. A person with a good heart, so helpful and good-tempered, but a heathen and scoffer, and it was hard to accept she might be lost. And she held Povl Vrist back so he didn't join in his heart with his compatriots either in his belief or anything else.

Certainly, the pastor answered. That's very good of you, Tea, that you nurture such concern for good friends. And I had already decided to look in on Povl Vrist. I knew him when he was a boy. He was a well-behaved fellow, but left home early and went out to dangerous shores. But we shall talk together, Mariane and I.

Tea felt heartily glad about the assurance. Now Mariane would get to feel after all that people existed who were smarter than she was. Tea felt like asking whether she might go along—but that wouldn't do. Yes, if Mariane's self-confidence were shaken—that would be a joy. Together they should extol and sing praises if she found peace.

The pastor said good-bye and left. Tea had tears in her eyes when the garden gate slammed shut after him. He was some pastor! Plain and friendly and with a word of consolation to whoever was in need. But also the sharp admonition to those who needed it. And he had drunk two cups of coffee and eaten her cakes with honest pleasure. Oh, it would surely be a long time before she had such an hour of joy again. And suddenly their poverty and misfortune stood before her like a threatening specter. She sat down and wept.

But Tea, Tea, Jens Røn said surprised.

Oh, we're miserable, she cried. What will it come to? You'll see, Jens, we'll end in the poorhouse, and no one will take notice of us any more. No, I had never thought we'd face such hard times.

Conscious of his guilt, Jens Røn bowed his angular head. After all, it was his fault. He had no luck. He was an inferior worker, who couldn't provide his family with food. The children sat quietly and dispirited. Now Little-Niels said in his slow child's voice:

You shouldn't cry, mother. We can talk to Jesus.

Tea raised her tear-moistened face and again heard the voice and truth of providence from the mouth of the innocent. Yes, there was Jesus! Of what importance were daily bread and livelihood in the short time of earthly life. Outside waited bliss on eternity's shores.

—In Anton Knopper's simple bachelor's lodgings there was only a chair and a bed. The pastor sat down on the uncomfortable chair, and Anton sat on the bed, where he sank down deep into the soft, heavy eiderdown. He was uneasy in his heart and didn't really know how to begin the conversation. But the pastor went right to the point:

So tell me, Anton Knopper, how are you doing with the temptations of the flesh?

Anton Knopper turned red as blood. The pastor was a smart man. No one could resist him. He looked into your heart and knew your most secret thoughts.

Yes, to be blunt, he said unwarily, I have many temptations, and I barely know what will become of it. I'm a bad one for thinking about womenfolk even if I watch out as carefully as I can. And when I dream, evil sneaks into my dreams. I'd be mighty glad if I could get some advice. It's not easy for an uneducated man to know what to do.

You must not yield to sin, the pastor said. That's the first and most important thing to remember. You mustn't even *think* impurely—it's the same as adultery...

No, Anton Knopper replied and cast his glance down. But I can say that with a good conscience. I haven't even once approached a woman in my life—and I'll soon be in my forties. And I watch out for my thoughts as far as I can.

Anton Knopper—it's foolish that you don't get married. Remember what Paul says about marriage. And marriage isn't just a makeshift—it's pleasing to God. You must get married and put children in the world, Anton, and you should have done that long ago.

That's true enough, but it's as if it gets harder every year that passes. I can downright start shaking when womenfolk come near me. Often my good senses shut down entirely. Surely I've become too old—that kind of thing should be done when you're young and more forward and straight on. But I want to be completely honest with you, Pastor Thomsen. I'm afraid: there's a young woman here in town I've certainly been looking at a lot.

Is she saved, the pastor asked.

No, unfortunately I have to say she isn't.

So in any case one thing is clear: You must first lead her to Jesus. Nothing good can come of marriage between God's children and the unbelievers. In that case marriage isn't at all what it was supposed to be. But there are also plenty of good, pious women. We Pious mustn't care too much about all that stuff about falling in love and love. Pray to God and ask his advice and take things the way he will have them, then he'll certainly take care of earthly love.

Yes, that's true, Anton Knopper said. I'll also lay the matter on Jesus. Then it will go the way it should.

Anton Knopper followed the pastor to Povl Vrist's house. They said good-bye at the garden gate, and the pastor knocked on the door. Povl Vrist had seen him from the shed and came, a bit embarrassed, and was welcoming him just as Mariane opened the door.

Good morning, Povl Vrist, Pastor Thomsen said. I just thought I'd look in on you since I'd come here to town. So, that's your wife—I can imagine. . .

He measured Mariane with a quick glance of appraisal. She was indeed an industrious woman and a hard flint—good Tea had certainly not gotten that wrong. She was standing with bare arms, and her cheeks were red and heated. She had just come from the washtub.

I don't want to disturb you, he said, when they had come into the drawing room, where everything was clean and tidy. But on the other hand—I come with greetings from Povl Vrist's kin, both from your sister and your aunt. Indeed, you of course know that Mama Vrist has grown old, and she's actually doing rather poorly. But she's a pious, old woman who knows the path to her savior and steadily walks that path.

Mariane had quickly slipped out and came back wearing a

black dress and with her hair arranged. She sat down a little apart from the men and listened with a vigilant expression around her mouth. Povl Vrist had got going and asked eagerly about people in the old parish. Mariane was out for a moment to make coffee and set the table. The pastor talked constantly; his deep monotone voice sounded like a rolling wheel on a road. Mariane didn't trust him much. He had surely come here for one thing, and in a bit he'd certainly come out with it in all seriousness. But so what: she wasn't some kind of mouse either—she was aware of that. After they had drunk the coffee, there was a little pause. Here it comes, Mariane thought and was ready.

You weren't at the meeting yesterday evening? the pastor asked.

Yes we were, Povl Vrist cautiously assured him. They'd been there, but there was so little room, and they had just barely gotten seats in the back row. Yes, yes, they were there—that was for sure.

The pastor calmly looked at Povl Vrist, and when he came to a standstill, he was silent for a long time. Only the clockwork's composed ticking could be heard. The pastor sat completely quietly and looked from one to the other. Povl Vrist nervously scratched his stubby chin. But Mariane stared immovably in front of her with just the faintest glimmer of a little smile at the corner of her mouth. The pastor got up and went over to her at the window.

Give your heart to Jesus, Mariane! he said firmly.

No, I won't do it!

She had also gotten up and they were standing face to face. Mariane was half a head taller than the pastor, but otherwise they were a good match. Well built, solid, with healthy, strong faces and the same refractory glow in their eyes.

Then you'll be lost, the pastor said darkly.

There are many who are lost if things happen the way you people say they do, Mariane answered. And if others can survive it, surely I can too.

The pastor stared her in the eyes sharply for a minute. He felt the need to take the intractable woman in his farmer-hands and squeeze her until she screamed. The clock struck—it gave Povl Vrist a start—but Mariane stared again obstinately. With heavy steps the pastor walked back and sat down on his chair.

Now I want to tell you two something, he said: You should think about the fact that the time will come when you'll have use for Jesus. But it may be that he won't have use for you. It may be you're such big people you take no account of a miserable Mission pastor's word. I've seen people just as rigid sigh and complain that they didn't yield when the time had come. Perhaps you don't believe in God at all, Mariane?

Yes I do, Mariane said. I'm no heathen, but I believe in him according to my understanding.

And you people have children! Don't you ever think about what a great grace God has bestowed on you? Healthy, active children, health and good conditions!

We're not complaining, Mariane said. But, so what, in the end we also have to use our hands to get it.

Complain! the pastor roared and hit the table. You don't complain when you eat your cake and have it too! Can't you use your eyes to see with. There—he pointed to the door—there outside the door misfortune and sorrow and sickness are standing and waiting to come in. Sickness will beat you into the ground, and sorrow stands and lurks to rip the heart out of your body. But you sit in your warm parlor and suspect nothing. Who will help you when the evil hour comes, and how will things go on the day of judgment. Look, when you're called up before the throne and the Lord says: Look, so there we have Mariane—what have you done in your life, Mariane, you'll answer: Oh, I've been a decent wife and taken care of my house and home and behaved myself. The Lord looks at you and shakes his head: That's all well enough, but have you been a child of God and gotten redemption from your sin, Mariane? Then you'll stand there and won't be able to answer anything. And you'll look over at Jesus, to see whether he can help you, but he'll look the other way and won't know you, because while you were alive, you didn't know him. So don't you believe you'll regret you defied and resisted Jesus? Answer me, Mariane.

Mariane had been looking stiffly straight ahead while the pastor was talking. Now she looked him in the eyes, and the corners of her mouth moved again a bit.

I just can't understand how you can know that things have to happen in this way in another world, she said quietly.

Taken aback, the pastor stared at her: How I can know...

He sat silently for a while—there was no dealing with this woman.

Povl Vrist tried to guide the conversation into other channels, but soon after the pastor said good-bye.

Thomas Jensen sailed the pastor across the fjord to where he was to speak at a meeting in a Mission parish. It was sad to see the motorboat disappear in the half-dark drizzle. Thomsen had come as a reminder of old days, and now it would surely be a long time until another such visit would warm the heart. In the afternoon Tea slipped over to Mariane. She was short of breath from curiosity. Pastor Thomsen had been there—what had he said?

Yes, yes, Mariane was full of admiration—he was quite a pastor. And not so quarrelsome as his reputation. He'd drunk coffee and talked about Povl's kin back home. It had been cozy.

A bit disappointed, Tea asked whether he hadn't said anything else.

Well, what should he have said? Mariane teased. Pastors always preach a bit in between—they're so used to doing it they almost can't let it be. I really can't remember the words. But you know what, little Tea, as light as he was on his feet—I believe he'd be good to dance a polka with.

That was a rude joke, and Tea, offended, said farewell. Pastor Thomsen and dancing—they couldn't even be named together. Tea felt it like a knife in her heart, and it was Mariane's intention to mock. That she understood.

— Easterly wind and frost set in; the sharp wind pierced through nerve and bone, and it was impossible to keep warm either outside or inside: the men had to sit with their work in the parlor. But otherwise it was a happy time: the fields were manured and the seed began to sprout. Pastor Thomsen's word had not fallen on stony ground, and the listeners began to flock to the meetings of the Pious. There was no space in the little fishermen's parlors, where there was room for at most twenty people. Thomas Jensen spoke to Aaby, and it was arranged to hold meetings in the school. Aaby paid for the light and fuel out of his own pocket.

Thomas Jensen gave himself no rest, and made house visits all over the parish. In many places he got empty words, but others were just waiting for a little push. Thomas Jensen had a bunch of tracts in his pocket and gave them free to everyone who wanted one. Once a week the tones of hymns could be heard from the school. The meetings were packed full. The saved stood up and bore witness, and the sinners admitted how they'd gone astray, and cast the burden from themselves. That was a life for Tea: her cheeks took on color, her life substance—there was meaning again in the world.

They were mostly common people, and many looked at revivalism with unease and repugnance. What kind of arts were they? Traveling missionaries had been in the parish before, but no one had taken seriously what came from outside and was untested. Now the meetings got heated up, and the lukewarm were thawed out. Women sobbed and men sat with stiff, clenched expressions when the missionary depicted hell's terrors and torments, and when a new convert, wailing, spoke of the puddles his lusts had wallowed in. People were accustomed to caution and reserve; they were bound to hundreds of secret rules—in every corner of the world an eye sat and spied. Now all chains were dissolved. It was freedom and relief. You could say everything when it happened for Jesus's sake. And status and wealth meant nothing against the burning, faithful heart. God's children fought as brothers and sisters against the world's deceptions and the stiff thorns.

The fields were hard as stone, and the wind was icy. It was only during long intervals that you caught a glimpse of the sun: the endless winter was oppressive and pressed down the soul. The meetings in the school were an opening in the ice.

Pastor Brink felt out of sorts. When he stood in the pulpit, he noticed the cold cascade against him from the Mission people's rows, and it made him insecure. His preaching no longer had the joyful radiating beam, like a message from the land of bliss. He was tired, but he held himself erect when he walked through town. They wouldn't bend him. He vouched for his personal way of looking at life—it was as good as theirs and he had fought his way to it. But the revival would surely drift away, just as the sun melted the snow in the spring. The good is victorious. Spring follows winter.

On the farms people did small chores, tended to things in the stalls and out-buildings and managed to pass the time. The evenings were long. The youth association had gymnastics in the assembly hall, but it didn't offer much variety. Then there was the hotel. It lurked like a temptation with its church gables and its nickelodeon. Thomas Jensen talked to Mogensen and tried to get him to do away with dancing, but the innkeeper shook his head: there were mortgages the interest on which had to be paid—did Thomas Jensen want to release him from them? That wasn't possible. Would the Pious hold their meetings here with a coffee hour after the speeches? No, Thomas Jensen answered. God's word shall not be heard in an inn. Then Mogensen knew no way out.

I want to tell you one thing frankly, Thomas Jensen said. If you don't keep to the closing times, you'll be reported to the police. We must have the law upheld—we can demand that. And now you can't complain you haven't been warned.

Every Saturday evening men and girls came in swarms marching from the parish farms regardless of whether there was a snowstorm or rain. The music made a din, and the floor rocked under heavy steps. One evening the men became unmanageable. They had bought spirits and brought them along and stood in small knots in the garden and drank in the black evening. Then they tumbled into the hall, tramped around like madmen, swung the girls and went out and drank again. Katrine was in hot water. She balanced trays full of coffee cups and soda water glasses among the crazy people. Arms kept reaching out for her. Appalled, Mogensen shook his head and saw how the cups were being smashed on the floor. Katrine's face was boiling hot and she held her own with sharp words.

As the evening wore on, the men became wilder and wilder. It was sheer madness: they roared like animals and filled themselves with spirits to excess. When the bottles were emptied, they were slung against the wall, and with bloodshot eyes the troop tumbled back in again. The girls stood in anxious groups and no longer wanted to dance, but the men were charged with energy—their looks were furious and they moved their limbs slowly. It was like before a thunderstorm, when the sky is black as night and dangerous. Then it all began exploding.

A man with a blotchy complexion embraced Katrine. She screamed and defended herself, and another person jumped in on the violent perpetrator and planted a fist in his face. The two men rolled over on the floor—entangled, and for a moment the hall was a battlefield. Screaming girls swarmed at the door, while the men tumbled about with blood flowing from their faces. The dull blows fell, and men sank down. The sober stole away, and a couple of reasonable men ran for the parish sheriff.

People gathered outside and looked in through the windows. Katrine had run out into the garden and ran right into Anders Kjøng's arms.

They're killing one another, she said breathlessly.

They've doubtless been drinking, Anders Kjøng said and kicked at an empty bottle. But so what if they didn't have more sense.

Katrine instinctively clung to him—she had gotten heart palpitations and breathed with difficulty. Anders Kjøng led her away to a bench and took her on his lap. The big, heavy girl leaned against him and sobbed.

They wouldn't leave me in peace, she cried.

Now, now, the man consoled her. Don't take it to heart. After all, no one was hurt. Just let them beat one another to a pulp.

They sat for a bit silently and listened to the seething noise from the hall. A man jumped out of the window and disappeared in the dark; you barely saw a scratched, bleeding face in a streak of light. A pane was smashed—the glass shards rattled against the wall. Outside on the road people moved in waves back and forth; the women stood with shawls around their heads and tried to catch a glimpse of the fight. Boys ventured up to the windows, while the elderly stood in small bunches and waited for the parish sheriff to come. Some had sticks and rope in their hands—things surely might heat up.

Katrine uttered a little shriek.

No, you keep away from me, Anders Kjøng.

Anders Kjøng held her more firmly and craned forward with his mouth toward her neck. She felt his hot breath and tried to get free.

Let me go, she begged.

May I lie with you tonight? he whispered breathlessly.

Oh, let me go, the girl wailed. I'll yell for help. Don't.

Anders Kjøng had lost his senses. He pressed his hand against her mouth to prevent her from screaming. Where's your room, he said. I'll come tonight.

It's there in the gable, Katrine whispered half-choked. But you mustn't come until everything is closed. When you knock on the window, I'll let you in.

She pointed to the window in the gabled end of the house, and after a hot kiss Anders Kjøng let her go.

Katrine slipped away while Anders Kjøng slowly sauntered out onto the road. Yeah, he was some guy! Now he had as good as seduced a girl and was supposed to lie with her tonight. Instinctively Anders Kjøng strutted and wished people could see it in him.

The parish sheriff came running followed by a band of out-of-breath men. Mogensen stood in the doorway and waved. Hurry up, he called. They've totally lost their senses!

Inside the hall chairs and tables were smashed to bits. A couple of the men lay on the floor—others propped themselves up against the walls. The parish sheriff thumped his cane on the floor.

What's going on here? he called. One roared back: What's it your business, you satan! The sheriff went over toward the man and gave him a blow to the head with the stick. You'll soon find out.

Two or three of them fell upon him. Their arms went like flails. But most of the brawlers quickly escaped out the windows, and those who stayed behind were soon overpowered. Three men were lying tied up on the floor, and the sheriff looked around in the hall.

I wonder what got into them? he asked.

They went crazy just all of a sudden, Mogensen complained. They were sitting and drinking in the garden—at least a score of men were lapping up cognac like milk, and then they got angry. And now they've splintered all my things.

It's surely the winter that does it, the parish sheriff said. They build up strength they can't use up. But we better take these guys here along.

The three bound men were lifted on to their feet and taken home with the parish sheriff to sleep off their intoxication. People now crowded into the battle place, and Tea and a couple of other women, who had been standing on the road, ventured to go along. What a puddle of blood there in the corner, she said and couldn't take her eyes from it. You might have thought they were wild animals. Pale and short of breath, she explained: I can't stand to see blood.

Anders Kjøng sauntered out on to the road, back and forth; he didn't feel like going home. What if she now became pregnant? Anders Kjøng felt a mild well-being at the thought. People would look to him and think he was a buck. And he'd lure other girls. Now he'd learned the art.

He was not at ease, but shuffled into the inn garden. It was drizzling, and it didn't take long before he was soaked through. Inside behind the black panes a light moved from room to room. It was Mogensen, who was looking after everything. He lay down on a bench and stared up into the rain-soaked clouds. As he lay there, he began to shiver in the cold night. The time passed slowly, but Anders Kjøng was determined to hold out. He felt gentle and in a good mood. Maybe he'd marry Katrine, who was a big and pretty girl—that wasn't at all out of the question. After all, he was no monster

Finally everything was dark in the hotel, and he sneaked over and knocked softly on the pane, waited a bit and knocked again. There was someone who turned in bed—he distinctly heard it creak and got hot in his head and knocked a little harder. The window was opened. It was Mogensen who was standing there.

What's this? he asked drowsily. Did you guys totally lose your senses this evening? Anders Kjøng jumped out of the garden. Rage pushed him to the verge of crying. Like a dog that had been flogged, he slinked home to his room.


The herring came. Early in the morning, while the air was still gray, the men set out to empty the nets. The fjord was dark and shiny; the nocturnal clouds were reflected in it coldly. But when the herring were scooped into the boat, they radiated a brilliance of colors. Silver and purple, red and blue shadows, and a rain of glistening scales gushed from the living pile in the boat. It was a piece of a rainbow that you had gotten in your net.

Over the meadows the dew lay white and steaming, and in the village the smoke rose from the chimneys. The exporter stood on the wharf and weighed the herring and threw them into boxes. A couple of teenage boys were his helpers; he was an island resident, and had a strange way of speaking, but his tongue was made for singing hymns. While he put ice over the herring and nailed the boxes shut, his voice resounded toward the sky. He sang and swung the hammer, and the boys struggled with the scales. Bucket after bucket of glistening herring was scooped up from the flat-bottomed sloop:

> If the world I would discover
> Going on its rose-strewn way
> Underneath the rosy bowers
> Where the serpent is not seen,
> And I would embrace the flesh,
> Then I see your troubles fresh,

> When my thoughts of you are constant,
> All I see is Satan plotting.

Not much went into Jens Røn's herring net, and the hymn the exporter sang over his herring boxes was rather brief. But he was satisfied so long as he earned food and payment on his heavy debt. These were good times for Jens Røn; he got money in his hands, paid off at the coop, and got clothes for the children.

There was growth in the air. In the warm afternoon sun the frost from the fields was steaming. Also the cause of the kingdom of God was growing—the Lord's fields were greening. More and more found their way to the meetings, which were packed full in the school every Saturday evening.

Thomas Jensen made trips to arrange the matter of the Mission house, and he came home with glad tidings. It could still be taken care of this summer. And collections were made at meetings. Everyone gave his portion according to his disposition and wealth.

Anton Knopper had become quiet and turned inward. He was no longer crazy about chatting about the wonders of the world and God's omnipotence, but attended mostly to himself and sat in his room in the evening. But he often had an errand in town, an errand at the coop or the baker. So it happened that he ran into Katrine. Every time he blushed and cast his eyes down, and if he tried to say something, it never failed that the wrong word came out of his mouth.

One day he discovered he was in need of spruce bars for the posts. There was actually no hurry, but just as well today as tomorrow. He shouldered a woodman's axe and went out to an estate where he had an agreement with the owner and could cut for his use. It was a misty afternoon. The trees were, so to speak, full of fine, white wool—they resembled animals that stood and crouched. The sun was only a pale gleam of light. The moss and grass were green and shiny with moisture.

Anton Knopper lopped off the twigs of the spruce trees with many thoughts going through his head. People are trees, and one day death comes with his axe. Something becomes timber in paradise's palace, and other things are kindling wood and only to be thrown on the hot flames. And righteous and unrighteous, we have our stake in the flesh. Original sin had its claws in him too. He had finished and was walking home. On the road he couldn't see many steps ahead, but he took his time. At the coop he had heard Katrine whisper she was going home today, and if he wasn't mistaken, she came back along the road here. Anton sat down with a sigh at the edge of the ditch and waited. It was the first time he ran after the girls, but now it would be the way Pastor Thomsen had advised. Anton Knopper was determined to talk with the girl and hear how things stood with her soul and faith.

On the estate the sparrows were peeping, and far off he heard a plowman call his horse. Otherwise the world was tranquil as if it were packed in cotton. He got up and walked back and forth a bit and sat down again. The mist was good—no one could see which path he was out on today. But he had never thought he'd be lying in wait for women on the highroad. Maybe Katrine had purposely given him a signal. I'll be coming back again in the afternoon, she said, and even if she didn't look over where he was—women just couldn't be figured out.

Someone was coming. Anton Knopper walked up to the road and waited. When Katrine stepped out of the mist, she gave a little shriek.

Oh, it's only you, she said. I was totally frightened. It's a nasty fog, and if I didn't know my way around, I would have gotten lost. It was stupid I didn't go the other way, but of course it's longer.

Anton Knopper couldn't find words to answer. He was overwhelmed by the big woman walking at his side. A warmth streamed from her that made him hot and cold. A wagon droned by; the steam rose from the horse's nostrils. They stepped out on to a side road, and Katrine sat down on a pile of spruce. Now I want to tell you like it is, Anton stammered. I came here to meet you. I thought you'd probably come this way, and there's something I wanted to talk to you about.

As long as there's no one to see us, the girl whispered. People are always such busybodies with me...

Well, but what I want to tell you, Katrine, I have honest intentions... Anton Knopper sat down next to her and took her large toil-worn hand.

Katrine leaned a bit toward him. She liked the big fisherman. And if he was a little up in years, he still was far from old, and earned his own money and was his own man.

It's a serious matter for me, Anton Knopper said. Couldn't you tell me whether you could imagine—if we otherwise believe it's God's will—we two should live together.

Yes, she whispered.

They sat a bit silently. Anton Knopper's heart was hammering away in his breast. So it was no worse than that. Now he was an engaged man and owned a girl from head to toe. But her heart! That couldn't be forgotten.

Are we going to have a ring? Katrine asked and looked up at him.

Yes, Anton answered. That's my thought. But there's one thing I want to ask you about, and it's just about the most important thing: what about Jesus? Do you believe you can give your heart completely to Jesus?

I don't know, Katrine said. You know I'm not Pious. But if you believe I can, I'll try.

Then you're on the right path even if you're still walking in the fog, Anton said with profundity.

Katrine snuggled closer to him and became a bit short of breath. If she was now an engaged girl and had a betrothed, then it was also part of the deal that he'd give her a kiss and take possession of her. Anton Knopper noted the gentle warmth from her body and felt her soft, full form. But even if his life depended on it, he couldn't touch her in such a way without further ado. He felt cold in his soul from horror and began shaking.

Yes, I suppose we'll first have a ring, Katrine said a bit disappointed.

They heard a man coming along the road. He coughed and thumped his cane hard on the ground. Finally he popped up out of the fog. It was teacher Aaby. He looked totally tattered—the fog hung from him in bits. He stopped and greeted them.

Familiar people are out and about, he said. The fog is truly not good for the chest. But, after all, one should get some exercise when one sits in school for so long. How are things out in the bog, Katrine?

Oh, the girl said, they say old Mikkel Frost will die.

Well, he's gotten worse, Aaby sighed. Yes, so he'll have to go. After all he's not young either. I wonder whether he's suffering much?

He's surely in much pain, Katrine answered. It's cancer and the doctor said he won't live out the week.

Yes, death is hard, Aaby said and gave a muffled cough with his gaunt, crooked hand in front of his mouth. One doesn't understand as long as one has one's powers, but only when one has become a lonely, old crow in the wild fields. But we have Jesus. I say we do *have* Jesus, and no fear of that. He hammered the cane into the ground to establish the words.

But we have to go under the earth, he added with a sigh.

He nodded and plunged into the fog again. The two of them wandered in toward the village. Everything was oddly remote and unreal and resembled a dream, it appeared to Anton Knopper.

— So the news spread that Anton Knopper had become engaged to the serving girl from the hotel. Tea kept wailing and Mariane teasing. So he's probably going to learn to dance, she said. No, Tea answered angrily. But if Anton chose the girl, she must have a good foundation, and so she can still be saved from the sinfulness she's lived in. But Tea didn't like that. It was not the Creator's intention that his children should marry sinners and bargirls. But otherwise the girl conducted herself decorously. She sat with her eyes cast down at the meetings and had a talent for singing.

Katrine gave notice at work. Mogensen took it coolly—he was thinking about finding a new girl in town. Fate had treated him harshly: the crazy people had smashed his nickelodeon to pieces, and he had to have a mechanic to get it repaired. There were no more dances in the spring; he wasn't going to be daring with those wild guys. Mogensen had new plans: there'd be a new beach hotel. He was fire and flame and went around with brushes and paint buckets smartening things up. After all, the hotel was situated near the water, and city people liked to swim.

Kock shook his head: people in town were not as easy to entice as one might believe; they certainly knew the way they wanted to have things. And they'd never come where they couldn't get alcohol.

Well, but the temperance people! Mogensen objected. Those sorts of people surely also want to go to the country.

People who can pay—they're seldom temperance people, the customs official declared. That's the reason.

But Mogensen wouldn't let himself be frightened. It would be accomplished. One evening he got an idea and sat up for many hours writing a poem. That was the way to attract attention to the place. The next day he read his verse out loud to everyone who came near him: Where the fjord reflects the beech tree, and the lark's sweet song resounds, there live I in summer's beauty, and rejoice in nature's grounds. Yes, but the beech? Kock asked. Yeah, okay, there aren't any there, but it's poetic speech, Mogensen answered. Perhaps I should rather write in the last line: where the Jutlander abounds? What do you think, Kock? — I prefer the first, Kock said: it raises an expectation in the reader. The poem was printed in many newspapers, and now Mogensen was owner of his own beach hotel.

The mornings were fresh and everything was moist with dew and night rain. The mold steamed off in the first sunlight, the young cattle roared in the pens, willow-catkins, green buds: it was spring. The light flooded down—clouds passed over the area. Wind motors flashed in the sharp sunlight. Dandelions and buttercups shone in the new grass. The farmhand who was plowing had fallen deep into thought and had to be awakened with a stud-stave, larks stood like little spots under the pale blue sky, and on the beach the sandpiper whistled in its sweet voice. Old people stirred out of the corners and breathed in the spring.

The herring swam in gleaming schools in the fjord. Jens

Røn's debt at the coop was paid, and a penny or two was left over. Now it was out of the question for the manager to give them moldy flour—no, he tilted his head and spoke sweet words. But Tabita wouldn't trust him for a second. I'd like to have flour, but not the moldy kind, she said, although the manager chatted and wanted to let everything be forgotten. And Tabita strutted out of the store.

One afternoon Alma came up to Laust Sand's and found Adolfine in the pantry. She was standing with a slice of bread in her hand.

You're getting yourself starchy food, Adolfine, Alma said.

Frightened, the girl turned and dropped the bread on the floor.

Hello, Alma, she said quickly. Please, come into the parlor. I had just gotten hungry—that's all it was.—

You dropped the bread, Alma said and picked it up. Bewildered, she stared at it. The slice of bread was smeared with a thick layer of green soap.

But in Jesus's name, Adolfine, what are you up to?

She cast a searching look at the girl and discovered she was pregnant. It's odd no one had noticed it before; Adolfine sat collapsed on the kitchen chair and looked vacantly in front of her. Alma felt dizzy for a moment and supported herself against the wall.

How did you let things get to this point? she asked without being stern.

Adolfine bent forward and sobbed uncontrollably. It sounded like a sick animal. Alma took her hard by the shoulders to get her to stop. The girl immediately calmed down.

Alma thought about the seaman who had visited in the fall, and asked: Is it Mads Langer who came too close to you?

I can't say anything, Adolfine answered and rocked back and forth. — — I can't say anything.

Oh, Adolfine, Alma complained. What is it you've gone and done, oh dear little child.

Adolfine's face became distorted from weeping, and the tears dripped down into her lap. It was as if the terrible, inevitable fate sat there and grieved over itself. Alma took her by the waist and helped her into bed. The girl fell asleep almost immediately. Alma sat for a while and looked at the tortured face and thought about what she should do. It wasn't possible to let her be alone now. She could do away with herself. She sighed: it would be necessary to reveal to the others what had happened, but she wouldn't talk about the soap. Adolfine had not been in her right mind.

When Alma came home, she confided in Thomas Jensen. He listened silently and seriously to her. What shall we do? Alma asked in doubt. Yes, the truth must out, Thomas Jensen answered. I'd have preferred it hadn't happened, because what will people think when that kind of thing happens with a believing girl? Things will also be hard for Laust Sand if he didn't notice anything ahead of time. He has a melancholy disposition.

In the evening Thomas Jensen assembled the West Coasters. There was talk about fishing and worldly affairs. Then Thomas Jensen said:

There's something we have to talk about. I'll tell it like it is: Adolfine has gotten into trouble and has confided in Alma.

The room became completely quiet. Tea's eyes were unnaturally big, and Anton Knopper had a melancholy expression, which made him seem strange. The lamp light fell soft and yellow over their features.

Yes, Adolfine is going to have a child, Thomas Jensen said, and she won't say who seduced her.

Out in the kitchen you could hear the kettle boiling on the range, and in the bedroom sleepy children's voices could be heard. Tea sighed anxiously. Poor girl, Mariane mumbled.

Now I think Adolfine should be ashamed of herself, Tea said after she calmed down a bit. — She went to meetings and played pious, and then she was intending the worst things. I know of course we're not supposed to judge, but I'm ashamed of her.

Now watch your mouth, Tea, Jens Røn's deep voice resounded.

But the father? Anton Knopper asked. I just can't imagine it's Mads Langer who treated her ill.

Thomas Jensen said quietly: It surely can't be anyone else. She's completely beside herself, and I think we should try to help her back to grace. But she must confess who led her into misfortune.

I never trusted Mads Langer, Tea declared angrily. — No I didn't. He was so full of talk, and he had odd opinions and gave himself airs with gold chains and cigarette cases—I could plain see in his eyes he wasn't to be trusted. And Laust Sand should have supervised them more—after all, he is Adolfine's stepfather.

No one answered, but Mariane said: It was good they got engaged. Because you have to assume Mads Langer will marry her.

Yes, but will he really? Tea said. When the fellows have gotten the girls to that point, they're wont to forget what they promised. And even if they do get married, she committed fornication. I'd never imagined that about Adolfine.

We'll be obliged to be with her in the beginning, Alma said. She's completely disturbed in the head, and something could easily go wrong. And Thomas thinks she has to admit it's Mads Langer so Laust can write to him and demand that he be honest with her.

That evening there was no joy in singing hymns, and everyone soon went home. In the morning Alma was with Adolfine. Laust Sand had gone to the fjord early and hadn't come home yet. Does he know? Alma asked. Yes, Adolfine answered. He knows everything. Alma was silent for a bit and said: Yes, I did have to tell the others. They would have seen it sooner or later, and we all want to stand by you, but you must say who the father is. Adolfine clapped her hands in front of her eyes: Oh, I wish I were dead, she wailed, I wish I were dead. I won't survive it.

Malene, Tea, and Mariane came one after the other. They took Adolfine's hand loosely without looking at her. How you have gotten into trouble, Malene whispered sympathetically. But we'll help you as much as we can. No one can help, Adolfine said flatly. Tea sighed. Now you mustn't let evil take power over you, Adolfine, she said, because we know there's nothing we can't go to Jesus with.

Adolfine lifted her gray blotchy face for a moment and looked at her with an anguished look. Then she collapsed on the chair again.

Malene took her hand. — It's a great sin you've committed. But you mustn't lose your faith. There's no one who says of you, Adolfine, that you've thrown yourself away frivolously: no, that's not our opinion, even if you have sinned. If you can repent, you will still get forgiveness. But you must confess who the child's father is.

I can't say anything, the girl wailed. I'd rather go into the fjord—then I'll have peace.

Don't pay any attention to it, little Adolfine, Mariane said in her friendly voice. There are girls who were seduced before you. You'll marry the fellow, and then it will soon be forgotten. Did you let him know? Otherwise Laust Sand has to write and tell him how things stand. And if he's the kind that seduces a decent girl and afterwards goes his way, then you really needn't shed any tears over him.

Tea didn't like Mariane's easy manner. You should be merciful, but the point wasn't simply to fawn over sin either. Adolfine was lying in the bed she had made.

There have been ugly acts, she said—I think no one can ever disregard that.

Oh, shut your mouth, Mariane said sharply. Is that your Christianity—to accuse a poor child.

Tea blushed and gasped for breath. Mariane was flighty in things big and small. She looked to Malene and Alma for support, but they cast their eyes down.

Is it Mads Langer? Alma asked urgently.

Adolfine threw herself forward. She knocked her head against the floor and screamed like a person in extreme distress. Mariane and Malene quickly took her by the arms and lifted her up. She had beaten her head bloody, and her eyes were wide open and wild. Together they carried her into the bedroom and laid her on the bed. She dropped off immediately. We have to switch off being with her, Mariane whispered. Now I'll be here for the time being if the rest of you will take care of Povl and the children.

It's no use at all trying to press her. She's really a sick person.

The other women quietly went home. Tea was melancholy; she regretted having been so stern with Adolfine. Even if the girl had sinned, it was obvious she was crushed by remorse. Oh, with the heart I have, she said to Jens Røn, I'll never become a real child of God. — That's hard for everyone, her husband consoled her. If Mariane had hit me on the cheek, it wouldn't have been too much, Tea lamented. I'd almost thank her for it. I don't deserve better. Now you mustn't take it too hard, Jens Røn said. All of us at some point can get too fired up.

For two days the women switched off taking care of Adolfine. She ate almost nothing, but lay and stared up at the ceiling. If someone spoke to her, she answered with a frightened look. The women quietly busied themselves around her, and no one questioned her about what had happened. When he wasn't on the fjord, Laust Sand walked about silently and tortured. Every time he came into Adolfine's room, she lifted her face from the pillow and followed him with her eyes. He sat for a moment on the bed and patted her on the hand. They both groaned while breathing and looked at each other in the eyes. When Laust Sand got up, drops of sweat covered his forehead.

On the third day Alma was with Adolfine. Laust Sand sat in the shed and mended nets, but in the afternoon he came into the room. Alma felt odd. He moved ponderously, and when he went over to the bed, he bent over Adolfine and stared mutely at her. Seized by a strange horror, Alma held her breath. Without saying a word Laust Sand turned and left. Adolfine got up in the bed and screamed: You mustn't, Laust, oh, you mustn't. Alma forced her back into the down quilts and prevented her from jumping out onto the floor, and wailing, she turned in toward the wall.

Laust Sand took his hat in the entry hall and walked through town. He walked stiffly and moved his arms mechanically back and forth. He stopped outside Thomas Jensen's house, and his eyes roved about the sun-whitened road. Some children were playing a little way off, and a high scolding woman's voice was heard from one of the houses. In a tree that was white from the dust on the road a flock of sparrows were chirping. Jesus! he groaned. Jesus! He stood for a moment as if he expected something would happen. Then he went into the shed where Thomas was sitting and working.

Hello Laust, Thomas Jensen said and nodded to his two boys. Can you go out for a while and stay away until I call. His lads let go of the trap they were repairing, and hurried out with a quick look at Laust Sand's distorted features.

I've come to tell you I'm the one who seduced Adolfine, Laust Sand said tired.

Thomas Jensen dropped what he had in his hands and stared at him perplexed.

It's you, Laust, he whispered. But in the name of our savior—

I alone am guilty, Laust Sand said.

With your stepdaughter, Thomas Jensen mumbled—to whom you were in father's stead.

It was like witchcraft—I couldn't resist, Laust Sand said flatly. I asked for help, but it was no use. And from the very beginning I've been so tortured by remorse I was close to dying. We kneeled together on the floor and begged Jesus to stand by us. It was evil that overpowered me, and now I've dragged the poor girl down with me.

Laust Sand tottered and was about to topple over. It's evil that has taken seed in me, he groaned. And the Savior had no help for me. Now the Lord must do with me as he will. But I beg you people to take care of Adolfine.

But what are you intending? Thomas Jensen asked terrified. Surely you don't intend to harm yourself?

No, Laust Sand answered. I'll let the whole thing take its

course.

Oh, Laust, Thomas Jensen complained. Pray to Jesus. As much as you've sinned, he'll still bestow his mercy on you. Just as long as you throw yourself at his feet and beg for forgiveness! I know for certain he will receive you.

Laust Sand shook his head: There's no saving me, he said. I clung to him, but evil gained power. I've forfeited my salvation. He turned and went. Thomas Jensen sat down and hid his face in his hands. He was shaken as if a great misfortune had struck him. He had known Laust Sand for many years, sailed with him, fished with him, and been his brother in the Lord. A terrible paralysis gripped him, a feeling of chilling dread. When one of the saved could fall so low, the world was a puddle of sin. The devil and evil powers raged in the souls—there was only one thing to do: throw yourself down on your knees and beg for mercy.

A little later he got up and went out behind the house, where his smallest children were playing. He took a little boy in his arms and chatted gently with him. He could surely see a bird was sitting in the tree. The little one pointed at it with his dirty hand and nodded seriously.

*Tabor* was what the Mission house was to be named. Craftsmen had begun work as soon as the frost had left the ground, and the Pious followed the way the walls grew from week to week. Everyone contributed his portion to the Lord's house. Now they were getting a place to be with their faith.

On warm summer evenings they gathered in small clusters at the building site. The house was lacking only the roof, and inside it smelled of whitewash and newly planed wood. The pastor came by every day on his walk. He wrinkled his forehead and set his cane firmly on the ground. Foreign priests and missioners were about to conquer his parish. Or was it the season of the year that made it seem that many people no longer sought the church? One evening when there was a meeting in the school, he shuffled by the illuminated windows and looked in. He saw a glimpse of a man at the lectern and serious, attentive faces in the room and hurried away so as not to be seen.

The spirit of dissension had sown its seed, and censoriousness and narrow-mindedness grew up in the fields. The pastor's wife sighed when they came home from the half-empty church. How unreliable the people are, she said. They used to be so glad for your preaching. — Yes, Pastor Brink said, but now they prefer to listen to tailors and fishermen, who can barely spell their way through the bible. The healthy folk-traits are about to fall into decay, but better times will come, and in any case I stand firmly on the basis of intellectual freedom. — Oh, that's distressing, the wife complained. You with your great abilities. And you understand so well precisely how to deal with little people and you can be something for them. — I'm not giving up the fight, the pastor said. Remember the words: He is strongest who stands alone.

Pastor Brink had, immediately after having come to the parish, founded a youth organization and had been elected chairman. It had quietly languished, but now he breathed life into it and planned a series of lectures of popular enlightenment. A people's high school superintendent, who was on circuit tour, spoke about Socrates's warm-heartedness and most deeply Christian personality. Know thyself, he admonished, and Pastor Brink nodded and looked about in the assembly. They were mostly young people who had attended, and afterward there was dancing at the hotel. The pastor himself read from Ibsen's *Catiline* and gave an account of the human personality's relationship to conscience. Kock sat in the front row. What was your impression? the pastor asked after the meeting. Did I manage to emphasize the main aspect correctly? Yes, Kock said. But it's a mistake in the lectures not to have discussion. There were certain things that needed to be explored and established more closely. I would have wished to make a connection with something. Really, the pastor said, it didn't fit your taste? There were especially many pertinent comments, the customs official thought, but one could have wished for a bit more precise account. — You must keep in mind that it was a purely popular lecture, Pastor Brink replied, a bit annoyed, and said good night. Kock nodded triumphantly: he managed to push the pastor into a corner. That was tit for tat. Kock hadn't forgotten the meeting with Thomas Jensen in the parsonage before Christmas.

Rumors began to trickle out about Laust Sand and Adolfine; people talked in muffled voices about what had happened, and before long the whole parish knew about their guilt. When the women went by the house, they cast a glance at the house where the curtains were drawn. It was as if someone lay dead in there. Indeed, it was more eerie than death. Adolfine was Laust Sand's stepdaughter, and what they had done was punishable by prison. Laust went stooped to the fjord and tended to his work; he had become old and bowed and hid his eyes. No one greeted him any more with a cheerful shout or even with a nod. If he went by a bunch of chatting men, they stopped talking and looked the other way. Everyone could see in him that he had sinned and had been struck by God's judgment. He was like a leper among people.

Pastor Brink had heard about the news and was in doubt as to what he should do. Actually it was his obligation as clergyman to visit Laust Sand and to speak a serious word with him. Laust Sand was Pious. The event would surely not favor his opponents. People would feel frightened and offended and have their eyes opened as to how much unwholesomeness and superficial divine worship the strict pietism contained. What was it he had said to Pastor Thomsen: The consequences of the violent suggestive pressure. Pastor Brink told himself he was right and explained the matter to his wife.

Then what will you do? Mrs. Brink asked. Can't you talk to the poor people and give them a little consolation? Right now a gentle and affectionate word could perhaps mean so much to them.

Yes, I may do it, the pastor replied and ran his hand through his hair. Psychologically it's certainly the right time now that their closest associates are turning their backs. And I believe it is plainly my official duty even if the purely human aspect doesn't prompt me to do it.

He considered what he should say, and decided to make the visit immediately. When he came to Laust Sand's house, he stopped for a moment and walked on down to the wharf. He needed to breathe fresh air and think over his words yet again. It was soon evening and out over the meadows the fog was steaming. A couple of boys came cycling at a wild full-tilt and turned in a hasty curve around him. At the very bottom near the wharf came a solitary man. It was Laust. His figure seemed dark and ponderous against the water and the pale sky behind, and the pastor instinctively stood still.

When the fisherman had come closer to him, he said: Good evening, Laust Sand. I was coming to talk to you—I've heard what happened and so I thought—Laust lifted his mildewed face and looked at him as if from far off. It's the pastor, he mumbled. Yes, Pastor Brink answered and noticed that his voice was shaking. I thought I could perhaps help. It could perhaps relieve you to unburden yourself, and — — He stopped and couldn't manage to say any more. Laust Sand's look contained a horror of despair, which he had never before suspected. I don't know, he stammered. Perhaps it's wrong of me, but I'd like to be of help to you. Laust Sand looked down at the ground. I must say thank you. But for me no help is to be expected. — He walked on along the road.

The pastor stood for a while confused and watched him. On the way home it became clear to him that he had been on the verge of doing something psychologically wrong. The man was in the midst of a rending, psychic crisis, and it was altogether unwise to intervene before he had calmed down and again tried to put down roots in his life. Pastor Brink felt relieved and gave up trying to talk to Adolfine. After all, it was first and foremost his duty not to cause humans harm. Suggestive pressure, he thought, that's precisely what one had to avoid.

No, no one talked to Laust Sand, who had forsaken his savior. The West Coasters were gloomy in spirit—in whom could you have faith? The point was to cling to grace and never let go.

The meetings in the school were full of people who bowed their heads under the speakers' sharp words. The women constantly helped Adolfine, who still lay in bed, but they avoided her look and asked her about nothing. Only Mariane sat on her couch and chatted as best she could.

Mariane—she didn't have much rest. When she was home, she washed until the soap foamed around her red arms, or tormented herself with the children and was in a humor that didn't resemble her. She lay on her knees and used the scouring brush and soaped the doors and walls and didn't have time to do anything but clean. When she came up to Adolfine's, she made coffee and pressed a cup on the girl. Mariane knew what she was doing. Coffee was good for sickness and misfortune and could never hurt.

Now you'll soon have to try to get up, little Adolfine, Mariane encouraged her. As soon as you get going and do something, you'll get the best of those gloomy thoughts.

Will I? Adolfine asked with a little hopeless smile.

You certainly will, Mariane assured her.

You shouldn't talk in such a friendly way to me, the girl said. I'm not the person I passed myself off as. It's my fault—if I only I could confess it in front of everyone. I want to tell you, Mariane, my whole being is bad, so full of sin and lewdness. If you only knew the thoughts I've had, you'd never speak a word to me.

Mariane poured a cup of coffee and forced her to drink.

You're really no worse than the rest of us, Mariane consoled her. Believe you me, little Adolfine, there's much madness in all of us, even in those who appear so well-behaved. Now just see to it you get over the bad times, and then everything will be alright.

Less and less went into the herring nets, and finally it didn't pay to have them in the water. The wear and tear on them was greater than the gain. Povl Vrist was the first to take his in, but it didn't take long before the others had to follow suit if the nets weren't to be destroyed. Laust Sand had, since his guilt had been revealed, tended his nets alone. No one liked to be in the boat with him. People wondered how he managed without help, but he got the fish on land. One day Jens Røn and Anton Knopper were out emptying the nets. It was early morning and there was little wind. The boat left a glistening stripe in the water, and in the east the rosy dawn was ablaze. They went into the yawl, and Anton Knopper lifted the heavy netting piece by piece, while Jens Røn scooped the fish in with a catcher. The catch was small, and they were soon done.

Tomorrow I'm taking my nets in, Jens Røn said. Maybe you'll give me a hand, Anton. I don't want to ask Laust Sand after what happened.

Of course, Anton Knopper nodded. What do you think is going to happen with him, Jens?

It's not easy to know, Jens Røn answered. Surely they won't avoid getting their punishment for the crime they committed. But Povl Vrist will probably go to town and talk to a lawyer. They can be given permission to get married if they apply to the authorities for it. That's what Aaby said.

So what will Mads Langer say? Anton Knopper asked. I think it will be hard for him to hear how his sweetheart acted.

I can't understand why Povl Vrist wants to interfere in this, Jens Røn said. It's probably rather Mariane. —

She's a capable wife, Anton Knopper asserted.

Yes, a clever and hard-working wife, Jens Røn readily conceded. And he's surely one of the most capable fishermen in the fjord. He always has luck, but he also knows how to make use of it. He's caught fish for a lot of money this year—you can scarcely imagine how it happens. It's as if he's blessed to excess even though he's not a believer, but strongly opposes God's kingdom.

Jens Røn was silent. It was seldom he said so much, but here was a thing that astonished him.

There's a lot we can't understand, he said.

But you still know things work the way they're supposed to, and there's a meaning in it — And we shouldn't interfere in what surpasses our understanding.

When they came back, Laust was sitting in his sloop at the

wharf sorting flatfish and codling from the herring pile. Thomas Jensen and Lars Bundgaard were standing on the wharf and had gotten their catch weighed, and the exporter was busy nailing the boxes shut. Suddenly Laust Sand slung a big silvery ray fish out into the water and looked carefully at his one hand.

That was surely a sting-bull, Anton Knopper mumbled. And he turned toward Laust Sand and asked: Did you get stung, Laust?

Yes, Laust Sand answered and lifted his head.

The fishermen looked at one another. So it had happened. The punishment had overtaken him. And Jens Røn said quietly: Suck it out as best you can, Laust. If you don't have turpentine, you can get some at my house.

I'm not going to do anything about it, Laust Sand answered and began to scoop the herring up for weighing.

When he walked home, he had his hand deep in his pocket. The others remained standing and watched him. It was God himself who had judged.

Laust Sand mostly kept at home, let his nets remain in the fjord and sat in the half-dark shed and didn't talk to anyone. When the women were with Adolfine, they sometimes heard him rummaging around in the kitchen; he was presumably finding himself a bit of food. They became still as mice and listened for his footsteps, but dared not go out there. No one had told Adolfine what had happened. Adolfine was thinking now mostly about the child, who would come in a few months. She complained to Mariane.

How will things be for a little child who was brought into the world in this way.

I'd prefer if the child died, she said.

And she nodded to herself: yes, if all three of us could die—and there wasn't anything afterward.

Mariane took her roughly by the arm:

Come to your senses, Adolfine, you're being unreasonable. It's the worst thing you can do to take it that way. You have to keep a stiff upper lip and see to it that you get over all this for the child's sake. But there's so much you don't know yet. Once you've had the child, you won't care the least bit about what others say. —

There was a knock at the door—Tea had come to visit. She gave Adolfine her hand, but she stared stiffly ahead, and when she sat down, she sighed full of cares. Previously Tea hadn't taken things so scrupulously, but when she went up to visit Adolfine, she had her black dress on, although it should actually have been treated with care. It wasn't because she wished to be arrogant about her clothes, but a dark solemnity hung over the visits in Adolfine's room. Tea knew she had a responsibility for the deceit that had been committed here. Many a time she had joked with Adolfine and taken everything too easy instead of having been vigilant and remembering what lurks in people. Tea had her guilt to beg pardon for, and it was proper that she showed her seriousness in her outward appearance as well.

Mariane chatted away; she chatted all too much, and Tea sat in all of her melancholy and felt above it. If she said a pious and serious word, Mariane would rush at her like a pole-cat and say things Tea could never get herself to answer again. But so long as she just sighed sadly and sat gloomily with her hands in her lap, she had the upper hand. Deep sighs rose from Tea's breast, but Mariane jabbered away and cackled cheerfully. She told of things she had heard of in her childhood—a long story about an old uncle, who was given to drink, and one evening he came home, went the wrong way and walked into the ram. The roar and hollow boom woke up the farmstead, and when they got out into the stall, the ram was standing over the uncle and had almost butted the life out of him.

Mariane noticed Adolfine was listening and talked on. Out in the fjord in the place where she was from was a tiny island where there were only a couple of small farms. On the one farm there lived a couple of old, sickly people, and on the other a younger married couple. One day the wife was about to be confined, and a messenger was sent to the midwife; she came and it was a difficult birth. The husband himself had to assist. Finally the midwife said: Yes, so it's a boy! Oh, it's a boy, the husband said. Yes, so thank God. — Don't say thanks yet, the midwife said: there are more on the way. — Oh, it's also a boy, the husband said. Yes, well then thank you. — Don't say thanks yet, the midwife said: there are more on the way. Yes, so I really want to say thank you, but now it's enough. There wasn't much life in the three little ones, and one day, when the pastor was over on the island to chat with the old woman on the other farm, the husband went over to the house where he was with the children in a basket and asked for them to be baptized. The pastor was an old man, and he didn't have any objections. The husband laid the children on a bed and came with them one after the other. The pastor baptized them just as quickly as he could, but when he had come to the seventh, he nevertheless became somewhat surprised and asked how many there were. There are only three, the husband said, but I've got them mixed up, and I don't know which of them were baptized. I've never heard worse, Adolfine said. But is it true? Yes, yes, Mariane assured her, I heard it when I was a child.

Tea looked at Adolfine: the girl was lying with a little smile on her faded face and felt well in the midst of her misfortune. So long as Mariane jabbered away thoughtlessly and told stories, which ridiculed baptism's sanctity, sin and guilt were forgotten and obliterated.

Now I think—she said quietly, but Mariane didn't let her finish speaking. Now what do you think, little Tea? she said with a dangerous glint in her eyes. You must absolutely not forget to say what your opinion is because otherwise the world won't exist another minute. Tea bowed her head and blushed. But she didn't have the audacity to dare an open fight with Mariane, who was rude and reckless and didn't treat people with kid gloves. Oh, it's nothing, Tea sighed. I'd hate to disturb you when you're sitting and telling stories—believe you me. Tea's voice was as sweet as syrup, and it was obvious she regarded Mariane as a frivolous person who merely gossiped away. But Mariane doubtless didn't notice it.

Mariane was telling a new story when there was a rustling at the door. Mariane stopped and stared over there. It was Laust Sand. His face was hot with fever, and he could barely get the words out. I'll have to go to bed, he said. I'm not all that well. And I beg you to send for Thomas Jensen.

Adolfine jumped up in her bed.

Oh, Laust, she called. There's nothing wrong with you, is there?

Lie down, Adolfine, and be calm, Laust Sand said, while he kept his sick hand hidden behind his back. After all, sickness can pass again. He nodded to the women and went into his room. Tea got up and gave a defiant look to Mariane.

I surely better go for Thomas Jensen, she said in a voice that was affectionate with humility. So you can continue telling Adolfine stories. Tea was sure again and knew where things were headed. The fire fell from the sky—a sinner was judged.

When Thomas Jensen came, Laust Sand had gone to bed and was lying, his face red and sweaty and eyes pale. He showed Thomas Jensen his hand, which had been struck by the sting-bull stinger. It was swollen and inflamed, and there were red stripes up along the arm.

But God forbid, Thomas Jensen said terrified. That'll never do. We have to send for the doctor—there's blood poisoning in there.

It's going the way it should, Laust Sand answered hoarsely. You surely know that it's not for nothing I was stung by the sting-bull.

Oh, if you'll throw yourself at Jesus's feet, Thomas Jensen said. Then he'd take your burden of sin from you. You've committed the worst thing a person can do, and if you were my own father, I couldn't find anything to say to excuse you. But Jesus can forgive if you go to him.

Laust Sand turned his head toward him: I can't pray any more. The devil has gotten his claws too deep in me. Now I'll take the punishment. I've gone and watched my hand every day and felt how it contracted.

But if you're going to die now, won't you think about the eternal torment? Thomas Jensen whispered.

No, Laust Sand said tired. I can't any more: God must judge me as he wishes—and I can surely see there'll certainly be no mercy for me. But if he'd only bear with Adolfine. I'd ask you, Thomas, to make sure you people help her with intercession and good words. . . He sank back in the pillows and closed his eyes.

Most of all I'd like to go away from here, he groaned.

Thomas Jensen sent for the doctor, who came in his car and wanted to have Laust Sand driven to the hospital immediately. But the fisherman didn't want to, and no one could force him. He sweated and was cold and was tormented by pains and then fell into drowsiness. Day after day went by. Adolfine had gotten up out of her bed and sat gloomy and desperate in the room with him. But she wasn't good for anything. Mariane took care of getting an old girl in the parish who was used to going out and caring for the sick. Laust Sand was gaunt and emaciated with an unkempt beard, and his eyes lay deeply sunken under his forehead. Outside it was summer now. The lapwings hastened away from the meadows. The sandpipers whistled and the ducks swam in flocks down on the low water near the beach.

Now it was again time to get the traps into the water before the autumn darkness came. Every morning people were up at daybreak and watched the weather. The days were sunny with wind that blew warm.

The nets were driven down to the wharf in wagons and loaded onto the prams. The wagon wheels rattled on the wharf's wooden planks, with a crash the stakes were thrown into the boats, men shouted and ran in resounding wooden shoes, the motors crackled, the town echoed with the tramping of horses and creaking wagon wheels. The work had begun.

Anton Knopper and Thomas Jensen stood in the pits and tarred the last traps. Anton Knopper had a large sackcloth apron around his waist and around his head he had wrapped a ragged piece of wool. The sweat rolled down his cheeks in drops. The tar bit into his eyes, and the heat glimmered from the bubbling vat. He tended the hoist apparatus and raised and lowered the net into the boiling tar. Thomas Jensen was in old clothes, which hung in rags on him, and his arms were shiny from the tar up to his elbows. On his head he had a broad-visored straw hat, which cut down on the sun. He carried the traps to the pots and spread them out afterwards to dry on the grass. They worked hard and without talking to each other, but once in a while Anton Knopper had to jump away from the oven and gasp for fresh air when the heat and the tar smoke became too strong.

A shrill howl sounded and Thomas Jensen hastily turned around. A little body came rolling down the steep slope with a cloud of sand after it. In one jump he was gone and picked up the child, while he quickly felt around to see whether the boy was hurt. Then he took the boy in his arms and dried his eyes.

But how in the world did you come rolling down, you little one, he consoled him. You could easily have been hurt, and you know very well you mustn't crawl up on the slope. Now sit down and play, and watch out the next time.

He set the boy on a grassy knoll and gave him a couple of round stones to play with. The urchin was covered with sand and sobbed, but soon he sat contentedly and chatted with the stones. They were cows and horses and were supposed to go into the pasture—that's what they were supposed to.

From the blacksmith's could be heard the cheerful clang of iron being hammered, and in the field behind the pit a plowman was shouting at his team. The hours moved at a snail's pace just like sluggish people in the heat. The men sweated at the tar-pots, and after midday the wind stopped blowing altogether. New wagons came with nets and traps, which were lowered into the tar and spread out on the grass. The men had cast off all their outer garments, and stood in pants and woollen jackets, their faces shining sweaty and black, and their arms were as if cut in shiny polished ivory.

They talked and laughed. Shouts could be heard from the tar-pots to fishermen passing by; old people came trudging by to see how the work was progressing. The children played, and tar smoke wafted everywhere. The iron on the wagon wheels gleamed; the smoke from the fire drifted black toward earth. It was a day of work, a sun-lit, sweaty time.

Once in a while a wife came to fetch her husband to eat. There was no time for rest. At most a pipe of tobacco and five minutes' nap with a jacket over their head in the shade of the hill.

Katrine took a walk to the sand pit to go see Anton Knopper. He greeted her a bit embarrassed, but felt proud deep inside. His sweetheart came and visited him. You surely had to believe the girl had a hard time doing without him for long. Anton Knopper totally forgot Laust Sand, who lay in the throes of death, and sat down a while in the grass with Katrine.

I would scarcely have it known that you're seeing me—after all, I look like a monster, he said and rubbed his tar-black face. But it was nice of you that you wanted to come.

I was just walking by, Katrine answered and cast down her eyes.

What do you think about Katrine? Anton Knopper asked, when she had gone, and Thomas Jensen nodded: really, there was nothing to find fault with in her. Now she had a job with a believing farmer and never went dancing, and at meetings she listened to the word and sang with all her heart. She was definitely on the right path, Thomas Jensen said and dried the sweat from his face.

Yes, Anton Knopper said. As soon as she in all earnestness has found Jesus, we'll have to see about getting married.

Toward evening a boy came running to the sand pit. Things were bad with Laust Sand, and Adolfine begged Thomas Jensen to come immediately. The people dropped their work and looked at one another. So Laust Sand was to go on the great migration and be admitted to death and judgment! Thomas Jensen nodded and heaved the last, newly tarred trap up from the pot. The boy had to go on to look for Lars Bundgaard to see whether he had come from the fjord.

You'll go along, right, Anton? Thomas Jensen asked and spread the trap out on the grass.

Anton Knopper looked at him terrified: I'd prefer to be free of it, he said. It's so terrible for me to see Laust Sand in torment;

and I'm an untalented man and can't at all find words that can help him.

Thomas Jensen didn't take time to go home and change clothes, but ran up to Laust Sand's house immediately. There was no one in the parlor or kitchen, and he went into the bedroom. The nurse stood bent over the bed, and in a corner Adolfine was sitting with her thin hands in front of her face.

Are things really bad with him? he whispered, and the nurse nodded mutely.

The air was heavy in the room, a vapor of death and dissolution, that was oppressive and made him gasp for air. The curtain was drawn, and in the semi-darkness Laust's face shone white and full of pain. Thomas Jensen went over to the bed.

Things are bad for you, Laust, he said. But the sick man was unconscious and only once in a while opened his eyes and stared ahead deliriously. The nurse made room, and Thomas Jensen sat down on the death bed.

Has the doctor been here? he asked.

Yes, the nurse whispered. He said he wouldn't live through the night. Instinctively both of them looked at Adolfine, and Thomas Jensen got tears in his eyes.

There was a soft knock on the door, and Lars Bundgaard stepped in.

He too had not taken time to change clothes when the message came, and was soiled with tar and mud from the stakes. The big fisherman stood for a bit near the bed and watched the sick man.

Did you send for the pastor? he asked.

Yes, he was here in the afternoon and tried to talk to him, the nurse replied. But he understood nothing. I thought it was right to ask you to come now that the time is drawing near because Adolfine is totally gone.

Poor girl, Thomas Jensen mumbled. Let's hope she doesn't lose her mind.

Lars Bundgaard went to the shelf on the wall and took down the old worn-out bible. After he put on the light, he sat down on the bed and read aloud. His voice was slow, and he took pains to utter the sacred words cautiously. He read about Christ's suffering and death and the thief whom God forgave in his last hour and took along to paradise. Down from the road could be heard the trample of horses and rattling wagon wheels; bicycle bells chimed, and children shouted to one another. But Lars Bundgaard conjured up sentence after sentence over the dying man's bed. The others sat with bowed heads and listened. Once in a while Thomas Jensen went over and dried the sweat from Laust Sand's face, which was as gray as a corpse. Lars Bundgaard's voice began to become hoarse and dry, and he stumbled over the words. Thomas Jensen came to relieve him. When he took the book, he said:

Look at her. It's pure misery.

Lars Bundgaard looked a bit reluctantly at Adolfine. You mustn't say that, Thomas, he replied. It's a terrible sin she's committed.

Lars Bundgaard went into the other room to wash himself and get something to eat, and Thomas kept reading, where he had left off. He had to have his glasses on: the tar and the sharp sunshine were hard on the eyes. He read very softly, and in his mouth the severe words became milder. Prophecies became admonitions, and as soon as he was finished with the chapter, he leafed on to the Sermon on the Mount. In his gentle, friendly voice he read the words slowly, and their power caused even him to get tears in his eyes. Perhaps there was mercy for Laust Sand despite everything. He had to stop a moment to overcome the emotion. Alma had come and stood silently for a moment at the bed.

Now you shouldn't begrudge yourself time to eat, Thomas, she said. There's food for you in the parlor.

Yes, would you read until I get back, he answered and looked up over his glasses. After all, we don't know whether he might not regain consciousness and hear just a single little bit.

Alma took the book and sat down by the bed. She read in her pretty, calm voice and pronounced every word with care. The light fell across the sick man's face; small pearls of sweat lay across his forehead. His facial features were dissolved, and his breathing was heavy and bubbling from inside of him.

After a half-hour the men came back in. They had been out in the scullery to scour the worst dirt off, and their faces were red and warm from washing. Alma got up immediately.

Shouldn't we sing a bit, Thomas Jensen whispered, and he had just taken the hymnbook from the shelf when old teacher Aaby entered softly. His face was anxious, and his eyes roamed from one to the next. Behind him came Jens Røn and Tea, solemn and quiet. Tea walked a few steps toward Adolfine, but she stopped at the sight of her pale, extinguished face. Tea felt a pang in her heart.

Lars Bundgaard distributed the hymnbooks, and they joined in singing, first very weakly, but then the singing took on force as if the point were to wake the sick man before death came. While they sang, they stared over at the bed:

O God, my God, my heart is fearful,
It sends its troubled sighs to you.
You know the source of all its sorrow,
You know why it is anxious, too.
You see our need, our darkened soul,
Oh, hear our prayer, be merciful!

For if the sun would lose its brilliance,
All flesh would soon return to dust,
Yet, worse, our souls themselves would perish
If your arm of mercy shut!
We feel it in our anxious souls,
And pray, O God, be merciful!

Lars Bundgaard prayed with his hands folded over his face. Old bible words were mixed in with fragments of sermons and everyday expressions, and he sang out the words in an odd, bleating tone. Thomas Jensen's eyes filled with tears, and teacher Aaby was pale and held his shaking hands squeezed together on his chest. Jens Røn stood with his calm, somewhat dull look and stared at the bed. Laust Sand had been his friend from youth on;

they had worked together for years, fished, and had a cutter jointly. Lars Bundgaard said amen, and for a moment there was stillness in the room. The sick man's eyes had slipped open, and his eyes stared emptily to the ceiling.

He's still here, Aaby whispered hoarsely.

Let's sing again, Thomas Jensen said and began singing:

Not a festival or honor,
Not a perfect day or time,
Can we find under the heavens
That is free from sin or pride.
None should think that they have won
In the evening, say well done,
For at daylight they may stumble,
Grave misfortune make them humble.

Not a grief, or any sorrow
Here on earth do you not know,
Jesus, you have known the sinner
All his treachery and woe.
Peter saw it when you marked
All the treach'ry of his heart.
He recalled your words with sorrow
When the cock crew thrice that morrow.

Tea's voice rang out above the others. Her eyes were shining and wide open, and she felt a shudder deep inside. Something dangerous lurked in the semi-dark, sultry room, which was the evil spirit hidden at hand to seize Laust Sand's soul when it departed his poor, dilapidated abode. Lars Bundgaard went over to the bed and got down on his knees, and the others knelt in a circle around him. Only Adolfine remained sitting in her corner with her eyes closed and head propped against the wall. No one could see whether she had fallen into a reverie.

Lars Bundgaard recited the Lord's Prayer out loud and mightily like a challenge. Then he was silent for a moment and began to pray very softly in his own words. Little by little his voice rose and filled the parlor; he roared and shouted and admonished with mighty words; he struggled in the face of God with the powers of evil for a soul. The prayer was chaotic. The sentences stumbled over one another, and the spit rolled in showers from his mouth. His eyes were fixed on Laust Sand's wan face—nothing more existed. Tea sobbed, half-choked, and Alma hid her face in her hands. Teacher Aaby groaned weakly and closed his eyes; only Adolfine sat by herself and noticed nothing.

Jesus! Lars Bundgaard shouted and stretched his hands ecstatically toward the ceiling. Jesus, come to us now and stand by us so we can rip the lost soul out of the devil's claws. Otherwise it will burn for eternity in the glowing puddle. Oh Jesus, be merciful! Once he belonged to you, and you can surely remember him even if he fell away from you and sinned so terribly. Oh Jesus, for the sake of your blood, you must help us drive Satan out. He's in here. Lars Bundgaard got up halfway as if he were talking to someone. — You're in here, Satan, he shouted. I know it. You've taken up residence in Laust Sand, you're sitting in him and lurking to take his soul. But I say to you in Jesus's name: Get out! When Jesus gave his blood for the sinners, you were overcome. Get out! Oh, dear, merciful savior, we pray to you with all our hearts that you rip out this poor person from the darkness and save him from hell. He's a sinner, and if you can't take pity, he must be lost. But let him just regain his senses again a single moment so he can name your name and cling to you. — Oh, Jesus, Jesus, Jesus!

Tea could no longer conceal her excitement and cried out loud and plaintively. Aaby whined in a tortured old man's voice, and Jens Røn rocked back and forth and mumbled Jesus! Jesus! Thomas Jensen prayed softly for reconciliation and mercy. But over their intercession Lars Bundgaard's voice resounded like a mill, which grinds, now wailing and doleful, now threatening, mocking, and raving. He got up onto his knees and broke out into mocking against the enemy and sank again to the ground and importuned for forgiveness and help. The salty sweat poured down over his face, which was scalded by tears and scorched by the sun.

Laust Sand trembled violently, and his moaning became a snoring. It looked as though he was trying to raise his head from the pillow and Lars Bundgaard bent close down over him and shouted into his ear: Jesus! Laust Sand, think of the savior! A weak spasm moved across his wan face, he blinked his eyes a bit, and there was a rattling in his chest. The agonies of death had begun.

He's going away now! Aaby whispered and squeezed his hands.

They sat a while without saying a word and stared at him and saw how life was yielding. One after the other, the tormented, stiff features became smooth. Lars Bundgaard shuffled over to Adolfine and placed his hand on her shoulder.

Adolfine, he said. Laust Sand has gone to his judgment. Adolfine woke up with a start and stared vacantly past him. But when she grasped the words, she ran to the bed and threw herself across the dead man.

Oh, Laust! Oh, Laust! she cried.

Thomas Jensen was praying. His voice was gentle and tranquil, and filled with a remarkable, great solemnity.

Oh, dear Jesus, he whispered. Now we thank you for all your mercy and for your holy blood, so truly we are your children. For if it's your will, you can take the poor, sinful soul in your care. Don't let it out of your hand if you can, for we will of course not set ourselves against your wisdom. You know how weak we are, and how much evil there is in our hearts. Take care of her, who offended together with him, and turn her away from the path of sin. Obliterate the evil act with your mercy. In the name of our Lord Jesus Christ, amen.

They rose and stood for a bit next to the deathbed. Adolfine had slid down on the floor, where she lay sobbing spasmodically. Tea and Alma bent down over her and dragged her into bed. Thomas Jensen watched her. The tears trickled down his cheeks.

So he has finished his struggles, Aaby whispered and could not take his eyes off the dead man.

Alma came into the parlor again. I'll have to stay here, she said to her husband. We can't just leave her here alone. She could hurt herself.

Thomas Jensen nodded.

They went out onto the road in the warm evening and walked for a bit without talking to one another.

Do you believe now Laust Sand will be damned? Thomas Jensen asked and stopped.

Jens Røn didn't answer, but Lars Bundgaard said seriously: I know nothing of course. But I believe so.


Adolfine walked about the house swollen and encumbered, but without a complaint. Her look was a bit disturbed, but no one knew what to say to her. But Mariane and Alma came every day, and Malene had begun to look through her children's clothes. There should easily be some things for the child when the time came.

Only the West Coasters came along to the funeral. Only one funeral guest had come from their home in the old district. That was Laust Sand's sister, Dorre. She was older than her brother, white-haired, and with features as sharp as a bird's. Her fate had been penurious. Her husband had been convicted of stealing shipwrecked goods and couldn't bear the shame. When he came home from prison, he hanged himself. She was a bit disturbed in the head and saw warnings, and ahead of time she had also known this misfortune would come.

The coffin was driven on a wagon along the dusty road to the church, and afterwards the mourners walked in heavy, black clothes. It was an oppressive heat, and the church stood blindingly white in the sunlight. In all the doorways people stood and watched the funeral procession. After all, everyone knew what Laust Sand's end had been like. The men unloaded the coffin from the wagon and carried it through the brown churchyard gate to the grave. It was a silent understanding that Laust Sand should not enter the church. The fishermen looked stiffly at the ground during Pastor Brink's speech. His words were very simple. *Here* there should have been talk of the Lord's heavy hand and vengeance and the horror of sin. But the pastor spoke only of death, which reconciles.

The earth struck hollowly against the box: From dust you have come, to dust you shall return, and from dust you shall again arise! Now Laust, whom they all had known and respected, was laid in the earth with his guilt. But another morning he would rise and wander to his judgment with his ledger book. Sinners are we, perdition lurks for us, and hell stands open with its blazes.

They sang a hymn, and those in attendance dispersed silently and earnestly. No one went up to the house of mourning, where Adolfine wandered about restlessly. She couldn't sit down and calm down, her mind was long gone, and her face stiffened in ash-gray desperation. Old Dorre shuffled at her side from room to room.

What's going to become of the child, when it comes? she asked in her deep, grating voice.

Adolfine looked vacantly at her and finally grasped the question.

I know nothing, she said.

No, we know nothing, Dorre mumbled. But it will doubtless go badly. I've seen a warning.

Have you seen a warning? Adolfine asked, suddenly all there.

The old woman nodded mutely and knew what she knew. What have you seen? Adolfine asked.

Dorre shook her head—it was smartest to be silent.

But the next day Mariane came and was like a boiling kettle; she chatted and didn't let Adolfine alone. Didn't we say the house had to be cleaned? That's what people generally do after sickness. She chased after Adolfine, they scoured and soaped, aired the bedding, and polished whatever there was of nickel and brass in the parlor. In the evening Adolfine went to bed dead tired in her head, and early in the morning Mariane was there again. And when the cleaning was over with, Mariane looked about and nodded contentedly: that thing was taken care of. But now what about the baby clothes? Yes, baby clothes, Adolfine said hopelessly. Mariane slapped her hands together and shouted: I've never heard the likes of it: aren't you thinking at all about the child now that the time is so close? We have to go sew and I mean immediately.

She forced Adolfine to go along to the coop and buy cloth and whatever else was needed. They rambled through the whole town. Adolfine walked stooped and said nothing, while Mariane chatted away. At the coop the manager, unsure of himself, cleared his throat, but Mariane stood stiffly and looked at him somewhat sharply, and there wasn't a word said that could offend Adolfine. But when the goods were to be packed up, the manager could no longer control himself; he tilted his head pensively and looked at Adolfine: I'll put a scriptural word inside. After all, it can't ever hurt the way we humans are, he said. Mariane quickly took the paper, crumpled it up and flung it on the floor. We came to trade, she said angrily. And we don't care about your little pieces of paper. It was only a text from the scriptures, the manager explained. We can get that from the pastor, Mariane said. That's not why we've come here. Yes, I'm a saved person now, the manager answered and bowed his head, and would like to do something to help my fellow humans. Mariane took the package: I don't know whether you're a fool or a scoundrel, she said. But when I've discovered which, I'll come and let you know.

One day Adolfine went to bed and was to give birth. It was a difficult birth. The doctor was fetched, and he took the child with the tongs—Alma shuddered when she saw the bright, shining instruments. Dorre was still there; she wandered about fidgeting while it lasted. The women ran back and forth with linen and water, and finally the child saw the light of day. It was a big boy, healthy and hardy. Mariane put him in Adolfine's arms.

Adolfine opened her eyes halfway—she was still in a daze.

Is there something wrong with him, she whimpered.

No, Mariane said encouragingly. He's the way he's supposed to be. Such a big and strong boy, Adolfine.

Oh, thanks and praise, the girl sighed. I've been so afraid.

After all, God could easily punish him too.

It was as if Adolfine had woken up when she had her child. When others talked to her, she looked down and could barely answer, but when she gave the child her breast, there was a little smile around her mouth. And the boy was big and beautiful. Alma, Malene, and Tea were surprised that it could be the fruit of sin.

Thomas Jensen had written to Mads Langer right after Laust Sand's death, but the letter had taken a long time to reach him. The child was a month old when he unexpectedly stepped into Adolfine's parlor. Terrified, she started up and nearly dropped the boy on the floor.

What do you want? she asked.

He answered: Yes, you might well ask about that. Otherwise it's surely me who should be getting answers. Aren't you my sweetheart?

Adolfine looked at the floor. The ring was lying in the bureau drawer, but actually Mads Langer was within his rights. She had offended against him. He must have believed she had agreed to become his wife.

But now you're going to go with me, Mads Langer said.

Adolfine was about to scream and thought her heart stopped beating. The seaman stood in the middle of the parlor with an evil look in his eye: Indeed, she had to go with him.

Mads Langer had been around town to his good friends and conveyed his decision. Everywhere he harvested praise: the act was worthy of a Christian man. He was taking the fallen girl patiently by the hand and leading her back to the safe path.

Now how do you suppose Laust Sand happened to do it? Anton Knopper asked in confidence.

I don't know, Mads Langer said. He must have lusted for her—there's no other answer.

Anton Knopper felt sheepish and didn't know what he should answer, and the stoker said in a dark voice: But now it's doubtless being burned out of him!

That gave Anton Knopper a start, and he was just about to say that the Lord alone decided that. But he was silent. After all, it was reasonable that Mads Langer was offended.

Where were you last? he asked, and Mads Langer talked about New York, where he had seen a man beaten into the ground so his skull split like an egg you drop on the floor. The gray-white brain could be seen under his bloody hair.

Mads Langer went to town and talked to a lawyer and probate court; altogether it took time to arrange. Adolfine was to have her share from her mother; otherwise Dorre was the next to inherit. Mads Langer reasoned with her and explained it was reasonable for her to leave her share to Laust Sand's child. Dorre said yes to the whole thing and signed the papers he brought. Mads Langer nodded nobly: I've become engaged to Adolfine, he said. And I won't run away from it. And I'll confide something to you, Dorre: if the authorities ask around too much as to whose child it is, I'll take the blame for it.—

Laust Sand left a little money: a bit in the savings bank, nets and equipment, boat and fishing rights in the fjord. Mads Langer traded and sold. The North Sea fishermen jointly bought the share Laust had had in the fishing waters. They got it on credit as solid people, but otherwise Mads Langer would have preferred money immediately, because now he and Adolfine were to settle down. Mads Langer had gotten a job as a stoker on land—he was tired of the traveling life.

Adolfine's pale smile had disappeared, and when she was in the parlor with Mads Langer, she started shaking. One day she said to Alma, crying: I'm so afraid of him!

Alma took her hand and tried to console her. After all, Mads Langer was a good and believing man, who wished her well, and what would otherwise become of her. Here in the parish only shame was to be expected. And Alma added without looking at her:

If you turn your heart to Jesus and repent of your sin, you'll surely find peace in your soul.

That was easier said than done. Adolfine lacked courage—she had not prayed in a long time. She was too insignificant to knock on mercy's door. Now Laust Sand lay in his grave, and she had no one to rely on.

The child sucked in milk and was almost impossible to keep away from her breast. Every week he increased his weight, but Adolfine became more and more slender. Mariane had never seen such a beautiful child—she, who herself had pretty, healthy young ones, was full of jubilation and wonder. But what should the boy be called?

Adolfine thought about it and asked faint-heartedly: it surely wouldn't be possible to call him Laust. Mariane turned serious: that name was impossible. It was better to name him after someone in Mads Langer's family. Then he'll surely come to like the boy, Mariane felt.

Adolfine got up and began to walk up and down the floor with the infant in her arms.

I can't stand it! she wailed. Mariane consoled her.

You'll see, when you just get away from the area, she said. Here they'll never let you in peace. But when you travel with Mads Langer, there's no one abroad who knows whose child it is. You're not going to like it here, little Adolfine.

No, Adolfine cried. But I'm afraid of him—he's a terrible person. Oh, Mariane, you're the only one who's good to me; can't you tell me what I should do.

Mariane embraced her.

You have to think about the boy, she said. If you don't marry Mads Langer, then the worst can happen; he's capable of going to the authorities and reporting you. But I'll tell you one thing, Adolfine, the man hasn't been born you can't get power over if you really want to. You must try it for the boy's sake; if you can't stick it out, then you should come back here, and we'll always stand by you.

Mads Langer had plenty of time and didn't think about traveling for two weeks. Old Dorre constantly went and pottered about, and when Mads was in the parlor, she didn't take her eyes from him.

It's an odd spectacle, he said to Anton Knopper. She's totally disturbed. She just goes and glares. But Anton shook his head: Dorre knew something others didn't know.

She had seen a warning for Laust Sand, he said.

Do you believe in that kind of stuff, Mads Langer asked arrogantly.

I believe there's a lot we don't know about! Anton Knopper replied. And we shouldn't rack our brains about it either. But Dorre has gotten the ability to see what's hidden.

Hah, Mads Langer laughed. Such an old bone. I'll soon have to disabuse her of that. But maybe she can also see where Laust Sand has gone to now. Because that must be something that shines in your eyes.

Anton Knopper became serious and said sadly: We really have to hope there's also salvation for him.

No, Mads Langer said. There isn't. He's in the puddle and will remain scorched. If you believe he'll get off, what's the point of hell! No, that's not the way it works, old man.

With shining eyes Mads Langer again talked about hell and the eternal torments. His voice became loud and ringing, and Anton Knopper didn't like it, although it was probably right.

As the days passed, Mads Langer nevertheless began to be bored. People were on the fjord, and in the boats he was only in the way. The summer was over, wind and rain started up, and Mads Langer had to go over to his new job. When he told Adolfine to depart, she took to crying.

Oh, let me just stay here, she wailed. I don't know what will become of me there.

Mads Langer took her roughly by the arm: So, you think you can get around it this way. But you'll see otherwise.

One evening, Anton Knopper came late from the fjord, and Adolfine was sitting cowering on a fish-chest that had been drawn up right next to the wharf. She had swaddled the child in a shawl and pressed him tightly against herself. Anton Knopper glimpsed her figure in the dark and thought something crazy was afoot. He went over there:

But why are you sitting here, Adolfine?

He now discovered the girl was crying. She tried to hide her face in the shawl, but her sobbing, half-choked, penetrated through it. Anton Knopper was frightened:

Well but, dear little child, he said. That just won't do, you sitting here with your boy exposed to the night-cold. You're not thinking about anything crazy?

Yes, Adolfine said and flicked the shawl from her face. I can't stand it anymore.

Anton Knopper didn't know what to say. What grounds for consolation could he advance? In doubt, he sat down and looked at the child, who was lying with his eyes open; then he carefully tickled him on his throat.

And you're not thinking of the little one there? he said gently.

Yes, I am, Adolfine wailed. I want to take him along.

How can you say such a thing, Adolfine? Anton Knopper stammered. It's a great sin, and you must think about the fact that you're responsible for his life. Now come with me: I'll go home with you. Anton Knopper took the boy in his arms and got Adolfine to get up. The child lay warm and fine in his embrace, and the fisherman walked carefully with him and was afraid he might get hurt: after all, he wasn't used to such fragile things.

Early the next morning Adolfine stole up to the churchyard and looked at Laust Sand's grave. It lay desolate and forsaken among the fine tombstones and crosses, and the earth was covered only by a couple of withered wreaths. Adolfine sank down and patted the grave with her gaunt hands.

Dorre departed, and some time afterward Mads Langer moved away with Adolfine and the child. He had borrowed a truck, which was to drive the furniture and fixtures to the nearest train station. All their acquaintances had come to say good-bye, and Mariane had tears in her eyes. Mads Langer went around and arranged for the loading, grumbled at the chauffeur, and chatted with the people. It wasn't easy to arrange, all the stuff here, and it cost money to get it transported such a long way. But as soon as they got to the capital and found a place to live, he and Adolfine were to get married; so the furniture had to come along.

After they had said good-bye, they crawled up next to the chauffeur on the broad seat. Mads Langer waved with his hat, but Adolfine sat tiny and cowering with the child on her lap and rode out into the world.

The Mission house was a large room with pulpit and bare, plastered walls. Only on the gable wall was there a large picture. It represented Jesus in the temple. The coop manager had bought it cheaply from a believing painter in one of the railway station towns and gave it to the hall as a gift.

Now the Lord had gotten his house, and more and more found their way to it. Some of the respected farmers had joined God's children. But things were always a mess with the young people. When the pastor's youth association had held a meeting with a reading and lecture in the assembly house, they danced afterwards to harmonica music. And now there was almost no end to the things the pastor lent his name to. One evening animated pictures were shown, and Tea and Mariane went there. Their enmity had been long forgotten.

The man who traveled with the pictures had put up placards saying scenes of missionary work in India and China would be shown. Those were beautiful fields for missionary work! When the hall was full, he stepped forward and explained that mistakenly the pictures of the missionary work hadn't made it into the trunk, but instead he'd show a piece called "Elf Hill," which was famous all over the country. He was a handsome man with a long, full gray beard and black frock-coat, but he was rather a wolf in sheep's clothing. The piece showed people who had nothing better to do than kiss one another. Mariane was amused and laughed and behaved affectedly—you could almost imagine what she was up to. Tea would have preferred to leave if it could be done without attracting attention. But men and girls were sitting behind her and laughing at the worn-out pictures. On the way home she met Anton Knopper and explained what kind of exhibition it was. Yes, such things are not much use, Anton Knopper said. Use, Tea ranted. It just seduces innocent people to commit lewd acts! Yes indeed, Anton Knopper replied quietly. After all, you have to make sure you don't fall.

Anton Knopper certainly knew what he was talking about.

Katrine sat with downcast eyes at the meetings, but people whispered all over that she probably flirted a lot with the fellows on the farm where she served. Anton Knopper wasn't suspicious, and he firmly trusted Katrine. He knew he behaved toward her the way he was supposed to, and neither kissed nor pawed her. Anton Knopper was not the man to offend a girl with shameless manners. But let him who standeth take heed lest he fall! Anton Knopper had agreed with Katrine it would be best if they postponed the wedding until spring so she could be completely certain she was at home among the Pious.

One evening when he had finished his work he went to visit her. There was no one home at the farm. Katrine invited him into her room. There was only one chair, and Katrine sat on the bed. Her dress slid up a little, and Anton Knopper couldn't avoid seeing her round, broad knees and firm leg. His blood rose into his head, he got up, half without knowing what he was doing, and sat down on the bed beside her. Wild and giddy, he hugged the girl and forced her back on the bed, and the terrible thing almost happened. But when clutching at her breast, he got something hard and cold in his hand and, terrified, started up. It was the silver cross. For a moment he hid his face in his hands, and when he looked at Katrine again, the blushing girl was like a fog in front of his eyes.

You must forgive me, Katrine, he stammered. I was just about to forget myself.

But we're engaged, Katrine whispered.

True, Anton Knopper said. But that doesn't mean I have the right to behave like a wild animal. I'd give anything if evil hadn't risen up in me. And what must you think of me now? But I promise you: you needn't be afraid—I'll certainly keep the sinful instincts in check.

Anton Knopper had tears in his eyes and was breathing heavily. Katrine was sitting blushing and flushed on the bed. Her breast rose and sank quickly.

It doesn't matter, she said.

That's nice of you to forgive me, Katrine, he said, moved. Most women would surely have been offended and never forgotten it. I would ask you if you wouldn't kneel down with me and pray to Jesus that he pardon me for the sin I nearly committed. And we must thank him many, many times because it was Jesus who let the cross touch my hand after I'd nearly laid hands on you.

Katrine didn't answer, but threw herself wailing back onto the bed, and, disconcerted, Anton Knopper stared at her. She squeezed her body down into the down quilts, bit into the pillow, and kicked with her legs; it was a wild sight, and Anton Knopper now understood the fright he had caused. The girl was out of her senses, but after all it was reasonable after experiencing how her own sweetheart had almost taken her by force. His weather-beaten face was furrowed by simple-hearted remorse, and his beard hung sorrowfully down over his mouth. Katrine, he said and pulled at her. Be reasonable. I promise you with certainty I'll never do it again. Come to your senses. Katrine got up and dried her red face.

By the way: I don't care, she said.

Anton Knopper stood there confused and didn't know in from out. Womenfolk were the strangest things in existence. First the girl screamed, and then she didn't care even though you'd expect it least of all in a serious matter. Anton Knopper understood nothing. He took his hat. Surely it would be better if I go, he said repentantly. Yes, just you do that, Katrine snarled. That's what you're best at.

— The eel went into the traps and the price was good. Jens Røn had luck and got some cash in his pocket, and Tea looked confidently to the future. She no longer longed for home, but felt well here, where she had found believing friends, and where she and Jens Røn were well-respected people. And the children were well behaved. Martin was a servant boy on a farm for the summer, and Tabita made herself useful making food and taking care of the little ones. But Tea got a shock she least expected: Tabita, who was to go to confirmation class in the winter, was seized by arrogance and cut her hair. One Sunday morning she cut it with a scissors and showed off her bare head to Tea in the kitchen.

Tea clapped her hands and almost sank onto the floor: But have you lost your mind, girl, she shouted. Tabita looked at her nervously, but pursed her lips. Never mind! For months she had pondered whether she dare, and now it was done. Tabita had found an example in the dairy manager's daughter, who went to school in town and had short hair, and now she was not to be outdone, even if she had a bit of a fringe on her neck.

Jens, Tea called. Hurry up out here, Jens.

Jens Røn ran out into the kitchen, thinking an accident had happened.

Can't you see what she's done to herself, Tea complained.

But what's this all about, Tabita? Jens Røn said, perplexed. Have you totally lost your mind?

Tea smacked Tabita across the face and sank down on the kitchen chair and cried.

Just look at you, she wailed. Now people are going to think the worst of us when our children dress up that way. No, I never expected that from you, Tabita.

That's the way they do things in town, and —

But Tea didn't let her finish speaking. Never mind what they do in town, she said in a shrill voice. But you have to know you've brought shame on your parents. Oh, what will people say now—don't you have a thought in your head?

Tabita cried, and Tea was going around laden with sorrow when Mariane came in the afternoon. She took a close look at Tabita and helped with her hair using an embroidery scissors and found it finally rather splendid and practical not to have plaits.

I might truly like having it that way myself, Mariane said pensively and with a remote look. But Povl probably wouldn't like it. And also I'm certainly too old. But it becomes you now, Tabita.

Mariane wasn't serious enough, but Alma and Malene said Tea was right.

Shouldn't you watch out a little, Tabita, Alma said. It can easily go badly once you've begun this way.

Tea blushed a bit: Tabita has a good disposition, she said. And ultimately they're nothing but childish tricks.

People came to the Mission house from far beyond the parish borders. And at the discussion meetings Thomas Jensen and Lars Bundgaard were the leaders. They were accustomed to bearing witness and speaking from the soul. Here wealth and earthly renown were irrelevant. Mercy made no distinction. They were a society, sisters and brothers in the Lord.

Among those who repented was Katrine's father, Dead-Esben from the fens. He had a little place called the Dead Man's House. Many years ago a man had hanged himself from the loft beam. Esben married the widow. There was a certain horror attached to the name, but he was an honest man, who did no more evil than a sparrow under the sky. He was a tiny, gnarled old man, who had become a bit remote from being alone a lot. His wife was dead, and Katrine had been at work from the time she was confirmed. He liked meeting people, and every time he'd been in town, he thought for a long time after about every word that had been said. One person had shaken his hand and asked in a friendly way: How are things, Esben? And another had offered him coffee. Esben nodded and answered and was nothing but smiles after so much friendliness.

Esben often came to the Mission house and sat in the good warmth and felt secure and well among the people. One evening Thomas Jensen came over to him in the back bench and asked gently: How do you stand with Jesus, Esben? Esben couldn't answer much, as he sat there, but he did manage to say: Maybe it's not as it should be. Well, if it isn't, Thomas Jensen said, then you have to find your way to salvation and get peace in your soul. After all, we're sinners—much more than we think.

How did things stand between Esben and his God and creator? Surely not much better than for the other wild heathen in his desolate place in the fens. Around the house he had planted flowers and bushes; they were still standing with their leaves in autumn's drizzle. But his soul was, to be sure, in poor shape. Thomas Jensen and the other good people didn't begrudge him that. Many was the time he was on his way to town, but he turned around again. After all, you shouldn't seem to be intruding. When he came home, he went out into the stall; people didn't need to know it, but Esben had his best hours there. It was warm and peaceful, and the two cows stood in the good warmth and chewed their cuds.

Finally, one day he went all the way to the village. It was windy, and out in the fjord the water was foaming white. Esben walked by Thomas Jensen's house, but couldn't get himself to go in. Didn't it seem odd to importune the man? And he set off toward home; it would have to wait for another time when they met accidentally. When he was nearly home, he resolved to turn around and go to Thomas Jensen all the same. After all, it could happen that the man thought it was strange that he didn't come. Again Esben walked the wearisome way, but just at Thomas Jensen's door he began thinking it was best to get the animals milked first. Should the poor creatures stand tense in fear and torment, while he himself sought peace with Jesus? Esben had to go back; it was almost evening.

So he got there at bedtime and knocked on Thomas Jensen's door. Thomas Jensen was up, and they had coffee. Do you long for Jesus now? Thomas Jensen asked. Yes, Esben conceded he'd prefer peace in his house and in his soul and with all people and creatures. But how did you get peace?

First you have to confess your sin to the Lord, Thomas Jensen said. If you don't do that, you'll never have peace, neither here nor the other place.

Esben brooded—he was a sinner: that was never to be denied. But it was hard to find out what he should confess to God. Esben sat and warmed himself in the company of other people. The lamp was of sparkling brass; it was from a stranded ship. How it could shine, indeed, how it could shine.

In the house everyone had gone to bed. From the nooks he heard the quiet breathing of sleeping children. Everything was quiet. Esben felt well in this warm world. Here was peace in Jesus. He became gentle and glad and repented his sins, to be sure.

Thomas Jensen's friendly voice came from deep inside and had an oddly distressed strength. Alas, repent, was all he said.

Repent and have peace in your soul; lay the cross on the Savior: he bears it and still more. Esben looked inside a beautiful and pious world. Jesus bestows peace, and the children are the blessed straw on the world's fields.

When Esben came home, he went out into the stall and sat a while on the old feed box. It was warm, and the cows rubbed their muzzles against his coat sleeves. In the stall among the simple animals the Jesus child had come to the world. His little face had been reflected in their eyes. The animals had sniffed at him and licked his body.

— Fog and sleet enveloped the house gables; the icy wind swept across the fjord. The nights were dark with ragged clouds and a drifting ghostly moon. On the field the crows fluttered, and the sparrows chirped, exhausted in the bare trees. At the wharf the boats clutched at their moorings, and the water rippled cold and gray against the planks. But in the evening the warm light shone from the Mission house. Town pastors and booming peasant missionaries came marching to it; gentle people and thundering priests bore witness of salvation, where the soul found its shelter.

Pastor Brink wandered on restless walks and thought through his sermons precisely. There was an election to the parish council, and Thomas Jensen, teacher Aaby, and a Mission farmer got in. Should he seek another call? No, no one should assert he yielded to superior force. But it wasn't easy to find new lecturers for the youth association; there wasn't much money in the treasury, and even the most idealistic people's high school directors didn't use their tongues gratis. The pastor was obliged to lower the level more than he actually cared to. And it was a dangerous game—he knew that for sure: if something bad happened, he was responsible. Often some of the Pious met in the assembly hall and listened to the lecture. The pastor felt as if the enemies were spying on him everywhere, suspicious eyes following him, spiteful minds weighing his words.

One evening he saw Thomas Jensen on one of the back benches in the hall. The lecturer was a lanky man with a huge bald pate and protruding, worried eyes. He was talking about spiritualism. The pastor was annoyed: the lecture was dilettantish, but the man had been so modest in his demands. It was just unlucky that Thomas Jensen happened to come precisely this evening.

When the lecture was over and people left the hall, Thomas Jensen walked over to Pastor Brink.

There was something I'd like to ask the pastor about, he said in his low, calm voice. Do you agree with the man?

Agree and agree, Pastor Brink replied evasively. I don't believe one can wholly reject spiritualism, and the Scriptures do speak time and again about spirits.

Now the way I've understood it, we mustn't concern ourselves with conjuring, Thomas Jensen said. And all I can see is that spiritualists do that. And I don't quite understand why the pastor brings the youth together to hear about these doings.

Are you speaking to me as a member of the parish council? the pastor asked. Even if you are, I reject your critique. I in no way vouch for this lecture, but I can't see that it can hurt the young people to get information about the spiritual movements that currently exist. You can't force me into spiritual one-sidedness; I won't let myself be yoked into some system.

Pastor Brink was red with anger and breathed heavily. Was this the signal for open struggle? He hoped so and was prepared.

There's no one who wants to force you, Thomas Jensen said calmly. I can't imagine there's anyone who has that intention. But I say what I mean—we Pious don't like this kind of speaker, and we hardly believe it's your task to arrange ungodly lectures. — And one thing you're not remembering: after the lectures here the young people go right down to the hotel and dance. —

Pastor Brink's voice trembled a bit when he answered: You're a quarrelsome person, Thomas Jensen. You may think what you will, but I won't deny the young people an innocent pleasure. I myself danced in my youth. It didn't hurt anyone.

Do you know how many girls dancing leads to misfortune? Thomas Jensen said. But you can't know anything about that. Otherwise you wouldn't accept the responsibility. —

I know about people who call themselves Pious and God's

children, but their deeds aren't done in the light of day, the pastor answered ardently. There are bad apples everywhere.

Thomas Jensen looked at him firmly. You shall not damn Laust Sand, he said quietly. He took his punishment in humility from God.


Toward Christmastime a guest came to Thomas Jensen's. He was a lean, slender man with a thin, yellow mustache and slanted teeth that protruded from his mouth. He stood his old bicycle up against the house, knocked on the door, and, a bit embarrassed, greeted Alma, who asked: But if it isn't Peder Hygum? The man bowed with a humble smile: Indeed, it was none other than Peder Hygum in his own insignificant person.

But what are you doing in these parts? Alma asked. I thought you were an assistant missionary in the Orient.

Peder Hygum was nothing but smiles and explanations. The horrible climate in the heathen countries had nearly destroyed him. And he added modestly: Now I serve the good cause here in our own country.

Alma invited him inside and gave him food. Peder Hygum was Thomas Jensen's cousin, and the fisherman gave him a friendly greeting when he came home from the fjord. Peder Hygum fetched a little handbag from the bicycle, and Thomas Jensen asked him to stay a few days before he moved on. Peder Hygum was a hawker and solicited subscribers to a Christian weekly. His wife was staying in a far-off town with her parents. These were difficult times, and Peder Hygum hadn't had it easy finding his way to something when he came back to his fatherland.

It was a gray and slushy winter—one day snow, the next rain, east wind, cold, and sludge. The sky closed off the horizon, making it heavy and gray. On the other side of the fjord the black hills were like a wall. The water entered toward the north across the broad meadowlands.

Anton Knopper had lost his internal equilibrium. He was like restlessness in continuous motion; his mouth went unchecked; he talked and laughed, but his face had aged. He played with the children wherever he went to visit, and whirled them until they screamed with delight. But at times he sat and floated off somewhere, even when others were present, and an odd glow smoldered in his eyes. He wasn't seen very much with Katrine. Tea suspected something had gone wrong between them, and wanted to say a consoling word to him. She thought she had a word to say about love and sorrow—she who had gone through so much in her youth. But every time she cautiously began, Anton Knopper closed himself off. He probably dealt with it best alone.

Frost and wind set in, and the snow piled up in drifts. It penetrated through all the cracks, and in the warm parlors the walls were dripping damp. After a few days of frost there was ice on the water, and the broad stretches of meadow were like an arctic field, where the snow whipped down and rose in clouds. People struggled against the storm. The sharp wind ripped down into the lungs and scorched the skin. The Sunday before Christmas there weren't many people in church. Thomas Jensen had been to communion and worked his way home laboriously through the snow, which lay two feet high out of the wind. Right outside of the Mission house a white figure was standing motionless. He recognized Anton Knopper.

There's a snowstorm, he called, but Anton didn't hear him. He went closer.

But what in the world are you standing here for? he asked.

Anton Knopper turned his face toward him. Clumps of ice hung in his beard, and he was pale from the cold.

What are you saying? he called.

Why are you standing still here on the road in this terrible weather? Thomas Jensen asked. The smartest thing would be to hurry indoors.

Oh, there was something I started thinking about, Anton Knopper replied. See where the snow is drifting across the roof?

Thomas Jensen looked up at the Mission house roof, where

the snowflakes were whirling around the cross.

Of course, I can see it's a snowstorm, but that's hardly so unusual.

Of course it's not; no, it can't be, Anton Knopper said absentmindedly. No, I started looking at the cross, and then I got lost in thought.

They trudged home side by side, while the snow lashed their faces. When Anton Knopper got to the house where he lived, he stopped for a moment at the door.

I'm afraid I'm going mad, Thomas, he said softly.

You know, something can always go wrong for people, Thomas Jensen answered, a bit surprised. And if I can be of any help to you, you know I'm ready. But I can understand if you were standing and looking toward the cross over there on the Mission house, your thoughts are on the right road.

Anton Knopper flinched and quickly took his leave. Thomas Jensen pensively walked to his house. What could be gnawing at the cheerful man?

He was barely inside the door before Peder Hygum came running out of the parlor and helped him out of his coat. After all, the hawker couldn't make any headway while the snowstorm lasted. He had taken some rest and sat in the evening and read aloud from the books he had in his bag. Peder Hygum was a peaceful man, humble in all his conduct and thankful to those who showed him friendliness.

I don't believe there will be any change in the weather for the time being, Thomas Jensen said when he came into the parlor. And if it keeps drifting, you'll certainly be forced to remain here over Christmas. You'd otherwise have visited your wife and celebrated the holiday together with her.

Peder Hygum sorrowfully shook his head. It wasn't granted to him to meet with his dear ones during the festivities. His father-in-law was an unbeliever and had forbidden him access to his house.

That's really hard on you, Thomas Jensen said sympathetically.

Right now during the holy Christmas time it really cuts a bit into my heart, Peder Hygum replied. I lead a life in which I get tossed about, like a bird whose nest evil people have torn down from the tree. I truly don't accuse anyone, but many times my heart becomes heavy with the way I have to scrape through life. But I think about the words of the hymn:

> I never get to spend much time
> Where joy is for the taking,
> I've spent too many thrifty days,
> And there are more in waiting. —

In the evening Thomas Jensen talked to Alma. Shouldn't they invite Peder Hygum's wife and child as guests for Christmas? If they arranged things, they could surely house them. Alma had no objections. It was reasonable for Thomas to invite people from his family. Peder Hygum got tears in his eyes when Thomas Jensen asked him, and blessings flowed from his tongue. Now the only issue was that the trains not stop running. But a few days before Christmas the snowstorm died down, and the weather became clear, glittering, and frosty.

Peder Hygum had borrowed a sled from one of the farmers and drove to the station and fetched his wife and child. When he came back he was in good spirits and paced the floor chatting, sat down for a moment, and got up again. At mealtimes he had the little girl on his lap.

Laura Hygum was a slender, somewhat grief-worn woman, with fair, almost colorless hair. When she talked with people, she looked past them, as if she were turning her attention to something in the room. She was quiet and retiring and seemed very cool toward her husband. The little girl was a bit misshapen and resembled her mother.

I really hope you'll feel at home with us, Thomas Jensen said to Laura. You're heartily welcome if you'll just make do.

Thanks, Laura said. I hope you people won't have too much trouble —

Oh, surely not, Peder Hygum interrupted. We'll try not to cause a disturbance. You've shown yourselves to be good relatives and pious brothers and sisters, and if all people were like you, our earthly journey would be easier. There's a little verse I recall:

> Seems it in my anguish lone
> As if God forsook his own,
> Yet I hold the knowledge fast
> God will surely help at last.

Those are good words, Thomas Jensen said.

Yes, and they fit me so wonderfully, Peder Hygum replied seriously. Many an hour I've felt alone and abandoned and believed God had completely forgotten I existed. And every single time the Lord has shown me his mercy anew and helped get me on my feet.

Peder Hygum fell silent. Then he turned toward the little girl, took her hands, and folded them gently.

You've grown, little Kirstine, he said. Yes, you've gotten big. Let me hear if you can remember the hymn we read together.

The child quickly recited by rote in a whispering voice:

> Who stands outside of Paradise?
> A cherubim with swords of fire.
> And why are things so quickly lost?
> Oh, Adam fell away from God.
>
> But was he in God's image made?
> Oh, he has lost his innocence.
> What glory crowns his sinful head?
> He's wraithed in fogs of mind and sense.
>
> What blinded him, who was so wise?
> His own dear wife, with women's lies.
> Why did he stoop to do these deeds?
> The serpent's wily vanities.

> How widely falls this curse of sin?
> On all of Eve and Adam's kin.
> How can this story be made known?
> That we have turn'd from God alone.
>
> Who says that God is filled with wrath?
> Our conscience speaks this bitter truth.
> But what if it is lost in sin?
> It must be woken up again.

Thomas Jensen turned to his own children, who were standing around Alma and looking at the unfamiliar girl.

You aren't that clever. You'd do well to learn from Kirstine.

I think that hymn is really very suitable for the little ones, Peder Hygum said. It talks of original sin and makes clear there's no hope without mercy. I believe early on we should teach the children to appreciate their conscience and keep it awake. I can remember two years ago, when Kirstine was only four years old, she said to me one day: Father, I'm so glad, because Jesus has taken my sin from me. That's a beautiful word in a child's mouth. And out in the Orient I knew a missionary; the first word he taught his little boy to say wasn't mother or father, or whatever children usually say, but Jesus. That little child went out into the world, so to speak, with the Savior on his lips. Kirstine, let me hear if you know your Lord's Prayer.

The child began: Our Father, who art in heaven— — —but Laura got up and picked her up:

She'd better go to bed; I'm afraid she's very tired after the trip.

— Christmas eve they were in church. Thomas Jensen couldn't pay attention while the pastor was speaking; he came to think about Laust Sand, who lay buried outside. No one had decorated his grave for the holiday. He looked about. Everywhere were faces he knew. People who came to the meetings and were saved. He heard Tea's voice ringing over the others singing the hymn; in the corner he saw a glimpse of Lars Bundgaard and Malene, but Anton Knopper wasn't there.

There was a hard freeze and the sky was deep and dark with shining stars. From the houses in town the singing of hymns could be heard; only Anton Knopper was sitting alone in his room. He didn't notice the cold, even though frost-flowers had formed on the panes. —

— Laura was good at helping Alma in the house, but she wasn't much of a talker. Kirstine went about quietly by herself and couldn't really become part of the group with the other children. After all, she was mostly used to being alone. But Peder Hygum was in high spirits and lively. On the holidays they visited Lars Bundgaard and Jens Røn, and Peder Hygum won them all over. One evening he spoke in the Mission house and reported on the work in heathen country.

When Christmas was over, he became fidgety. There was still frosty weather with high snow, but one day he packed up his books and announced he would venture out to trade.

I hardly think you can bicycle the way the roads are, Thomas Jensen said.

Of course, the hawker replied. I've been out in it when it was worse. And you have to do something if you're going to earn your bread for yourself and your family. People don't want to sacrifice money, even for good reading. Yes, I'm truly not accusing anyone—most of them can't afford it. But I think I have to go out to my work. I often think about the fact that such a little pamphlet perhaps helps a soul that is just in need. I recall a little verse:

> Although you seem to suffer,
> Still all the soul is glad.
> Should bread be all you're after,
> In hunger, wrangling, hate,
> With you they will discover
> In spite of all your gold,
> In heaven, it will be clearer,
> That God is all you hold.

Peder Hygum bicycled out every day. Thomas Jensen tended to his work, and Laura was alone with Alma. When she talked about leaving, Alma turned it down. There was no hurry, and there was surely no prospect for the time being that they could set up their home?

Laura shook her head: that wouldn't happen for a long time. She'd been with Peder Hygum in the Orient and talked about it, but otherwise she wasn't very communicative. Alma understood that her father had a store with wooden shoes and wooden articles and was a rather well-off man.

He's not saved? Alma asked.

No, Laura said. He's an Adventist. And he and Peder can't be together.

Is it because of their beliefs that they're enemies?

No, Laura answered hesitating. There's so much else. Peder's been unlucky since we came home from the Orient. He was the head of a seaman's home for a while, but he couldn't stay there: it wasn't for him. Since then he's looked for all sorts of things. With his manner it's not easy; there's so much he has going against him.

Yes, yes, Alma consoled her. Surely better times will also come for Peder Hygum.

Anton Knopper no longer went to the farm where Katrine worked, and people seldom saw them together. There was whispering that the engagement was about to come to naught, and the women followed Anton Knopper with searching looks. The change in his manner became clearer and clearer. He was silent and turned inward and looked after himself.

The ice on the fjord had become so thick you could walk on it. The fishermen marched out with axes and eel-prongs, and the ice resounded hollowly under their feet. Anton Knopper and Thomas Jensen walked together. It was tranquil frosty weather. To the south the hills rose white and glistening in the sun, and to the north the meadows merged with the ice-covered fjord. The air was cold, and people's breath froze.

That's nice to see, Thomas Jensen said. If you had skates,

you could skate clear across the country.

Yes, Anton Knopper replied, as if his thoughts were far away.

Thomas Jensen was standing with his eel-prong at the hole in the ice and was so close to Anton Knopper he could follow all his movements. Suddenly he saw him thrust down the eel-prong and at the same instant pull the pole up and throw it on the ice. Then he began tottering toward land.

Anton! Thomas Jensen shouted. There's nothing wrong, is there?

Anton Knopper didn't turn, but tumbled off like a sick man, and Thomas Jensen ran after him while the ice sang under his feet. When he caught up with him, he said out of breath: You haven't gotten sick, have you, Anton? Anton Knopper turned his gray face toward him.

I don't know what it is myself, he said.

Why did you fling the eel-prong and walk off? Thomas Jensen asked. There must be a reason.

It's not easy to understand, Anton Knopper answered, and his teeth chattered. But when I wanted to thrust the iron down into the hole, I was gripped by a strange fright. I don't think I dare spear eel any more.

But there's no danger in doing it, Thomas Jensen said.

No, I know that too, and I can't say either what it's supposed to mean. But I'm really bad off. If you'll listen to me, Thomas, I'd gladly seek advice from you, because after Pastor Thomsen you're the smartest man I know. I have to say things bluntly the way they are. In the fall it happened that I almost laid hands on Katrine. At the last moment my hand hit up against a little silver cross she wears on her breast, and I definitely understood the sign, and no one was hurt. But you can surely imagine I was very remorseful and did everything I could to wash off the sin.

So did you receive forgiveness? Thomas Jensen asked softly.

No, it got worse and worse for me. I couldn't overcome my sensuous lusts. And you have to understand it really got bad. Every time I prayed, unchaste pictures popped up before me—and finally I couldn't see a cross without having the most sinful thoughts.

Appalled, Thomas Jensen stopped. But what are you saying?

Can you remember that day you met me outside the Mission house where I was standing and looking at the cross on the gable? I had just been walking by, and accidentally I looked up toward the cross—and immediately evil got hold of me and wouldn't let go. I don't know where it will all lead. Because if the cross, which the Savior died on, excites unchaste thoughts in me, then it surely can't be anything but the devil that's in the picture. If I died now, I'd sail straight into hell's fire.

You mustn't talk that way, do you hear, Anton, Thomas Jensen said. There must be a way we can find. Are you sure you didn't let yourself be seduced by lusts of the flesh when you became engaged to Katrine?

Of course I believed she could become one of God's children, Anton Knopper replied.

You believed it, but are you sure you didn't deceive yourself? I'm afraid you haven't kept your eyes open as to what was driving you. I don't trust the girl even if her father is a believing man, and I believe it's reached the point that you've forgotten Jesus for your lust. And now God's giving you a sign. See, you grabbed for the girl and got the cross in your hand! Now you have to choose which one you want.

They had come to the shore, where the brittle ice crackled under their feet. Anton Knopper walked with his head bowed.

I think you're right, he said. And I want to say thanks, Thomas. I'd never have figured that out on my own. I'm not a gifted man.

With a heavy heart Anton Knopper went to see Katrine. The girl fumed and cried, but Anton Knopper insisted it had to be over between them. Then Katrine became gruff and turned up her nose: by the way, I don't care a fig for you. I can find another sweetheart. You're the worst guy a girl could have. You mustn't bear a grudge against me, Anton Knopper said. I certainly know I haven't been to you the way I should have been.

The weather broke—there was a thaw. The snow melted, and people saw the ground again. One night the ice broke up with a hollow drone, the posts cracked like matchsticks, and a piece of the wharf was ripped away. The highway was a bottomless puddle, and the ditches overflowed with water. It wasn't possible for Peder Hygum to travel out on his bicycle. He and his family were still enjoying Thomas Jensen's hospitality, and every time they talked about leaving, nothing came of it. It was reasonable for them to stay as long as Peder Hygum could sell something in the area. He also earned a bit on his trips. But it wasn't much, the hawker sighed.

He was a speaker in the Mission house and was able to report on his travels around the parishes. He had passed by inns where screams and roars rang out in the dark. He had heard about drink and lewdness and ungodly priests. A shower of spittle sprayed from his mouth when he became animated.

At a meeting Anton Knopper happened to sit next to a woman he hadn't seen before. She was tall and strong, had a somewhat lanky figure and deep pock-marks in her face, but her eyes were pretty and her lips red and full. She sang in a high, penetrating voice. When Anton Knopper walked home together with Thomas Jensen he asked who she was.

Her name's Andrea, Thomas Jensen answered. Her father had a small farmstead, and they now have a house east of town. She just recently repented. To speak bluntly, she also has a child. Her father is old, up around eighty, and they say he's a bit odd, and her mother is dead.

So, she has a child, Anton Knopper said.

Yes, but otherwise she's a capable woman as far as I've heard.

Anton Knopper was busy; he toiled from morning till late in the evening and didn't allow himself any rest. Evil lurked—he noticed it; one look at a woman could lead him into misfortune. In church and the Mission house he sat in the front row where he had no one in front of him. But when he saw the cross on the altar, he had to close his eyes and became dizzy.

As soon as the weather permitted traveling on the roads, Peder Hygum pushed his bicycle out of the shed. He had gotten a new shipment of books and pamphlets and they sold well. Alma gave him food for the road. As a rule it was late before he came home, and sometimes he stayed away for several days. One night Alma heard loud voices and crying from the guest room, which sounded like Laura wailing. The next day Peder Hygum said she'd been plagued by toothaches and hadn't been able to sleep a minute. Alma looked at her—she was sitting looking at the floor and was a little pale, but she bolted up with a nervous start when someone knocked on the door, and Anton Knopper entered. He was invited to sit down.

I've gotten a letter from Mads Langer, he said quietly.

Really? Thomas Jensen said anxiously. But there's nothing amiss, is there?

You better see the letter for yourself, Anton Knopper replied and handed him an envelope.

Thomas Jensen got out his glasses and read:

Good friend.

When you get this letter from me, it's because Adolfine, whom I married, is dead. In a delirium she plunged into the harbor and drowned. It began with the child's getting sick in the fall, and when it died, she became totally mad. She was in an institution, but they couldn't keep her any more and doubtless felt she could be at home. But you couldn't talk to her, and if you said a word to her, she was like a person possessed. I know I indulged her and said to myself: she's insane—you have to be gentle with her. I've had to spend a lot of money on her, and I'd appreciate it if you and the rest of you good friends would send the money still owing to me from the water rights you all bought. Sickness and burial are expensive, and I've gone into debt. It's written that their worm dieth not, and the fire is not quenched; the words fit Laust Sand, who is to blame and will be called to account on judgment day. He dragged Adolfine down with him, and I did what I could to drive her away from sin, but it wasn't to be. I won't write about how she often behaved; she had an evil nature because she was an insane person, and that's also why she flung herself into the harbor. But I ask all of you again to send the money because my debt is large, and I'll need it. Greetings to all my good friends and to you, good friend, in the name of Jesus, our savior and redeemer, in whom we shall find help both here and when the time comes.

*Mads Langer*

It was quiet in the parlor because he had read the letter aloud.

So Adolfine has found peace, Thomas Jensen said.

Yes, so Adolfine was dead and had taken her own life. Mariane cried when she heard the news. I should never have let her go with him, she said. He was a foolish person, and she was afraid of him. But I thought it would be alright once she had the child. — There you can see what comes from lewdness, Tea said. But she went up and placed a wreath on Laust Sand's grave. Where might Adolfine have been laid to rest?

There was a meeting in the Mission house; an unfamiliar pastor had spoken, and a man took the floor to bear witness. The door was opened a bit, and a cold draft swept in and made the candles flicker. People in the back rows turned around. Peder Hygum had come. He had been out for two days.

His feet dragged a bit when he walked up the center aisle, and he looked tired and pale. In the front row people squeezed closer together to make room for him. But Thomas Jensen had scarcely asked whether there were more people who wanted to speak when Peder Hygum was already at the pulpit. There was something wrong with him. His eyes, hazy, stared down randomly in the hall, and he swayed back and forth like a tree in the wind. He began to speak in a hoarse whisper. People bent forward to hear, but no one grasped what he was saying; slobber dripped in streaks from his mouth. Thomas Jensen went up and took him by the shoulder.

You're sick, Peder, he whispered. Come, it's better that you sit down.

A vapor of alcohol wafted toward him. Peder Hygum was

drunk.

Thomas Jensen and Anton Knopper got him out. They had trouble dragging him, and his lips moved as if he were giving a talk.

It's strange he was able to ride his bicycle, Anton Knopper said shaken.

He did fall, Thomas Jensen answered. I immediately noticed his clothes were soiled.

They carried him halfway home and put him in bed. Laura stood stiff and pale and watched. She had immediately put the child out in the kitchen with Alma.

You better go along into the kitchen, Thomas Jensen said without looking at her. There's nothing to be done here.

They went into the kitchen, and Laura stood for a bit and looked out the window.

It was wet and windy outside. You could hear the cold roar from the fjord, which was still full of sheets of ice. Alma came in and sat down without saying anything.

So now you know! Laura said and turned. When it comes over him, he can't stop drinking. That was why he was sent home when he was a missionary. He drinks up all the money he gets in his hands.

Oh, Lord, Anton Knopper said compassionately—the poor man.

They were all silent for a little bit; then Thomas Jensen said: It's terrible for you, Laura, that he can't hold himself in check. Otherwise there's so much good in him. But maybe he'll get the strength to overcome the evil inclination.

Laura was standing and leaning against the wall. Anton Knopper said good-bye, and Thomas Jensen did an errand outside the parlor. Alma got up from the sofa and went over to Laura. She had tears in her eyes and gently put her hand on Laura's arm. It's happened before that such things get onto an even keel again, she said. But I know how it is. My own father was a drunk. And he recovered.

Every time he's been drunk, he complains and wails and promises to turn over a new leaf, Laura said flatly. But there's no escaping it.

You shouldn't talk that way, Alma replied in her gentle standard Danish. We mustn't oppose fate, but bear the cross we get.

I'm not someone who can forgive everything, Laura said, and her face had stiffened in cold serenity. I don't trust him, and I don't set much store by all his words and assurances. No one can demand that I forgive him, and I won't do it. Oh, if you knew what I've gone through with him.

The next morning Peder Hygum got up late. Alma poured him coffee in the kitchen, and he slurped it down quickly with brief sidelong glances at her. When he was done, he went out into the shed, where Thomas was sitting in his jacket and mending seine nets with his cold, stiff fingers.

You certainly got an odd impression of me yesterday evening, Peder Hygum said and made his voice sound candid. And I can surely understand you expect an explanation. The thing is, I got a fever in the Orient, they call it climatic fever, and it can come over me at any moment. Yesterday evening I had an attack while I was in a house; I was shaking and half unconscious and about to fall over. The people led me over to a sofa, and one of them poured a regular swig of cognac down my throat. They wanted to drive me home, but after I regained some of my strength, I felt I could probably pull through on my own. But after I got on the bicycle, it hit me that, you know, I'm not used to strong stuff . . . and the fever. . . Thomas Jensen looked at him fixedly, and his voice became more and more uncertain. When he fell silent, there was a long silence. Thomas Jensen didn't stop looking.

You should go to Jesus, he said. And pray for him to help you. And you mustn't lie to me. I've behaved decently toward you.

Yes, sure, of course, Peder Hygum said humbly. I've prayed to the Lord and clung to him . . . but I'm weak, and at times I fall. . . I know it so deeply in my heart. . . I'm just a poor wreck . . . No one can get anything out of knowing me . . . Instead I should move away . . . And try to recover and find peace again.

I'm not saying anything about your having fallen, Thomas Jensen said. I won't judge. But you've hidden it and pretended to be better than you are. I think we should part without bad words, but you better leave as soon as you can. . .

— But before Peder Hygum left, ugly things were heard about his doings. He had gone on a spree in the inns in the area and drunk whiskey. That's what was being spread about now. But the hawker went around to friends in town and said goodbye. After he talked about leaving, he laid the package of books on the table, and it wasn't easy to say no to him. Peder Hygum almost managed to sell them all off and took all allusions with humility. Tea bought a little book about missionary work in China; it cost a crown, and that was too much. But Peder Hygum got an admonition for the road.

I wonder if you're one of God's rightful children, she asked him in a low, stern voice.

Peder Hygum sighed and got tears in his eyes. He was just a poor, fallen man, who fought his fight in private. He was just about as wretched as a person could be.

Yes, Tea said. Whiskey is an ugly thing, which leads people to ruin. But is that the only thing, Peder Hygum? I've also heard tell of things I'd scarcely want to imagine. They say you were very fresh with a girl in the Voldum inn.

The tears trickled down Peder Hygum's gaunt, stubbly cheeks. Tea was sorry for him, but lewdness had to be punished.

I know I'm a sinner, Peder Hygum said. Everything I've done happened without my own will. When the whiskey devil gets hold of me, I don't know what I'm doing. Could I have sunk so low I violated a girl in Voldum inn? It's odd, Tea, I don't remember anything about a girl in Voldum inn. Maybe I should bicycle over there and see to making good what damage I caused in my wretched condition?

No, Tea said. If you go into the inn again, you could easily do something crazy again. I think it would be better if you repented of it. —

No one regrets every mistake the way I do, Peder Hygum

bemoaned. After all, I have a wife and child, and I so much want to be a pious person. But if you will all pray for me, then maybe the cross will be taken from me.

I'll do that, Peder Hygum, Tea said touched.

Again Peder Hygum took the book bag out and asked Tea to take a little book as a momento. It was called The Path of Sin and dealt with the world's dangerous paths, and she was to have it gratis for her good words. But Tea thought twice about it—she couldn't very well accept gifts from a poor man. — If I want the book, I'll also pay for it, she said.

Yes, Peder Hygum sighed, the book is really worth the money, and it costs only one and a half crowns.

Laura had her father to take refuge with, and Peder Hygum wanted to accompany her on the way and try his luck some other place in the country. They went on a little motor schooner, which was to go down the fjord, and Thomas Jensen and Alma accompanied them to the wharf. Laura stood silent and stiff on deck holding the child's hand. As the boat glided from the wharf, Peder Hygum began to sing. His loud, thin voice was audible above the crackling of the motor and the wind:

> I walk in danger all the way;
> The thought shall never leave me,
> That Satan, who has marked his prey,
> Is plotting to deceive me.
> This foe with hidden snares
> May seize me unawares
> If e'er I fail to watch and pray:
> I walk in danger all the way.
>
> I pass through trials all the way,
> With sin and ills contending;
> In patience I must bear each day
> The cross of God's own sending;
> Oft in adversity
> I know not where to flee;
> When storms of woe my soul dismay,

I pass through trials all the way.

Thomas Jensen listened to the hymn, while the tub disappeared in the foggy day.




The herring nets were out there; showers and storms swept through when they were to be emptied. But it was spring. The sun became more powerful and shone yellow in water puddles and ditches; it glittered on the wind motors, and white clouds drifted across the pale-gray sky. The plow turned the shining wet earth, and the gulls flew screeching down onto the furrows.

At Easter Tabita and Maren, Thomas Jensen's oldest girl, were confirmed. Tabita resembled a little woman in her black clothing, and Tea saw how fine and elegant she seemed among the others, whose shape was big and coarse. So Tabita was now grown up and had to go out and earn her keep. Thomas Jensen had already gotten a position for Maren—she was to be nurse-maid on a farm in the parish. But Tabita wanted to go to town and get a job; she insisted on that, and Tea couldn't contradict her.

It was cold when the men went out to the fjord in the damp mornings. The foamy waves were shining white in the semi-darkness, and the motor hissed with an odd, cold sound. They went out into the broad waters—so far you could barely catch a glimpse of land. But when the seine net was lifted, the herring in the boat shone with fantastic tinges of silver and purple. Often the crew was soaked through despite sea-boots and oilskins, and still it was nothing compared to the sea the way it was in a spring storm. Yes, the sea!

No one had been back home in the old parish since they had moved away. It was a long and expensive trip, and they had enough other things to spend the money on without it. But now Thomas Jensen suggested making an excursion to the sea when the herring fishing was over. It was only a six-mile drive and it couldn't cost a fortune to rent a big truck from a hauler in the nearest town with a railway station. The children would also come along so they wouldn't forget where they came from. They discussed all the ins and outs of the plan. They all longed to see the sea and feel the salt air in their lungs once again.

Anton Knopper was still melancholy—he said neither yes nor no. He didn't tell any jokes, and when he wasn't on the fjord, he mostly sat at home and mended nets. Many an evening Alma sent for him, and then it almost always happened that Andrea was visiting. Alma had been spending a lot of time with her recently, and Thomas Jensen surely had been thinking about her and Anton Knopper. As a rule Andrea had her child along. The little girl had developed an odd trust in Anton Knopper, and he liked to sit with her on his lap.

Andrea was by nature reserved, and there was something, as it were, broken about her. When people talked to her, she looked up with a terrified look, but Anton Knopper felt at home in her company. He certainly understood what the point was of inviting them together—Anton Knopper wasn't blind. And he'd gladly admit Andrea was a woman for him. She didn't arouse wildness and desire. He could look at her for a long time without having terrible thoughts arise, and no silver cross on her breast led his thoughts to sin and perdition.

One evening he was sitting at home in his room when Katrine came to visit. Anton Knopper's head got hot, and the girl stopped in the doorway, embarrassed.

It's crazy for you to be visiting me here, Katrine, he said. What in the world won't people find to say?

Are you still angry at me, Anton? Katrine asked, looking at the floor.

No, no, dear Katrine, Anton Knopper said insecurely. I have nothing to be angry about—and we talked at length together about what happened between us.

So things can't be good again between us? the girl asked.

Confused, Anton Knopper looked at her. He had never before experienced a girl coming and courting him. Katrine was big and shapely. Anton Knopper squeezed his hand hard on the bedpost and couldn't take his eye off the cross on her bosom. It was resting so securely between her breasts—the cold silver against the warm, sun-browned skin. The heat rose to his head, he breathed heavily and took hold of the bed till it creaked so he wouldn't jump at the girl and grab her. But if he fell now and abandoned himself to fleshly lust, then he'd defile the sacred cross and would have to be thrown into the eternal flames. He bored his fingers into the wood and collected all his thoughts about Andrea, who was a child of God and a woman for him. Finally he gained power over himself. I liked you a lot, Katrine, he whispered. And I want to wish you all the good in the world. But it just can't work between us.

I've done everything I could to become pious, Katrine said humbly.

But it's me there's something wrong with, Anton Knopper answered. I look at you with unchaste eyes, and you yourself know how close I came to violating you. It's not your fault I'm a lewd man, but I want to beg you from the bottom of my heart to go. Just looking at you arouses everything that's sinful in me.

Katrine turned without saying a word and left. From the window Anton Knopper saw her walk down the path and was on the verge of running after her and catching up to her.

The next day half the parish knew Katrine had visited Anton Knopper, and Tea looked to see whether the ring might have come back on his finger. She sighed in relief. Anton Knopper had survived the conflict. In Tea's estimation Katrine was a calculating girl who pretended to be pious to dupe a good man into marriage. It almost seems to me it's time for him to get married, Mariane said.

Yes, but not with a nonbeliever, Tea replied.

Come on, Mariane said. I don't believe there's a big difference between the Pious and the rest of us when it comes right down to those things.

That startled Tea. You ought not say that, Mariane, she answered in anger. Because there's a difference if you treat people with Christian decency or if you're like the heathen, who think only about the lust of the flesh...

I don't know what you call it, Mariane said. But I believe it happens the same way with everyone.

Tea got angry: You don't *want* to, because otherwise you certainly can see the difference between Christian love and sinful lust of the flesh. You're also always making yourself out to be worse than you are.

Believe me—I'm bad enough, Mariane smiled. The children I have—they truly didn't come on their own.

Jens Røn came into the parlor, and Tea couldn't respond. She was boiling: Mariane was a sensuous woman. But she herself knew of a much greater happiness than what could be found in earthly desire. She understood Anton Knopper, who had chosen the right path, and said it straight out to him one day they were alone:

I say what I mean, she said hesitantly. And you mustn't think I'm trying to interfere. But I'm glad it didn't get serious between you and Katrine.

You really mean that? Anton Knopper asked.

Yes, I do, as surely as I'm sitting here, Tea said. Believe you me— temptations can take the form of flesh and blood. It's good you resisted, Anton.

Anton Knopper cast down his eyes. I think you're wrong; Katrine is good by nature, even if we're not made for each other. And I'm not as solid as you take me for. No, I'm worse by far.

Curiosity made Tea's eyes big. Something had happened, she suspected, but she couldn't get herself to ask. Had Anton Knopper fallen? Then he ought to stand up and confess his guilt.

Yes, there's a lot of sin in the world, she said sadly. But I'll never believe anything bad about you, Anton—nobody will get me to believe that.

Anton Knopper didn't answer. Tea felt bitter and disappointed. She understood Anton Knopper was brooding over something. But what was faith worth when this kind of thing was to be hidden in the dark?

They got serious about the sea excursion in May. All the West Coasters and many of the believers in town wanted to go along, and they rented three big trucks, which came early in the morning. Fog, wet and cold, still lay over the stretches of meadow, but when they got inland, the weather was mild with sunshine and warm wind. They had taken songbooks along, and in the lead wagon they began to sing in the fresh, dew-moistened morning.

When they came through the big, prosperous villages, where the mansions stood with the sun shining against the tinted windowpanes, Thomas Jensen struck up a song again, while people came to the windows, and yelping dogs darted at the wagons. They rolled past the inns and assembly halls, where God's spirit definitely didn't rule, but other places there were Mission houses with a cross on the gable and an admonishing word over the door. Not everything was bad.

— It didn't take long before they got to the areas where there were only heath and dunes. The houses were low and windswept, with black, ragged straw roofs. Here and there a couple of sheep were grazing and screeching gulls flying over their heads. Over the noise from the motors they heard the roar of the sea, and the trucks plodded their way along the sandy road between the dunes.

The trucks stopped in a trough between high dunes; they all got out and walked the last stretch on foot. But the West Coasters didn't have the patience to wait. With Thomas Jensen at their head they crawled up on a dune and looked out. Yes, there was the sea. The sound that droned toward them was like music to their ears. Lost to themselves, they stood and looked at it. Thomas Jensen said quietly: Well, we got to see the sea again.

They went down to the shore. The men in groups and the women behind them two by two. Instinctively the West Coasters kept a bit to themselves. They became, as it were, a bit more straight-backed, and memories of sea excursions in the past surfaced. It was a good time, Anton Knopper said. You could almost wish it back again.

All the same, we have it good where we are, Lars Bundgaard said. Afterwards we can easily forget how hard it often was.

But the salty wind swept toward them like an old acquaintance, and the birds' shrieking and the roar of the breakers on the beach were intimate sounds. Yes, well, Jens Røn said, the sea is a lot different than the little fjord. But it gives us food, Thomas Jensen replied. The sea wouldn't do that. No, that's true, Jens Røn conceded. I don't want to find fault with the fjord either, but we were born and grew up near the sea.

It was time to eat, and they sat down on a dune, away from the wind. Thomas Jensen said grace, and the food baskets were unpacked. Anton Knopper happened to sit down next to Andrea, and Tea had some misgivings: it looked almost as if Anton Knopper was about to become a skirt-chaser and couldn't let the women alone. But Anton was in good spirits today; he chatted it up with Andrea: Had she ever been to the sea before? It was many years ago, just after she had been confirmed, Andrea replied, and she really felt like getting in the water. Tea and Malene looked at each other. That didn't sound good that a girl sat among menfolk and talked about going into the water. Next she'd probably take off her clothes and reveal herself in shameless nakedness. Doubtless it wasn't by pure chance that Andrea had had her child of sin.

They didn't intend to return home before evening, and the whole afternoon they sauntered about the shore. Thomas Jensen and Lars Bundgaard had gone over near a fisherman's settlement behind the dunes. Suddenly Lars Bundgaard stood still and listened.

I think it sounds as though someone is singing hymns, he said.

They climbed up on a dune and caught sight of a little group of people, who were sitting up along the sides of a dune pit.

It must be a meeting, Thomas Jensen said. It was good to hear the word of God.

When they had come a bit closer, the preacher began to speak. Thomas Jensen took Lars Bundgaard by the arm. I'd be much mistaken if that isn't Peder Hygum, he said surprised.

It was the hawker. He looked more gaunt and rumpled than he usually did, and his clothes were old and tattered, but he was undaunted in the struggle for the Lord's cause anew, and the fishermen sat down and listened. Peder Hygum spoke with furious speed, and his words had power and fire. When the speech was over, he came over to them and greeted them.

I caught a glimpse of you immediately, he said and smiled placidly. Yes, I gathered some of the friends here for a little edification. They have such a long way to church and a Mission house, but it's a faithful little flock who like to hear the word.

And how are you, Peder? Thomas Jensen asked.

Well, in the purely worldly sense, not so well, Peder Hygum replied sadly. I ride around on my bicycle far from wife and child and earn my bread by selling publications, and when it's required, I can also say the Lord's word as you heard here. But in spiritual respects—there I can say truthfully I've had joyous experiences.

Now have you after all! Thomas Jensen said. I've found peace and forgiveness, Peder Hygum explained. But let's sit down—I've been standing up so long. Yes, the last time you saw me I was in a state of degradation. Hard times came, when I knocked and knocked on mercy's door, but, as it were, couldn't come in. But I didn't let go. And now I can say in the words of the psalmist:

> God be praised for all his mercy,
> He has given me such pow'r
> So that I can face the sorrow,
> Grief and fear of every hour!
> Therefore I will daily play
> On my harp new songs of praise,
> And in joy or bitter sadness
> Sing my hallelus with gladness.

Those are good tidings, said Thomas Jensen, who was moved. I've prayed a lot for you.

Peder Hygum held out his hand with a humble look.

I'm also in need of it, he said. You may be sure I know how terrible it is in the puddle of sin. If it isn't arrogant, I can perhaps say I'm an example of Jesus's infinite mercy. If I could receive forgiveness, there's salvation for everyone if only they want it.

Thomas Jensen invited the hawker to join them for the rest of the day. Tea was startled when she saw whom the two men came with. Peder Hygum greeted her and sat down next to Tea. He told her in a half-whisper what had happened to him since his departure.

You said some good words to me, he said. That was a good seed you placed in my breast, and I thank you for it. You reproached me for having been fresh with a girl in Voldum inn. It was hard for me to hear that I'd been so deep down in the puddle. So I think I'll tell you I've been in Voldum and talked with the girl, and I had in fact not behaved the way I should have, even though no one was hurt. But now she's forgiven me—she's a decent and good-natured girl, even though she works in an inn, and now I want to ask you if you too would forgive me as a sister in the Lord.

Tea's heart swelled: that was remorse by a Christian spirit. But Tea still wanted to know what had actually gone on in Voldum inn. Since Peder Hygum showed confidence in her, it would also be arrogant to reject him.

So what did happen with the girl?

Full of remorse, Peder Hygum looked at the ground.

I won't conceal what I did in my degenerate state, he said. She said I had pushed her over to the wall and grabbed hold of her breasts somewhat violently. But nothing more than that happened. And by way of excuse I can say she was far from being pretty in appearance. So it was presumably the spirit of drunkenness and not lewdness that took hold of me.

They commonly go together, Tea said somberly.

Yes, that's true, Peder Hygum admitted. But now I think it was first and foremost drunkenness because otherwise I've been a moral man all my days. Will you now forgive me, Tea, for having caused offense?

Yes, Tea nodded, I surely will.

And just tell other people how heavily I feel the guilt, the hawker said. I'd hate for anyone to bear a grudge against me.

— Anton Knopper and Andrea wandered along the shore. They walked all the way out to the edge of the beach, where the sand was firm, and a few times Andrea had to step to the side to make sure the waves didn't spray on her shoes. She happened to push Anton Knopper—he felt her warm body against his. Andrea, too, was a woman of flesh and blood. But he didn't feel the voluptuous impulse that seized him when he looked at Katrine. No, Andrea was quiet and modest and didn't excite sinful thoughts. That was surely because she was one of God's children.

There's one thing I'd like to tell you, Andrea, he said stammering a bit. I've come to like you a lot. Now maybe you think I'm fickle because I was engaged to another girl before. But I definitely believe this time it's serious. And that's why I want to ask you whether you could imagine marrying me?

Andrea stopped and didn't notice that a wave washed up over her feet.

I'm a girl who was seduced, Anton Knopper, she said. You know that.

Yes, Anton said. I don't think we should care about what can't be undone. After all, you've found the way.

Andrea began to cry, and Anton Knopper stood there perplexed. Does anyone understand the female mind's odd game? But Andrea quickly composed herself.

I'd very much like to, she said. But the day you regret it, just say so. After all, we don't know each other well yet.

He took her hand, and Anton Knopper felt a profound serenity in his heart.

Andrea walked tenderly and sweetly at his side. Suddenly she stopped.

But Karen? she asked, and her face twitched.

I like your daughter a lot, Anton Knopper said. And I'll try to see whether I can't be a father to her.

Andrea gave his hand a grateful little squeeze.

But I have to confess something to you, Andrea, Anton Knopper stammered. You know I was engaged to a girl, and I didn't act toward her the way I should have. I'm afraid I'm a sensuous person, and if I should ever come to offend you, when we get married, I want to beg you to bear with me.

Surely I'm no better, Andrea said.

You were young back then when you erred. But I should know better at my age—and with the faith I live in. I was on the verge of going to perdition, and sin still has its hold on me. I don't think I can completely overcome it before we get married.

Now they had come back to the others. The women were unpacking the dinner, and the children, who had played on the beach all day, put on socks and shoes. Peder Hygum was sitting and having an intimate conversation with Lars Bundgaard and had been completely taken into his good graces again. Anton and Andrea sat down among the others and listened to Peder Hygum's words. But Tea couldn't restrain herself—Andrea deserved a taunt.

That was a long walk you two were on, she said.

Yes, Anton Knopper said. And I almost think it's going to get even longer. Because Andrea has promised to marry me.

It was just like Anton Knopper to blurt out what should be prepared and said quietly. The women sat there surprised, but Mariane crowed: Then we'll be going to the wedding before long. You two don't have anything to wait for.

I'm sure it will be very private, Andrea said embarrassed.

Oh, don't you two want something, Mariane shouted. Why should it go off quietly? I mean, all the girls in town have been lying in wait for Anton, so you really can be proud of him. He's also too big a fellow to get lost in the bed-straw.

Several of the women smiled, but the others sat with uncommunicative and serious faces. Peder Hygum took Anton's hand. Those were good tidings, he said. Two Christian people who want to wander the same path.

Yes, the rest of us also want to wish you all the best, Thomas Jensen said.

Peder Hygum soon took leave.

If you come to the parish, you're welcome, Thomas Jensen said and shook his hand firmly.

Thanks, the hawker answered, but it's still not time. I offended all too grossly even if you good people have forgiven me.

Darkness began to fall on the cool evening, and it was time to drive home. They rolled through the villages where the light shone through the windowpanes. The children were tired and slept soundly.




Tea had responded to an ad in the newspaper, and now Tabita was to go to town and be a parlor-maid in the home of a believing dry-goods merchant. Tabita flew out of the nest and moved to foreign shores. Tea's voice became muffled as she explained to her the dangers that lurked. The only salvation was to close her eyes and stick to her faith. Then nothing would go wrong. But Tabita got up on her high horse and said there wasn't anything she couldn't deal with.

The last evening Tabita nevertheless spoke tenderly. She sat meekly and quietly in her all too big, grown-up clothes and listened to her parents' words. In the afternoon she had gone around and said good-bye. There was a solemn mood in the little parlor. In the next room the smallest children had been put to bed. Now Tabita would no longer be little Niels's keeper. At bedtime Jens Røn took down the bible and read the passage about Martha and Mary. One thing is needful—Tabita took these words along with her from home. Afterwards he folded his hands and meekly asked God to help the little child, who was to go out among strangers. Then everything burst in Tabita: she forgot she was grown up, and cried like a little girl. Tea took her in her arms and consoled her. It was hard to send your children off.

Oh, dear Jesus, keep her on the right path, Jens Røn prayed. And make sure that some time we all can be gathered in your glory.

She was to leave in the morning. Jens Røn had borrowed Povl Vrist's motorboat to take her to town. Tea wanted to go along: it was reasonable for her to get to see what kind of people she had entrusted her flesh and blood to. In the boat Tea chatted the whole time to keep her grief in check, but in the market town there was noise and traffic, whizzing cars and many people, and it was necessary to watch out. After a long time they found the dry-goods business. *P. L. Fabian* was written in large golden letters on the house. Tea hesitated a bit and looked at the big plate-glass windows. It was odd enough that a believing dry-goods merchant would exhibit these kinds of half-naked figures. A long silk leg jutted out in the corner.

They ventured into the store. A bald-pated little man with pale, gloomy facial features was standing behind the counter. It was Fabian himself.

What may I do for you? he asked and affably extended his hand.

Tea explained why they had come, and the dry-goods merchant's face became a bit stiffer. Oh, so that's the new parlor-maid. With quick steps he went ahead up the stairs, which led to the apartment. Mrs. Fabian was sitting in the parlor next to the window-mirror. She was fat with white, elegant hands. With a quick look she mustered the strangers and greeted them smilingly and condescendingly.

Jens Røn and his family were invited to sit down, and Tea looked around. On the walls hung edifying pictures in black frames, and a Christ figure with outstretched arms stood in a corner. She surreptitiously touched the chair's covering, which was smooth like silk. Mrs. Fabian asked what Tabita could do. Her eyes glided appraisingly over Tea. They stopped at her boots, and Tea instinctively drew her feet in under the chair. She was walking around in an old pair of Jens Røn's boots, and they were a little too big, but her own were no longer serviceable. Short of breath, she explained that Tabita was used to cleaning and knew about cooking, and Tea believed she could surely fill the job. She was just on the verge of crying—it was shameful that the fine lady should see her boots. She probably believed they were absolutely nothing. But among God's children that type of thing didn't count at all. We're a believing people, she said.

Yes, the wife said, that's precisely why I chose your daughter among the many applicants. There are really enough who would like to have a position here: we have no children and pay very high wages. But I only want to have servant girls I can rely on and who don't run out in the evening or have sweethearts. She looked at Tabita with her protruding blue eyes, and Tabita blushed. I believe you can be sure of Tabita, Jens Røn said quietly. It would be better if I used the familiar form of address, Mrs. Fabian said. You're so young. There was a brief silence, and Tea understood they were now supposed to say good-bye.

They got up. Oh, the girl's room is being painted, the wife said, so it's a bit inconvenient to see it now. She extended her hand. Tea saw there were two diamond rings on her fingers—*that* was arrogance! It would be better if you just stayed here right now, Mrs. Fabian said, and Tabita's face twinged a little. Good-bye, Tabita, Tea said and couldn't get herself to kiss her while the stranger was watching. Good-bye, little Tabita, Jens Røn whispered, his voice a bit rough, and can you remember — — — Tabita's shoulders shook, but no words came from her mouth.

When they got down to the street, Tea couldn't get control of herself. Let's go into a doorway, just a moment, she cried. I can't stop.

In the half-dark doorway Jens Røn consoled her as well as he could. We'll get to see her again, he whispered. And surely they're good people... Come to your senses, Tea. Tea realized she was taking it too hard. After all, Tabita had to go out into the world just like other people. She dried her eyes.

They could easily have let her go with us down to the wharf, she said.

Her mouth quivered again, and Jens Røn stood there helplessly. It was as if something evil were happening to Tabita. Their child was now under other people's will, and she was so slender and intrepid and could be broken like a straw. Tea felt like sitting down in a corner and crying. A man came in through the doorway and looked at them astonished.

Come on, dear Tea, Jens Røn said. We truly can't just keep

standing here. Many people come by here, and they don't want to see you standing and crying.

They went out into the sun-drenched street, people hurried by them, the stores had all manner of wares in the windows, wagons rumbled off, and cars tooted. Tea saw nothing. She was abandoned and old. Jens Røn furtively touched her hand.

We'll pray together for her, he whispered.

Tea nodded with her tear-moistened, round face. Jesus would help Tabita. She had forgotten that. Her belief was so weak that her grief made her lose it immediately. Suddenly her heart became gentle and warm.

Thank you, Jens, she whispered.

Jens Røn thought they should go drink coffee at a hotel since they had come to town, but it should be a place that wasn't all too fashionable. Finally they found an old-fashioned cafe down near the harbor. A stout innkeeper was standing behind the buffet, and in the corner several longshoremen were sitting with their lunch bags. Jens Røn ordered coffee and coffee cake. They drank their coffee without talking. Loud voices could be heard from the next room.

Tea looked over there and saw Peder Hygum come out with his pack of tracts under his arm. When he caught sight of them, his face stiffened for a moment in surprise.

Hello, if it isn't old acquaintances, he said and came over to their table. You've come to town — — How are things?

His face was flushed, and Tea thought Peder Hygum had once again gone astray. But he had an explanation ready to hand: he was here on good business—to speak the Lord's word with sea crews, who were holding forth in the other room.

But it doesn't help much, he sighed. They almost threw me out, and they were hardly completely sober.

Jens Røn offered him coffee and Peder Hygum sat down and got to hear why they had come to town. He knew Fabian and said he had a good reputation among the Pious.

That's good to hear, Tea said. I was beginning to have my doubts when I saw she had jewels on her fingers.

Well, that's the custom among city people, Peder Hygum

explained. But Fabian tithes all his income.

Does he really? Jens Røn burst out.

Yes, Peder Hygum said. Of every crown he earns in his business, God gets his share. This way he gets Our Lord as his partner and is certain of temporal profits. But it's not us little people who can do that, no matter how gladly we would —

Soon after Peder Hygum got up and thanked them for the coffee. He still had many things to do that day. Did he ever visit Fabian? Tea asked when they were standing outside the inn. But Peder Hygum didn't: compared to Fabian he was only an insignificant man. But if he saw Tabita, he'd certainly say hello.

On the trip home Tea's thoughts were again melancholy. This is the way all the children would leave her when the time came. The parlor was desolate without Tabita. How was she doing now? But Tea promised that Tabita would always find her home here no matter how the world was treating her otherwise.

Several days later a letter came from Tabita: she longed for home and looked forward to getting a free Sunday in the summer. Mrs. Fabian demanded that the work be done to a T, and Tabita didn't know anyone she could go out with her free afternoon. Tea wrote back and admonished her to obey the slightest wish of the mistress of the house, which was her duty, and to watch out for all the dangers found in the big city. There was nothing good to be learned out in the streets.

Katrine had gotten a job at the inn again and was totally unruly when the nickelodeon was turned on. She threw down whatever she had in her hands and rushed out to dance. But when she met Anton Knopper she looked the other way and didn't say hello. One day he stopped her on the road.

Are you angry at me, Katrine? he asked.

Angry! Katrine said and looked him up and down: what should I be angry about?

I don't know exactly, Anton Knopper answered. But it seems to me you hardly want to say hello to me.

If people see me saying hello to you, they'll just believe I'm thinking about making things good again between us, Katrine said. You should never have gotten engaged to me.

Anton Knopper didn't know what to say. It was true he had made the girl a subject of town gossip, and that couldn't be undone.

I'd be very sorry if you have to listen to nasty things as a result, Katrine! he said.

Angry—Katrine turned up her nose. I'm just glad it's all over. I'd rather be engaged to a telephone pole than to you.

Anton Knopper didn't get the point. But he hadn't broken the girl's heart. It should also be taken into account that he was a middle-aged man, who wasn't familiar with the female sex. It was truly a good thing Andrea was one of God's children.

Anton Knopper and Andrea got married as soon as the herring fishing season was over. It took a while before Andrea's father, Martinus, grasped what was to take place. He had a hard time in old age. One day Anton Knopper and Andrea explained it to him. He stared from one to the other with his pale eyes and nodded a couple of times.

Well, he said in his muffled voice, well so you're going to marry her anyway, you bull.

What? Anton Knopper asked appalled.

So you're going to marry her anyway, he mumbled. Such a rogue, who seduces decent girls!


Toward summer Tea got a letter saying her brother Kjeld wanted to come and live there. Tea clapped her hands in dismay: what could they possibly live on here?

Don't they have anything? Mariane inquired.

Not that I know of, Tea replied. He was a farmhand up in that area where she was from, and they met there. Her father owns a small farmstead inland, but he's a horrible person. They say he had his daughter work like a farmhand on the farm. I'm sorry to say it, but she had two children before they were married. But she was probably engaged to the son of a large farm owner, and they couldn't have each other —

That was surely bad for them, Mariane laughed. But they were able to have children.

Well, go ahead and laugh, Tea said offended. But I'll tell you: otherwise she's a nice girl.

Now don't get hot under the collar, Mariane answered. I have no intention of ever doubting it.

She has repented, Tea explained. Though I don't like these Free Mission people who live up there.

Jens Røn was to rent space for Kjeld and found a few small rooms in a dilapidated farm right near town. They were actually set up for retired farmers, and the space was cramped.

One day Kjeld came with all his furnishings and wife and children. He was a small, compact man with twinkling eyes and hair in unmanageable whirls. He had lost one finger in a machine. His wife, Thora, was big and powerfully built. She had red hair and regular white teeth. Her facial features were as if carved with a knife. The children resembled her. They were a boy and a girl.

Well, Kjeld said, when they were sitting in the parlor at Jens Røn's house. Surely it must be possible to earn something here. After all, there's both land and water to work on.

It's still not so easy, Jens Røn responded. We put up with a lot to get food. But you can always get a job as a fisherman's helper.

I don't know anything about that work, Kjeld said. But surely it can be learned.

Tea butted into the conversation: I'm glad you've come, she said. But I think it would perhaps have been smarter if you'd stayed where you were.

Well, but that just wasn't possible, Kjeld said. The old man was totally unreasonable, and he had title to the place. Thora had spoiled him: you know, for many years she had gone and done farm-hand's work without getting wages for it. Every time we needed a penny, he scolded us, and so we quarreled.

Well, he is old, you know, Jens Røn said by way of excuse.

That he is, Kjeld admitted. But that's no reason to flay other people's hides. I said to him: either you give up the title or we won't stay here any more.

That was hard-nosed, Jens Røn mumbled.

Well, Kjeld is right, Thora said and showed her white teeth in a smile. It just wouldn't do.

Kjeld reported how Thora had walked behind the plow with her skirt tucked in around her waist, or thrashed rye like a man. That was before I came, he said. I was working on the neighboring farm and went and looked at her.

Tea cast a surreptitious glance at the big, strong woman. She was large-bosomed with firm arms, and her skin shimmered with freckles. Tea felt restless in her soul; she had doubtless experienced a lot.

Yes, okay, she said. Then we certainly hope everything will work out for you.

For the time being, Kjeld got a job with Anton Knopper and was to help him repair traps. He sat and did his work credibly, but his hands lacked practice. Anton Knopper indulged him, and they engaged in small talk all day long—Kjeld came from an area that was far off and had many things to tell about life there. Besides, he had, after all, joined the Free Mission just like his wife.

It seems to me there's something odd, Anton Knopper said. The doctrines you people have. What can Our Lord have against us smoking tobacco? Whiskey I can understand—but tobacco? Especially when we do it in moderation as with everything else.

Kjeld had the explanation at hand. It wasn't right to pollute the body, which is the soul's abode.

Anton Knopper nodded: maybe there was something reasonable about it after all. But he added: I think I've noticed you're addicted to chewing tobacco.

Kjeld explained that chewing tobacco was more innocent and didn't percolate through the person like smoking. It was actually nothing but a kind of candy. And Thora didn't like him smoking tobacco, so they agreed on his doing it this way.

Anton Knopper was now a newly married man and had happiness under his roof. With horror and amazement he thought about how close he had come to perdition. The saying was true that the devil went around among people and confused their thoughts and caused their fall. Anton Knopper folded his hands and gave thanks because God had given him aid. His mercy was eternal.

Andrea got some color in her cheeks, and she moved about the house gently and quietly. Karen tripped after Anton wherever he went or stood. Whenever he came back from the fjord she trundled toward him on the way, and Anton Knopper felt well in her company. The greatest difficulties were with Martinus, who sat all day in the little room next to the parlor. Anton Knopper often considered whether it wasn't his duty to talk to him about death, which lurked outside his door. But every time Anton Knopper came near him, the old man looked at him angrily: You were surely forced to take her, you goat, he mumbled. Anton Knopper tried to explain he was innocent, but the old man wouldn't let himself be persuaded. He looked scornfully at his son-in-law and squeezed his hand around the cane: I say you were forced to take her, you goat. He didn't understand anything, and Anton Knopper took comfort in the thought that if God had clouded his mind, he also made no demands on him.

The harvest was over, and it was the middle of Indian summer. Now they were busy again tarring and preparing to get the traps in the water. And in the midst of it all Alma sneaked into bed, without anyone's really noticing it, like a cat about to have kittens, and gave birth to a son to Thomas Jensen. A big, strong boy, healthy in body and without defects. A new life in the world, a new soul to watch over. Thomas Jensen stood in the heat at the tar-pit and felt his heart swell in a song of praise.

— Tabita had three days off from her job and unexpectedly came home to visit. Tea could hardly believe her own eyes, but Tabita rushed and embraced her. That was nice of the mistress, Tea said. That shows she's considerate of others. I'll never forget her for that. Tabita had become a bit pale—her skin so sheer and delicate; that was probably the city air. And she reported on how she'd been doing. It was a strict workplace. Mrs. Fabian watched her minutely to make sure she didn't go out in the evening, and always had something for her to do. Tabita was a bit aggrieved, but Tea thought things were the way they were supposed to be. Surely they take you out with them? she asked. Yes, Tabita said—not when their company was other fine people, but mistress demanded that she come along to the meetings. That must be nice for you to hear so many preachers and missionaries, Tea said. It's a better life than running around in the streets where you can only learn folly and finery. I'm very glad she's looking after you and seeing to it that nothing bad happens to you. Tabita pursed her lips, but one evening she blurted out her feelings.

I can't stand it any more, she cried with hot tears. She's so wicked, and I can't do anything right for her. She's tormenting me to death—can't I look for another job?

But Tabita! Tea said appalled. What are you talking about? People will say you can't stand it anywhere, and people will believe you had a bad upbringing. No, you're not going to bring that kind of shame on us—you have to promise.

Tabita cried, but Tea consoled her with kind words. We humans put up with evil for our own good so we can learn to submit to the law. Tea's speech became stern: it was terrible that Tabita didn't get more profit from the meetings the mistress took her along to. Because if you don't believe with a humble heart, it's not easy to resist the world. She recalled her own youth: Tabita would hopefully be spared what she had to struggle with. When Mariane heard Tabita was dissatisfied with her job, she sided with her completely without thinking about what harm her words could cause. What do you want to be in that job for? she said. You know, you're not learning anything, and a shopkeeper like that—what's the point? No, you should go out to a big farm where there's life.

I don't care a thing about that, Tea said.

Oh, nonsense, Mariane said bluntly. What should such a little girl be looking for in town? No, she should go out to a big farm, where there are men and apprentices, so she can get herself a sweetheart.

Tabita smiled in embarrassment and blushed. But Tea didn't give up: Tabita had to stay at her job, and Jens Røn sided with her.

— Pastor Brink held a harvest festival in the assembly hall, and it was full to the very last seat. It was young people who attended. As an introduction the pastor gave a lecture, which dealt with the harvest, where the grain is gathered in the barn. With the kernel and the golden straw and with the bristly thistles, which also grow in the fields and believe that only they are nutritious grain. Do you suppose they understood the point? he asked his wife. I'm absolutely sure they did, his wife said. I noticed how they all followed your words. Yes, it's a challenge, the pastor said, and now they can give whatever answers they wish. Afterwards there was a man who showed remarkable magic tricks, and it was especially to see him that the young people had come.

The Pious shook their heads. Humbug and religion, preaching and magic tricks—they didn't go well together. At a meeting of the vestry Thomas Jensen mentioned it. The pastor got hot under the collar: he was aware of his responsibility and stood accountable to the dean and bishop.

Well, I was thinking more of Jesus, Thomas Jensen said calmly. I know Jesus as well as you do, the pastor said angrily. And I'm not going to put up with any interference with my spiritual freedom. I'm open about my conduct, and if you want to know what I talked about, it was about the stiff thistles in the grain field, which don't bear seed for people. That was a metaphor, Thomas Jensen said, and next time pastor can name the flower that people call buttercup—it doesn't give butter either. And then there are many among us who don't match the name they have gotten. I wouldn't have thought a clergyman would lead the young people out onto the path of frivolity.

Now you're going too far, the pastor said angrily.

What I'm saying I'm not saying for my own sake, Thomas Jensen said, but you can surely recall that once when we talked, you advised us Pious to dissolve our parish ties. Now I'll be just as honest with you: I think you should look for some other place.

That time hasn't come when you can dismiss me, the pastor answered curtly.

— If the older people forsook him, a group of vigorous young people grew up around him. He had to guard them against the obscurantists like a priest of life. That was his idea. And now before the summer was completely over, he wanted to organize an outing to one of the fjord towns.

One August morning boys and girls bicycled in from the distant farms with their lunch on their handlebars and full of great expectation.

The motor cutter was docked at the wharf, and the pastor was standing at the railing and greeted everyone who came with a smile and handshake. The weather was good, though the wind was blowing a little. By the time they had agreed on, thirty people had come, and the pastor gave the signal to depart. As the ship was casting off, a fellow came whizzing along on his bicycle. He was red as a beet and bent over the handlebars to speed it up. A short distance from the wharf he tossed the bicycle aside, and took a running start and jumped. He tumbled in among a group of screaming girls. That's the way it should be, the pastor smiled. They are truly the youth. On the shore people were standing and watching the departure. The pastor saw many of the Pious among them. Let's sing now, he shouted. I want to hear whether you can use your lungs. He struck up:

I love the green groves —

The boat glided away from the coast. The town turned into a heap of small, scattered houses. The boat rocked a bit, but in the bow a man was sitting and playing harmonica. A couple of the boldest men broke out of the group, grabbed the girls by the waist and began to dance on deck. The sun burned, and the men tossed their jackets and vests off and danced in shirt-sleeves.

That's a beautiful sight, the pastor said to his wife. The green shore over there and the blue sky above us. And the ship here with its dancing youth. It's almost like a symbol of everything that I believe and want. Yes, a symbol: the ship of youth, you could say.

His wife nodded with a little smile. Pastor Brink took her by the arm:

I think we should dance, he said cheerfully.

Can we really do that? she asked anxiously.

Of course, the pastor answered. Let's be joyful with the joyful. No one can find it improper for a clergyman to dance with his wife. We're still young, Sofie.

They danced out on deck; the other couples stopped one after the other and watched them. Keep it up! Pastor Brink shouted. Come on, keep it up, folks! When the music stopped, he dried his warm face and took off his jacket. He was wearing a white vest with a slender gold chain around his neck. A moment later he asked Katrine to dance. She turned flaming red and cast her eyes down. It wasn't any everyday event to dance with a clergyman. But the pastor grabbed her by the waist and swung her, while he stamped like a farm laborer on deck. The silver cross bobbed on the girl's breast.

You're enjoying yourself, his wife smiled. Who is that girl?

She's a splendid girl, the pastor replied. She works at the hotel and is a daughter of the people, healthy and native. Look—she's wearing a little silver cross on her breast. A poet could almost speak of faith's cross on flesh's heights.

But Henrik, his wife burst out. Now *that* seems to me blasphemous.

Not in Brorson's or Grundtvig's mouth, the pastor said.

In any case it's vulgar, his wife replied angrily. And that big, fat girl reminds me of a cow more than anything else. I don't think you should dance any more.

The sun got hot, and the warmth rose up from the tarred deck. It stank of petroleum, and an odd musty smell rose from the cargo hold. Several men talked to the skipper. So could they get beer?

Yes you can, he said. I always have a couple of cases along. You know, people as a rule get thirsty when they see all that water.

The men clinked the necks of their bottles and then grabbed the girls again. The motor pounded, and the boat shot forward in the blue water.

After a few hours' sailing they came alongside the jetty. With the pastor and his wife in the lead, they walked up to the pavilion. Anders Kjøng happened to walk alongside Katrine. They hadn't talked to each other since Katrine had maliciously made a fool of him. But she had been silent, and he hadn't been mocked and ridiculed by her, which is he what he had most feared. She had to be given credit for that. Well, you've come along, Katrine? he said.

Surely you can see that, Katrine replied, and Anders Kjøng didn't know what else to say. They walked silently for a while. Katrine was busy window shopping. Anders Kjøng glanced at her from the side. She looked big and beautiful in the light summer dress, which precisely outlined her full-bodied shape.

I guess nothing came of it between you and Anton Knopper, he said teasingly. Katrine got stuck up and angry. That's none of your business, she said. No, no, Anders Kjøng responded. But you've really become arrogant since the pastor danced with you.

Katrine didn't answer, and they walked behind the others up to the pavilion. There was already activity. The men were playing leapfrog and singing and making a din. Soon they took out their lunch packs and some ran for beer. Afterwards there was dancing on a stand, but when the pastor entered the pavilion, he saw seven or eight men sitting at a table and drinking coffee and cognac. He became a little suspicious, but didn't think it was worth intervening. After all, they were grown-up people, and they'd surely act in moderation.

It was warm even under the beech tree foliage, and the young people were soon tired of dancing. In couples or in small clusters they sneaked off. Anders Kjøng had danced with Katrine and didn't let go of her. They walked into the woods, and sat down on the grass in a sunny place. Katrine poked an anthill with a stick while Anders Kjøng followed her movements. It was really hot! When she bent forward, her summer dress slipped to the side, and he got a glimpse of her breast. It gave him a little start. He moved surreptitiously to take her round arm and fondle it. It didn't seem to be unpleasant for her.

And why should it be, he thought, and took courage. He was as slim a fellow as any and pleasant looking. He became warm and wild and stuck his hand down onto her bosom. Katrine struck at him, and they rolled huffing and puffing in the grass. The girl was strong; she turned him over on his side and got up quickly.

Can't you control yourself, you milksop, she said angrily. I want to be able to go in peace, and now you've ripped my dress to shreds.

I didn't mean to, Anders Kjøng said with a guilty conscience. But up in the pavilion you can surely borrow a needle and thread.

Can't we be sweethearts, Katrine? he asked after they had walked part of the way without talking. You're the most beautiful girl I know.

No, Katrine said, sulking. I don't trust you to marry me. And I don't want anything if I don't get a ring.

Anders Kjøng sighed. Katrine was a robust girl, and he'd never get anywhere with her.

At the pre-arranged time the fellows and girls came sauntering down to the harbor. Appalled, the parson's wife grabbed her husband by the arm.

They're drunk, she whispered. Oh good God, the pastor said flabbergasted. What's this coming to?

There was no hiding that some of the fellows had had a drop too much and were in high spirits. He quickly got them on board and counted them up. They were all there, and a moment later the boat sailed out.

We have to have them dancing all the time, Pastor Brink said. That's the only possible way to burn off this inebriation before we land.

He rushed over to the fellow with the harmonica and gave him orders to play and keep playing. At the same time he remembered with a sigh that he had actually intended to gather the group around him to read to them. He had "A Happy Boy" in his jacket pocket.

The dancing began, but the girls quickly became tired and sat down in groups in the bow with regretful looks. The men were too violent. They tumbled about on deck and roared and sang. But soon they disappeared, one by one, and when the pastor went to look for them, they were sitting down in the cargo hold and drinking. The skipper had provided a new supply of beer, and Pastor Brink thought that down in the semi-darkness he had glimpsed a couple of cognac bottles. Shaking with anger, he went to the skipper.

What's going on here? he said heatedly. Seven or eight men are sitting down there and drinking. Who gave you permission to sell alcohol?

The young people are out to have a good time, the skipper said. And I usually have a couple of cases of beer on board in case anyone gets thirsty.

I'm making you responsible, the pastor said threateningly.

They're all adults, the skipper said calmly. The pastor went over to the hatch-way and shouted down:

Please be good enough to come up immediately!

No one answered. But Pastor Brink heard them amusing themselves. It was unthinkable that they'd move before the drinks were all finished off.

He went to his wife.

It's terrible, he said and dried the sweat from his forehead. Now they're sitting in the cargo hold and drinking. What in the world am I going to do? He didn't wait for her answer, but paced the deck with a gloomy face. The girls anxiously stole glances at him. Once again he was over at the hatch and shouted down. But the men were singing and didn't hear anything.

Land was now in sight, the water was calm in the warm summer evening, and from the meadows you could hear the cows moo. The church bells rang down the sun in his own church. But the pastor knew nothing good awaited him on shore. He came sailing back a defeated man.

It's not your fault, Mrs. Brink said. Her eyes were red from crying.

But I'll get the blame for it, Pastor Brink answered. Well, I know my conscience is clear—I only wanted the best. They must surely be able to understand that. And no matter how it ends, I have to meet my fate with head erect like an honest man.

The ship docked at the wharf, and the men came up from the cargo hold. A couple of the wildest ones hooted and roared toward land. The girls kept their anxious distance.

We must sing, the pastor said. Sing, join in all of you. Now:

Lift your head, brave boy!

The girls sang for their lives, several fellows joined in, and the song drowned out the drunken roar. They walked up through town, the pastor and his wife at the front, and sang with all their might, and as soon as one song was over, they began the next. The drunken ones stumbled forward as best they could. People appeared in the doorways and looked in astonishment at the procession. All the attention had its effect: one after the other the girls stopped; for a moment only the pastor's ringing voice could be heard; then he too stopped. Now everyone could see how things stood: the young people had come home drunk from the outing.

In a moment the road was alive: people streamed out of their houses, children, old people, women, farmers, and fishermen were standing and gaping or shaking their heads. Then there was a road of laughter: it was a joke on a large scale. The pastor came home leading the drunken men. They had surely amused themselves. But the Pious were grim and silent. Now it was clear to everyone who had eyes and intellect that the pastor was leading the young people into ruin and misfortune.

Pastor Brink was pale and stirred up; he was shaking in all his limbs and felt like running—just to get away and home. But he stood erect and looked straight ahead, while he mechanically moved his legs. Without saying good-bye he turned up the road to the parsonage, and when he came into the parlor, he was agitated and kept pacing, while his wife sobbed in the chair.

The beasts! he said hoarsely. They were like wild animals. And to think I trusted the young people.

But it's not your fault, his wife cried. Oh, it was terrible running the gauntlet through town. The way they stared at us!

The pastor stopped in front of her and put his hands on her slender shoulders.

Poor Sofie, he said. Do you know from now on I'm a lonely man?

You *must*n't say that, Mrs. Brink sobbed.

Yes, I have to, the pastor said and began his restless wandering again. I had put my trust in the fresh, untouched youth, and now they failed. Do you remember what I said: The ship of youth; no, that wasn't the right expression—*we sailed with a corpse in the cargo hold!*

How could that person think of taking alcohol on board, the wife said.

Yes, that was just insane! Pastor Brink answered angrily. But let's not reproach others. The fault is my own. If I had possessed authority, they would never have dared. My position is undermined, and now I've fought my fight and lost. You can rely on the Pious not to let me off lightly.

Can't you talk with them, the wife sobbed, and explain how it happened. Maybe things could be put right again between you and these people. Oh it's a pity they'll reject you—you who of all people were made for the ministry.

The pastor shook his head sadly.


At Anton Knopper's big things were brewing. Old Martinus was to be honored and get the cross of the Order of the Dannebrog. People had begun to think about Martinus's having taken part in the 1864 war and deserving his reward. It was definitely a day when the county magistrate and chief of police would be coming; Andrea was busy cleaning the house: after all, these were important strangers for simple people.

Martinus sat in a corner, gnarled like a tree trunk and overgrown with a green beard, and let the world go its way. Now he'd have to be spruced up a bit: it wouldn't do for him not to look nice on such an occasion. Anton Knopper talked to Andrea:

they mustered the old man and decided there were no two ways about it—his hair and beard had to be clipped. Anton Knopper approached him with nice, friendly words and scissors in hand. But Martinus resisted and wouldn't put up with tomfoolery. He grunted like a furious bull—there was no alternative: Anton Knopper had to hold his hands while Andrea brandished the scissors. It was like clipping a stubborn sheep. The deed was carried out. The old man got a couple of nicks on his ear, but the hair came off, and Martinus sat there genteel and washed and resembled a human being. Anton Knopper tried from morning till night to explain to him what was going to happen. Martinus understood nothing. If only it had been possible, it would surely have been useful to pour a half-pint of whiskey down him. But Anton Knopper of course was not the man who resorted to that kind of expedient.

Everything was nicely fixed up long ahead of time. Anton Knopper had whitewashed the house and painted windows and doors. The authorities would find everything in order as far as it was in his power. Now the question was: who should be invited to attend the event? If the county magistrate and police chief announced they were coming, they of course had to be honored with the presence of many good people. Anton Knopper invited the parish council chairman, the parish constable, and teacher Aaby—after all, they were themselves officials. But what about the pastor? Anton Knopper didn't like having him in his house. He spoke to Thomas Jensen about the matter. No, Thomas Jensen said, after what's happened, I think we should act as if he just doesn't exist. But he is our pastor, Anton Knopper said, and if the county magistrate takes a mind to asking about him? Then, Thomas Jensen said, we'll have to make him understand how we feel about him. To put it bluntly, I regard him as an impious person. So Anton Knopper decided to invite his closest friends, the people from the West Coast—Jens Røn, Thomas Jensen, Lars Bundgaard, and Povl Vrist and their wives. But what kind of food and drink should the strangers be treated to? Here Alma was consulted: she was from the city and knew all about fancy people's ways. Well, on this kind of occasion people probably are accustomed to drinking a glass of wine. Anton Knopper was shaken. So was he obligated to pour a sinful drink in his house? No, Alma said, no one could demand that; it would probably be alright if you served hot chocolate of the best quality that could be gotten, and many kinds of cakes, and afterwards coffee. Alma came over to help Andrea with the preparations; Mariane was also called in. They kneaded dough and baked: no effort was spared.

On the day of the event the guests appeared ahead of time in their best clothing. A guard was posted to announce when the distinguished people came driving up; a swarm of boys tumbled down from the church hill: they're coming across the meadows. A moment later the car was there. It was a closed car, bigger than any people had otherwise ever seen; there were flowers in it, whatever the purpose of that might be. The sheriff opened the door and welcomed people. People swarmed all over the windows and doors. The county magistrate was in a long coat, but the police chief was wearing a uniform with a saber and cap. He didn't look very warlike—tall, thin, and near-sighted. No, the county magistrate was an impressive fellow—stout and authoritative, with a dignified, blotchy face. You certainly knew from looking at him he was the biggest man in the county next to the king; indeed, no mistake about it: he was very powerful.

The two officials came in and greeted everyone. The county magistrate gave every single person a solid handshake: it was obvious he was not arrogant. Martinus was sitting in his armchair in the middle of the floor. He was holding his cap in his brown, gnarled hands.

How do you do, Martinus Povlsen, the county magistrate said, extending his hand.

How do you do, the old man replied as if from the bottom of a well and then didn't see the extended hand. He was almost blind, his eyes were like pale milk, and his skin lay in brown folds around his face. With time his clothing had become rather too big for him, and it was green with age. But it was an expense to buy new clothing for someone close to the grave. Anton Knopper felt sheepish: it was unlucky enough that Martinus didn't give the county magistrate his hand. But the county magistrate acted as if nothing had happened. His eyesight is probably bad, he said. Yes, that's what happens with age; we can't last forever.

The county magistrate cleared his throat and turned to the others. He then gave a speech. It was as if he were exhibiting Martinus and explaining his virtues and characteristics. Look, there sits Martinus, an old warrior who had served the king and his country in their hour of danger. The county magistrate spoke of the flag and fatherland, the rediscovered sister to the south, the rural soldier, and the warrior spirit. Tea, who had stolen inside with the other women, was moved. Gosh, the way such a man could speak—like a bishop; it was a day of honor for Martinus—if only God had granted him the ability to understand the beautiful words. But it was not to be. Tea eyed the police chief, who was standing a little behind them with his hands on his back. He looked as though he were bored. His face was distorted as if he were about to yawn. He was probably a grumbler, even though you shouldn't say that about someone who carries the sword of authority at his side.

Old Martinus was sitting there with a dull expression and immovable and stared, while the county magistrate spoke of the virtue which is its own reward, and peaceful occupations, which also serve the fatherland. The men were standing at a respectful distance and listening. Anton Knopper nodded thoughtfully. It was easy to understand that such a man could go far and had something to say in the king's council. The words came fine and effortlessly, as if he stood in a black frock-coat every day and said great things.

The county magistrate turned to Martinus, who was sitting patiently and letting everything take its course.

You were one of the men who fought for our old mother, our dear Denmark, when she was in need, he said. You are one of the last of the generation whom we all honor and admire. I therefore now pin the cross of the Order of Dannebrog on your chest.

He searched a bit in his pocket and didn't find the cross.

Everyone anxiously held his breath. Had the county magistrate forgotten to take it along? He felt in his pants pocket and vest. The chief of police stepped over to him.

Mr. County Magistrate stuck it in his top-coat, he whispered. I'll go get it.

The chief of police returned with a little package; the county magistrate cleared his throat earnestly and attached the cross to the old man's frock-coat.

And I bring you a greeting from His Majesty the King, he said.

Suddenly the old man's face came alive as if a fly were crawling all over it.

In his muffled voice Martinus wheezed:

We're the ones who killed King Canute!

A bit confused, the county magistrate straightened himself up and had no answer. Anton Knopper was ashamed and blushed. It was shameful that something like that should happen at a solemn moment, but, after all, the old man was out of his mind and didn't know what he was saying. The county magistrate smiled in a friendly way and clapped Martinus on the shoulder.

Of course, he said. You're certainly right about that, dear Martinus Povlsen. That took place a long time ago, yes, indeed, many hundreds of years ago, but I've been asked to give you greetings from the king we now have in Denmark.

Martinus didn't move a muscle in his face; he reverted to his rock-hard serenity and sat bent forward a bit with the shining cross dangling in his frock-coat lapel. Anton Knopper hastened to say that lunch was served at the table set in the other room if the officials would make do with it.

They went into the drawing room, and Andrea poured hot chocolate. Only the men sat at the table. Both the county magistrate and the chief of police drank two cups and afterwards coffee. Yes, the county magistrate was a man of the people and a simple man. He talked a lot of nonsense and wanted to know everything about agriculture and fishing. He praised the cakes and asked for the recipe for one of them for his wife. Tea got all excited behind the door where she was listening: it was an honor that was bestowed on Andrea. A moment later the county magistrate had forgotten the cake and was talking politics with the chairman of the parish council. But the chairman of the parish council was a believing man and not so bad off that he couldn't use his brains. The county magistrate had been a cabinet minister for a brief time, and would doubtless like to get back into politics again. The chairman of the parish council was reflective and slow in his answer and didn't say too much. After all, here in the parish, people preferred to elect believing and good people.

Actually the chief of police was more dignified in his appearance. The county magistrate was a speaker, but he chatted too much; here during the coffee hour he wasn't the man you thought he was. Was it proper for people in such positions to be interested in cakes? Maybe the county magistrate was one of those who make a god of their belly? But the chief of police sat there calm and erect with the saber between his legs and drank chocolate. You could understand that: he was girded with the law's sword and had important things in his head. There was no room for cake recipes and parish politics.

The two gentlemen rose and took leave and went in to say good-bye to Martinus.

Farewell, Martinus Povlsen, the county magistrate said, and after he had let his eyes sweep over the men in the back of the room, he added earnestly: And God bless you.

After the officials had driven away, the women came in to drink the hot chocolate.

That was a nice speech father got, Andrea said, very moved. If he could just have understood what was being said.

What he wished him at the end wasn't honest, Thomas Jensen said heatedly. I don't think he meant anything by it. That kind of fancy people, they use Our Lord's name, but you shouldn't trust them too much.

The county magistrate had been weighed and found too light. But still, it had been an experience that created new things to talk about. Was it really true the king had sent his greetings to

Martinus? It was hard to believe he knew the names of those who had been in the war. No, Anton Knopper said, that wasn't likely. And now that they had seen so much of the world's power and glory, it was necessary to remember there was only one king who knew our name, indeed, every thought in our heart, and that was Jesus. Maybe the county magistrate could have learned more here among the plain people than cake recipes. They had a brief period of edification, and before they left, they sang a hymn. When Thomas Jensen came through the room where Martinus was sitting, he spoke to him briefly.

That was a nice ceremony, Martinus, he shouted. And now you've gotten a cross, but there's another cross you'll get more happiness from.

What? the old man asked and blinked with his eyes.

I say, you should make sure to win the cross of *mercy*, Thomas Jensen shouted. Because you surely know you're going to die soon.

The old man stared threateningly at him. Then he said in a muffled voice:

If I get sick, I'll hang myself!


In the dark, wet autumn the parish was closed off from the world. Nothing happened. The broad inland stretches of meadow were inundated, the fjord was cold and black, and the trees stood bare in the cold wind. The roads were slush, the days gray and rainy; there were weeks when the sun was scarcely to be seen. Only in the Mission house was there warmth for the soul.

Pastor Brink put his coat collar up over his ears when he went walking. He had become gaunt and looked tired and had gotten into the habit of talking aloud to himself. One day he met Thomas Jensen. They hadn't talked since the outing. The pastor stopped. His face was wet, and the rain dripped from his hat.

Do you have time? he said. I'd like to talk to you briefly.

Thomas Jensen immediately agreed and accompanied him to

the parsonage. He put his wooden shoes in the entry and carefully stepped onto the floor. Wet spots appeared where he had stepped. The parson's wife appeared for a moment at the sitting-room door, and an anxious shadow glided across her face when she saw who the guest was. But the parson quickly closed the door and drew the curtain. Thomas Jensen stood for a moment and looked out into the big, desolate yard. Behind the old barn the wind ripped into several tall poplar trees with black crows' nests. The steel door rattled on its hinges.

The pastor sat down on a chair and asked the fisherman to take a seat. That chair over there, I believe, is the most comfortable one, he said. Thank you, Thomas Jensen said. I'm truly not so spoiled. Yes, it's fall now, Pastor Brink said. It's a bad time for the people, but on the other hand perhaps a time for reflection when you consider this year's harvest. There are many things I'd like to talk to you about. I don't want to get into the unfortunate outing at all. I relied too much on the young people's moral health and strength, and I was mistaken. But there are other things I've considered and view with much concern. You know, I no longer mean anything here. The parish is changing from day to day, and I can certainly understand that it's you and your people who will be victorious. But I want to ask: are you aware of the responsibility you have assumed?

Yes, Thomas Jensen answered firmly.

Yes and yes, the pastor said a little irritated. It's easy to take responsibility, but it's hard to bear it. You're a sincere and zealous Christian, but the soul is a delicate plant, and a clergyman is like a gardener, who tends to it and trims it and provides the nourishment it needs. It is my conviction people should first and foremost ask a pastor: do you possess humanity? Because without humanity the work will remain without a result. Now *you* have taken my work from me here in the parish, where I was called to act, and now I'm asking you: do you know what your responsibility is? *Do you possess humanity?*

I do what I can to be rid of it, the fisherman said.

What are you doing? the pastor asked.

We probably look very differently at this thing like many

others. I feel the human condition is the evil nature we've received with original sin.

You don't see anything valuable at all in humans?

No, I know for sure we owe the good that is in us to grace. And even if there is good in the unrepentant, what use is it? It's lost in our sinful nature. I believe Jesus himself gave his opinion when he said that there was more joy in heaven over one sinner who repented than over ten just persons, which need no repentance.

The words came calmly and well-considered, but Pastor Brink's face twinged, and he stood up.

I'm tired of strife and discord, he said. If it was your intention to drive me away, you've succeeded. You mustn't tell anyone, but I intend to seek another post. Let's use up the remaining time to make it as bearable as we can.

Thomas Jensen couldn't hide his surprise. Are you glad? the pastor asked.

I'd have been gladder if you had found another way, the fisherman answered. I can truthfully say we would have been glad to have you as clergyman—if you were a believing man.

On the way home Thomas Jensen went up to the church and stood a while and looked in through a rain-covered windowpane. His hand slid carefully across the wall moldy with dampness. Now better times were approaching. The word would be spoken in God's house.

— In the Mission house the singing took on a deeper tone, but the assembly hall door was closed with lock and bolt. The pastor had long since resigned as chairman of the young people's association, and now Kock was not unwilling to take over the leadership and responsibility. Kock agitated. His plan was for it to become a kind of discussion club where all intellectual currents wrestled. But the Pious also had to be represented. Kock thought it was smartest to speak to Anton Knopper and put out feelers. He leaned back in his chair and took a piece of paper out of his pocket. He had already worked out his program.

Look, the first question I thought we should set up for debate is about the Jews, he said.

The Jews—what about them? Anton Knopper asked in amazement. — Yes, alright I know: they killed the Savior. So that's doubtless what we're supposed to talk about?

No, it's the Jews in our time, Kock answered. The Jews, you see, are one of society's most difficult problems. I say that truly not to boast, but I've studied the problem very thoroughly and read many books. The fact of the matter is the Jews are at fault for most of the misfortunes that have befallen the world, and it won't get better until we yield to the results of race science. That's the point.

Well, I don't know about all that, Anton Knopper said. I've only heard there are two kinds of Jews: slow-eating Jews and noisy Jews, but I don't know if that's true.

Scientifically that doesn't hold water, the customs official replied. But it might very well be good to disseminate information about how things stand with the Jews. Later there will be other questions, for example, about this socialism they're screaming about—I'd like to drive a stake through it.

— Kock was like a fly in a bottle: now the intellectual life was to be ushered in. He got a meeting called in the youth association so a chairman could be elected. Only a score of people showed up, and Kock took the floor and explained how he imagined the future. He stood blissful in the pulpit and foreign and strange words flowed from his lips. When he walked down to his seat, he was satisfied with himself.

The hall was lit only by a smoky petroleum lamp, and teacher Aaby popped up out of the dark in the furthest corner. When he went up to the pulpit, his shadow hopped oddly on the whitewashed wall. His clothes hung loosely on him, and one side of his jacket was pulled down by the Bible in his pocket. He stood for a bit and listened to the rain beating against the windowpanes. Yes, he said, before you know it, you're an old man, and death is knocking at the door, and so the point is where we're going. That's what we should always remember. The old teacher's language was gentle: He didn't rely on book-learning and warned against those who came with half-digested wisdom.

Is it me you're referring to? Kock shouted down from his

seat.

Yes, it's you, Aaby answered and winked a bit.

You don't count as far as I'm concerned, Kock said. You're opposed to all intellectual freedom and think we should always be sitting in school. I think you're senile.

I'll soon be an old man, Aaby answered calmly. And maybe I'll soon be used up and won't be able to go on. But one thing I know about you is that you're a dilettante. And it would've been better if you'd never learned to read.

Kock sprang to his feet, but couldn't say a word for all his agitation. Wasn't he a man with a well thought-out view of life, indeed with many views of life—life seen from all sides?

I nominate myself as chairman, Aaby said, and I think we should take a vote without any further discussion. Those in favor of me, raise your hands.

The customs official angrily looked around the hall. Two-thirds of those present had their hands raised. So, that's it, he said and stood up. I just want to propose we convert the youth association into a burial society.

That startled Aaby a little: Burial society, he mumbled.

That was the word, Kock said and walked toward the door. Because there won't be any intellectual life here when you're in control.

A cold draft blew into the hall when he opened the door, and the petroleum lamp flared up in a smoky flame.

Let's sing a song before we part, Aaby said and struck up in his old man's voice: A mighty fortress is our God.

— The fall storms roared across the land and tore at roofs and trees. The wind wrapped itself around house gables and rattled the doors. People struggled on against it: this was no weather for human beings. The traps had long since been taken in from the foaming fjord, and eel fishing was over. The catch had been moderate for most of them and beyond all measure for Povl Vrist. He was growing head and shoulders above the rest and had almost twice as many nets as anyone else.

For many months Kjeld had been working for Anton Knopper. He was industrious, but headstrong by nature. Anton

Knopper treated him with kid gloves and closely watched his own tongue. And still it ended badly merely because he gently said that a net hadn't been mended well enough.

If I can't do the work right, then I'd best go my way, Kjeld said and threw the net down.

Now don't act hastily, Anton Knopper said. After all, you know very well I've no reason to complain about you. That's not what I meant.

But Kjeld wouldn't change his mind; he stood his ground and left. Anton Knopper felt bad; it was as if he would bear the responsibility if Kjeld didn't have food in the winter. One day Thora was walking by and he called her in and talked to her.

I truly don't know what I should do, he said. Couldn't you give me some advice?

Thora shook her head:

He wants what he wants, and there's no use interfering.

For the time being Kjeld got work in the coop. He had good schooling and could serve as a clerk; he calculated, and wrote, and packed up goods. Toward Christmas it got busy in the store. Goods were sent out to people's houses in big boxes: oranges, apples, and prunes, and grapes in cork dust for those who could afford it. Kjeld was in his element: he flung boxes around and dragged sacks from the store room. But his stubbornness was unreasonable: one day he had a disagreement with the manager over a rotten orange. Kjeld had bought it Saturday evening, and Monday morning he showed it to the manager and wanted compensation.

What's supposedly wrong with it? the manager asked.

Come on, you can see it's rotten, Kjeld answered. And I feel you should give people a replacement for goods that are no good.

Of course, the manager said, if something's wrong with the goods, we give compensation, but they have to be returned in the condition in which they were supplied, and as far as I can see, this orange has certainly been peeled, and three sections were taken.

Kjeld got hot-headed and took a step closer: Don't play games with me because you're not the man to do it. How am I supposed to know there's something wrong with the orange without tasting it?

That's none of my business, the manager said stubbornly. It's not the money, it's the principle, and you have to bear the loss yourself.

He turned to go, but Kjeld grabbed him by the shoulder and wiped the orange all over his face. The manager coughed and got the burning juice in his eyes and mouth. With a roar he tore himself loose, and Kjeld smacked the squeezed-out fruit against the wall.

His wife appeared in the doorway: But what's wrong? she asked.

Oh, that crazy guy—he doesn't respect life or property, the manager said and dried his face. He wasn't far from choking me with an orange. But you can go now. Imperiously he stamped his foot on the floor. I don't want to have you here in my store any more.

I want my wages for today, Kjeld said snappishly.

Do you have to be different in everything? You haven't even been here an hour. But maybe you want to use violence: you know, you're one of that kind that isn't ashamed of it.

I don't use violence if I'm not challenged. But I want my wages for today, and I'll stay here till you pay.

The manager went into the office and took his time, but when he came back, Kjeld was sitting on a sack and waiting. Customers began to come; they stole a glance at Kjeld, but he was minding his own business and took a new plug of tobacco every hour. After lunch there were a couple of quiet hours when the manager sat and took a nap over his newspaper behind the counter. Kjeld wasn't having a good time, but no one was going to say that he gave up when he was in the right. There was a black circle of bits of spit around him. Not until it was closing time did the manager open his mouth.

We're going to have to be closing now, so you'll have to leave.

First I'm going to get paid, Kjeld responded.

Then I'll be forced to get the sheriff to put you out, the manager said. What you're doing here isn't lawful.

Kjeld walked slowly to the wall, where a row of oak canes were hanging, and chose the thickest one. The manager watched him a bit uneasily, but Kjeld went back over to his sack and sat there and weighed the cane in his hand. After all, that business about getting the sheriff was hardly meant that seriously. When you were a Christian man and respected in the Mission house, you had to proceed cautiously.

The manager yanked the money drawer out with one jerk and flung the money on the counter. His eyes flashed wickedly, but his voice was flexible:

You have a hard heart, you do. Now you can leave with the money you've gotten with your threats, but I'll tell you what I'm going to do: I'll pray for you. Because if there's a miserable person in need of intercession, it's surely you.

Kjeld turned his back and went home.

There were no complaints from Thora; on the contrary, she just smiled and showed her strong, white teeth. Christmas approached along with very hard frosts at night; there were frost flowers on the windowpanes and the frost pricked like a nail. Kjeld walked to the fjord as soon as it froze over, and used his eel-prong. But things were tight for them.

Christmas was over, and a thaw set in. When Thomas Jensen went by the hotel one morning, Mogensen was walking in wooden shoes across the slush in the yard with a board and a hammer in his hand. He stopped at the gable and began to hammer the board firmly onto the big wooden sign where there stood "Temperance Hotel." Thomas Jensen could scarcely believe his own eyes. In large letters was painted on the board: "Closed."

What in the world is that supposed to mean? he asked.

Mogensen turned his head toward Thomas Jensen: It means I've done my duty, as much as anyone can demand, he answered. I've tried both the beach hotel and dancing, but business was just lousy, and now the creditors have evicted me.

No, what do you know, Thomas Jensen said. So it's going to be closed?

I don't know anything about it, Mogensen said. But I've spent every penny, and let them open up the hotel themselves. I'm just glad to have been spared all the speculation.

Mogensen banged the last nail in and stepped back and contemplated his work.

Let them do it themselves, he said. They can easily say it's simple when they've never tried it—

He nodded and went in.

Mogensen hadn't managed to pay his interest installments, and the hotel was to be sold. His wife's family wanted to help them get a laundry in town. His wife was to take care of it, but Mogensen felt it would probably be his job to write the bills and supervise. He had already familiarized himself with prices of washing machines and coal. It was a profitable business.

Thomas Jensen spoke with him briefly before he left: So you can see where dancing and frivolity lead. They bring no happiness.

No, Mogensen conceded. But you know I had to pay interest on the capital and indecent things didn't happen in my house. But I've learned that running a hotel is a rotten livelihood: to begin with it doesn't pay, and second, people don't like you much. No, a laundry is a socially useful thing.

But we should also include Jesus in our earthly work.

We should, Mogensen replied. My wife is religious, even if she isn't outright Pious. And I myself—you must be sure not to think I don't trust God. If I'm leaving the hotel, there's also a meaning in *that*. You have to be tested—*that*'s what you have to be.

Thomas Jensen looked at him penetratingly: If you could just find mercy, Mogensen, he said softly.

— Dancing was over with at the inn, but the young people found shelter under another roof. At the merchant's east of town a speakeasy was set up. The coop had almost taken all trade from him, and so they danced evenings in the store. The bawling and noise could be heard out on the road when respectable people went by along with harmonica playing and stamping on the floor, and alcohol could surely be had. But people didn't know anything for certain, and no one cared to report it without proof at hand.

When Mogensen left the hotel, Katrine got a job with the baker.



When the man with the bagpipes came into the yard, you knew winter was over. With his foot he beat a large drum: dum, dum, dum; it was the ice breaking up, and the bagpipe wailed a brittle, little tone like newborn lambs and croaking frogs, and way in the background a cuckoo crowed. He rattled on a brass cymbal, which strangely recalled the shining melt-water in the bogs and the cries of the lapwing over its nest. The children stood around him and followed him from place to place. Then he moved on with his bagpipes.

White clouds drifted across the immense sky that almost enveloped you. The air was warm despite the night frost and easterly wind, and the newly tarred boats came in from the fjord. The herring nets were set out, and in rapid turns the gulls sailed down after the fish. There was life in the meadows with chirping birds in the green grass, but things were also sprouting in people's houses: Andrea revealed to her husband she was with child. Anton Knopper heartily thanked God and was doubly gentle to Karen. She would not be less dear to him for that reason.

When the children came from school, they played at the wharf, and when they could get away with it, they splashed out in a pram and ventured to raise a piece of sail on an oar, although that was otherwise prohibited. But in the middle of the beautiful spring, two of Lars Bundgaard's boys drowned.

There was pale sunshine with fluttering wind and small-rippled waves on the water. Ten boys were out on one of the big fishing prams and had gotten some distance from land. None of them was over twelve years old. A little kid leaned over the railing and splashed a piece of netting on a stick into the water. It was fishing gear he had made himself to catch stickleback.

Suddenly he lost his balance and fell out of the boat. They saw a glimpse of his face before he sank, and his brother, Teodor, who was eleven years old and could swim, tore off his shirt and jumped in after him. The boys struggled with the oars to get the boat turned around, but the big pram couldn't be mastered. Teodor emerged, a shock of his light-colored hair was on the surface for a moment, then he disappeared again and was lost in the cold water.

The others crawled down into the bottom of the pram, scared to death, and didn't dare look at one another. The boat drifted with the current.

Anton Knopper was in the fjord and found the pram drifting out into the broad waters; he wasn't thinking about any accident, but shouted to the children:

How much would you give to come on land, kids.

A little kid answered:

You can have my piggy-bank, Anton Knopper, because Karl and Teodor fell overboard.

Anton Knopper took the boat in tow and quickly went back to land. Lars Bundgaard was standing near the shore tarring a boat, and Anton Knopper ran over to him as quickly as his legs could carry him.

Oh, Lars, he whispered. It's just terrible. The boys say Karl and Teodor drowned in the fjord.

Lars Bundgaard stared at him for a moment with his eyes wide open, but then set off running out to the wharf and untied a boat. He had the tarbrush in his hand—now he flung it away and pushed off from land. Anton Knopper shouted to the men on the wharf to prepare the motorboat. But Lars Bundgaard rowed out into the fjord with long strokes.

Anton Knopper didn't know what to do. Who should inform Malene about the accident? There was probably nothing else for it—he did it himself. He hurried up to the house. Malene was washing and up to her elbows in foaming soapy water. With cautious words he explained what had happened. Malene said nothing, but dried her hands on her apron and kept drying them. After Anton Knopper had gone, she wandered around restlessly in the rooms without tears. Lars Bundgaard came home and nodded to Malene without meeting her eyes. He went up to the loft to be alone. In the pigeon house the pigeons cooed, and the chirping swallows flew in and out of an open trap-door. They had nests under the beams. Two lives had been extinguished—two children had gone home to God.

He lay down on a pile of traps under the rafters and turned his head toward the dark. Why had his children been taken from him? It wasn't his intention to take the Lord to task or doubt his wisdom, but he thought through his life: what was wrong with him? Had he been arrogant or relied on himself? Oh, never again would he feel Karl's soft hand in his.

Heavy steps sounded on the stairs. It was Malene. She went over to him and touched his arm.

Can't we be together on this? she asked helplessly.

Lars Bundgaard got up:

Can you understand why it had to happen, Malene?

No, Malene answered. But we have to trust in God's wisdom and mercy.

Yes, we'll do that, Lars Bundgaard said softly. I was just thinking about whether there might be some warning in it.

— After Lars Bundgaard and Anders Kjøng had emptied the herring nets at dawn, they rowed about in the fjord to find the boys. Lars Bundgaard was lying in the bow and staring down at the bottom. He had one hand over his eyes so the sun wouldn't blind him. In the other he was holding a boat-hook; once in a while he squeezed the wood with his fingers. The seaweed was dark green in the sunshine, with greenish-yellow specks of sand in between; everything glimmered and became blurred in the rippled waves, and on the surface the sky was reflected with its white clouds. The small fry glided like shadows over the light spots at the bottom and disappeared in the seaweed. Each time Lars Bundgaard blinked his eyes. They rowed across all the bottoms into the small inlets. Somewhere the children were lying and staring up through the green water.

Anders Kjøng rowed the boat slowly while small gleaming drops dripped from the oars. He couldn't bear to think about the moment when they'd find the children. Two rascals, fast on their feet and quick-tongued, little critters, and plump. Lars Bundgaard had admonished them and chastised and disciplined them, and carried them in his arms. And now they were lying, cold corpses, in the fjord.

They had their food along in the boat and searched until late in the evening. The full moon rose yellow from the hills, and in the shallow water a flock of big, dark birds was standing motionless, with their beaks lowered. They were gray herons. Gulls and lapwings fluttered over the beach in the evening light in long arcs, and the fog was steaming over the meadows. The lights were on in the village and gleamed in the semi-darkness. The wake drew streaks in the fjord, which was now completely black.

— Lars Bundgaard didn't find his children's corpses, though he searched east and west and sailed for miles in the motorboat. The current had surely taken them and carried them to sea. Malene went around restlessly and couldn't think about anything but the children who were rocking lonely in the cold water. She knew well that their souls were in a safe harbor, but she couldn't get any peace until their little bodies were laid in the earth. If only they were lying in a grave in the churchyard, they'd be home. Alma had to help her every day in the house. Malene couldn't manage anything any more. Around her the little children, who didn't understand anything, made noise. The older ones were silent and red-eyed from weeping. Lars Bundgaard's new house had become a place of sorrow.

For every week that passed, Lars Bundgaard became more stooped and ponderous in his features. The others helped him search, but no one could give him a word of consolation. Lars Bundgaard himself knew the way to his savior, and what he had to bear the others couldn't put on their backs. Teacher Aaby came to visit and spoke with Malene.

We must accept our sorrow with humility, he said. After all, we know it's all for our best.

Yes, Malene answered.

You've received so many blessings—all of life's blessings,

Aaby said. Now God wants to test your faithfulness—that's what we have to believe.

Aaby took her hand: Death strikes young and old, and is bitter at every age.

Thomas Jensen was working on one of the traps one evening, and the oldest children weren't in bed yet, but were sitting at the table and grinding away at their lessons for the next day. Alma was mending an old jacket. There was a knock at the door. It was Lars Bundgaard. He had to stoop under the low door frame.

Good evening, Lars, Thomas Jensen said softly. That's nice of you to want to look in on us. Please sit down.

He pushed the table to the side, and Lars Bundgaard sat down on the green plush sofa. Alma got up quickly and put down her work. I guess I'll go take care of the coffee, she said, and gave a signal to the children to follow her. When the door was closed, you could hear one of the boys out there reciting a verse from a hymn in a high, monotonous voice:

> Arise all things that God has made
> And praise His name and glory;
> Each leaflet and each grassy blade
> Do tell a wondrous story — — —

You've been in the fjord, Lars, Thomas Jensen said.

Yes, Lars Bundgaard answered softly. I didn't find them today either. The current must have taken them. But it's odd they haven't been found now that there are so many fishermen out there.

He was silent for a while and bowed his head so that it rested on his large hands.

I wanted to ask you about one thing, he said. Do you believe providence is at work?

We can't have any doubt about that, Thomas Jensen answered. We know there's a will in everything that happens.

Lars Bundgaard looked up: We children of God must speak frankly with one another, he said. I'm afraid grace has been taken from me.

You must never think that, Lars, Thomas Jensen answered, frightened. Look there—he pointed to a framed scriptural text on the wall. "Suffer the little children to come unto me"—you must never forget these words. And you must not take God to task. That's a terrible act. When he tests us with sorrow and misfortune, it's only because he loves us. —

I'm not opposing God, Lars Bundgaard answered. And I certainly know he must take what is his. It's not the children, though you can't deny it's the worst test that can befall you. — But I mustn't say that either because maybe something could happen that would weigh even more heavily on me.

He was silent for a while.

We're searching for them every day. And the only thing I'm praying for is to get them in from the fjord and laid in their graves. Malene is going downhill: day and night she thinks about how they're lying out there. — Do you remember four years ago when your brother was lost at sea?

Oh yes, oh yes, Thomas Jensen mumbled, moved.

There was a lot of talk about how concerned you were about where the body had washed up. And I thought you hadn't completely bent your will to God's will. It was the soul that mattered, so I didn't feel it was right to grieve over not being able to find the body. And I said that to you because I felt I was obliged to warn you if you were on a wrong path. Do you think that was wrong?

In truth I dare not say, Thomas Jensen replied. It was hard for me to hear that back then—you can surely understand that now. But maybe you were right. Ejler died an impious man, and it would have been better if we'd taken more care of his soul while he was alive than of his body when he was dead.

Lars Bundgaard rocked back and forth as if in torment: If I can't find my children, it's doubtless because back then I condemned others for the same thing —

Oh, dear Lars, you should talk with Jesus, Thomas Jensen said.

I did. Both day and night I've prayed for him to forgive me my sins. But it's as though he has turned his back on me. It's written: And with what measure ye mete, it shall be measured to you again. Now I'm harvesting what I sowed in arrogance.

Thomas Jensen got up: Let's pray together, he said quietly. All we know is that Jesus will help us if he wants to. And that's the only thing we need to know here on earth.

He bowed his head and prayed. Lars Bundgaard moved his lips while he stared up at the white circle of light on the timbered ceiling. His face was strangely moved. Alma came in with the coffee cups, but put the tray on the table and remained standing with her hands folded. Thomas Jensen's voice rose, and fell into the Lord's Prayer.

Thank you, Lars Bundgaard whispered.

Alma spread the cloth out over the flowered oilcloth, but Lars Bundgaard got up.

You mustn't take it amiss, Alma, he said. But I won't be having coffee.

When he got home, Malene was sleeping on a chair in the dark kitchen. She propped her head against the wall, and her cheeks were spotted from weeping. She awoke when her husband lit the kitchen lamp.

Did you get to talk with Thomas? she asked in a voice hoarse from night cold.

Yes, Lars Bundgaard answered. And I know now that Thomas has forgiven me. You'll see, Malene, now we'll soon get them on land.

He took the lamp and went ahead into the bedroom.

One day a man was standing in Tea's parlor. He was wearing old-fashioned ceremonial black clothes, and his face was hard and wrinkled with small blinking eyes. Tea asked him to sit down—he wanted information about Kjeld and Thora.

Yes, who is this man here? Tea asked. I don't think I know your face.

I'm Thora's father, the stranger said. My name is Mogens Koldkjær. I'd like a little information before I knock on their door. And of course you're Kjeld's sister.

Tea became short of breath. Had the old man regretted his

hardness and had he come to put the title and property in Kjeld's hands?

I wonder how things are with them? Mogens Koldkjær asked.

Well, they've had a hard winter, Tea sighed; Kjeld has been without work, but they've made it. He speared eel and did a day's work here and there, and for the time being he's working on the road for the municipality.

The small farmer blinked his eyes a couple of times; it obviously didn't suit him. He had possibly expected to find them in such great poverty that Kjeld had perished from it. Could Kjeld behave himself among the people here with all the craziness in him?

Yes, Tea said bitingly. All I can say is we're believing people here who treat one another with kindness.

Well, the small farmer said. Yes, that may well be. But if you want my opinion, I don't think very highly of the faith they have in this area.

The small farmer stared over at the chest of drawers. Tea followed his look. Jens Røn had forgotten his pipe; she was annoyed: there wasn't any point in his letting his things lie around. Mogens Koldkjær belonged to the Free Mission people inland, who considered smoking tobacco a sin. Tea felt caught up in something unlawful, but pulled herself together; it was all exaggerated: how could smoking tobacco in moderation harm the soul? The man was still staring at the pipe with his small, sharp eyes, and Tea blushed and became angry. She wasn't used to being called a nonbeliever. In a humble voice she said:

You know, it's written: There is nothing from without a man, that entering into him can defile him.

Mogens Koldkjær directed his sharp glance at her.

You're well-versed in the Scriptures—I can understand that, he said. Yes, I certainly know you people are busy quoting it.

Tea gasped and began crying: was she to be considered a hypocrite, she who had the gentle light of grace deep in her soul? But she remembered not to get hot-headed; it wasn't proper to argue with an old man, who had traveled from far away. Now she understood it had been hard for Kjeld to get along with him. He was one of the self-righteous.

Won't you have coffee, she asked with gentle friendliness.

No thanks, the old man said. Thank you so much. But I'd better see about finding where they live. If you'll just show me the way.

Tea went out with him and explained where the house was situated. He trudged off, short-legged and crook-backed like a subterranean. Even his cane looked threatening. It was thick and wax-yellow with knots and furrows, like a twisted tree.

When Kjeld came home from work, the old man was sitting in the parlor. They greeted each other like enemies.

So, you've come, Kjeld said curtly.

Yes, I've come, even if I'm not welcome, Mogens Koldkjær answered. And it's most of all the children I want to look at. Surely that can't be any skin off your back, and they're well off. He patted one of the landowner's children on the head with his broad hand, made crooked by arthritis.

Yes, we take care of them, Kjeld said sullenly.

Thora calmly walked back and forth while the men grumbled at each other. When Kjeld was outside washing, she turned to her father:

I'm telling you, Kjeld is good enough.

Of course, her father replied peevishly. I know him well. But haven't you people thought about coming home? I can scarcely manage the farm alone; farm hands are expensive: it's just terrible what they can demand for their labor, and then with the food they demand—it would never pay.

Thora shook her head. Only if he retired and gave Kjeld title would Kjeld return. The old man growled: nothing would ever come of that as long as he was above ground. Then everything would just stay the way it was, Thora said.

The small farmer looked over at the children who were playing in the corner: Surely I'm allowed to talk to the children, he said. They aren't his workmanship, as big as he is otherwise.

Thora showed her white teeth: Now watch your mouth.

Mogens Koldkjær stayed overnight, and the men talked with

strained politeness and watched every word. The next morning, before he was to leave, he found in his jacket pocket a bag of candy that had melted into one clump.

Can you share it and enjoy yourselves, he said to the children. And obey your mother in everything she tells you.

And your father, Thora added.

And I want to see you become well-behaved people, he continued unfazed by the admonition. So everyone can see you come from honest people. Mogens Koldkjær returned home.

— One Sunday in early summer Tabita had off and was home. The first thing she said was she had given notice at work.

But Tabita, Tea said, did you give notice at work without speaking to anyone about it?

I can easily get another job, Tabita said. But she gave me a letter to take along. She doubtless didn't write anything good about me.

Tea read the letter:

Fisherman Røn's wife!

Your daughter Tabita gave notice yesterday, which she surely has told you. Col. 3,20. I can't give her any recommendation. Although she comes from a believing home, Rom. 2,28, she has a hard time submitting to the will of others. I know I've been good to her, as if she were my own daughter, John 3,21, and only tried to protect her from the dangers that are found on a young girl's path, Matt. 7,13, Jas. 1,14-15.

With greetings in the Lord

Mrs. Maria Fabian, née Buncheflod

Oh, dear child, Tea wailed, what will become of you? You must have rebelled against your mistress. You have to look into yourself and ask her for forgiveness. What will other people say when word gets around you couldn't be with good, believing people? I'm sure she didn't do anything to you but what was her duty. Oh, you really know how to give us grief.

Tabita's breasts were fully developed and she looked like a mature girl. But now her face twitched and she was on the verge of crying.

I can't stand it, she said. If the mistress discovers I talk to the other people in the house, she becomes angry and says I should beware of gossip. I have to clean, and she helps only a bit with the food, and if I happen to break a saucer, she doesn't scold—she just sighs as if I'd done it on purpose to torment her. I don't have anyone to talk to—there isn't even anyone to scold me. And I'm never allowed to go outdoors.

Jens Røn had listened to the conversation in silence. But it's for your own good, he said to console her. There's much evil in the city you don't know about.

Tabita got up on her high horse: If you just knew her the way she really is. She's wicked, and I'd rather die than stay there another year.

Maybe you aren't the way you should be either, Jens Røn said. It's so easy to see the errors in other people. And we mustn't forget that both the husband and wife are pious people.

Pious, Tabita replied. Don't believe it. Because mistress and the clerk are sweethearts.

What did you say? Tea shouted, appalled.

It's true, Tabita said. She doesn't think I know, but the girl next door told me. She visits him in his room in the garret. All the people in the street talk about it.

God forbid—I'll never believe it, Tea said and clapped her hands in dismay. I thought she looked like an honest woman. But I was suspicious of that splendor she had on her fingers. But I'll say this: if she's one of that kind, you have to leave her house immediately.

Jens Røn put his shag pipe down.

Now don't get too zealous, he admonished her. People like to say whatever bad things they can about God's children. And it isn't certain it's anything but idle chatter.

But Tea was almost sure Tabita was right. She read the letter again and didn't like it. I think she makes too much of a show of how pious she is, she said, and it's no use for her to assert that Tabita is obstinate because she's never been that way.

You can't find mistakes in your own children, Jens Røn said.

Yes I can, Tea flared up. I'll never defend them when they do something wrong. But I certainly know Tabita. And it isn't nice either the way she shows how little she respects us. She calls me fisherman Røn's wife, but she calls herself Mrs. If that isn't arrogance, I don't know what is—No, I don't care a bit about her religion.

A week later Tea went to town to find out about the matter. She decided to visit the Mogensens. Maybe they knew something about Fabian and his household. The laundry was situated in a narrow side street. It was hot and humid in the little store, where Mrs. Mogensen and a young girl were standing and ironing when Tea came. Tea was invited for coffee, but Mrs. Mogensen kept rushing out into the ironing room.

I have to watch out, Mogensen explained. If a shirt gets destroyed, we have to replace it—in deference to our reputation. Tea nodded. It was reasonable for the elegant things to be treated carefully.

Mogensen went about without a collar and had felt shoes on. He had gotten a bit fatter. On the table paper, bills, and accounts flowed in abundance. Can you make a go of it with the laundry? Tea asked.

Oh yes, Mogensen answered. You have to say the business is really cleaning up—haha—that's pretty funny: *cleaning up*; you can also call it a business that has washed itself. Mogensen clucked. But it's a whole lot to watch out for—bills and calculations and purchases of soap and starch and fuel. I have to take care of all that.

Tea said what she had come to town about. Did the Mogensens know whether Mrs. Fabian had good morals? Mrs. Mogensen hadn't heard anything one way or the other. People surely talk a lot about her, Mogensen said. But I never take gossip seriously and haven't paid close attention to it. But we can soon find out. I just need to ask the policeman's wife next door. She knows everything of that sort that happens. Mogensen went out to find out about the matter, and in the meantime his wife complained about her troubles to Tea. It wasn't easy with the girls; many of them lolled about at work and were a pain to have around.

One of them I chased away a little while ago, Mrs. Mogensen said. No, these people can't be relied on. Do you know what she did? One day I come in, and she's standing and ironing a pair of men's pants—

I never heard anything so crazy! Tea said, irritated.

A pair of men's pants! Mrs. Mogensen nodded. I say to her: what in the world kind of pants are they, Karla? They're my sweetheart's, the wench answers; he asked me to press the creases on them—he's sitting in the laundry and waiting for them to be finished. We're going to the ball tonight. Well, what should I say? I didn't think I wanted to forbid her—that could look cantankerous. But then I keep catching her ironing men's pants, and every time she explains it's her sweetheart's. So I get suspicious and begin watching, and Mogensen's also watching. You can see he drilled a little peep-hole in the door. And in the week before Easter she ironed ten pairs of pants. Karla, I say to her, you lied to me: Don't tell me your sweetheart has ten pairs of pants. So she made a clean breast of it and admitted she got 35 øre for every pair of pants she pressed—I mean, it was her sweetheart who got the money, and it was his chums who owned the pants. Such young louts have to have creases.

That was an ugly prank, Tea said.

I'd like to have honest girls, Mrs. Mogensen explained. And so if it turns out that Tabita gets another job, I think it would be smart for her to be an apprentice with me. You know, she can live here—there's a room next to the kitchen—and she can cook and clean and be useful that way, and when she's learned to iron, she'll get a good wage.

Thank you for the offer, Tea answered. But I don't dare say anything.

Mogensen returned. Yes, now I've got the answer, he said. Mrs. Fabian doesn't have a good reputation. They say she has sweethearts, and she doesn't let the young people they have in the store in peace.

Isn't she a believing woman? Tea asked and cast her eyes down.

She speaks of God alot, Mogensen said. And she goes to meetings and gives donations to the Mission, but to put it bluntly she's definitely lascivious.

Then Tabita shouldn't be there either, Tea said angrily. But I always thought there was something wrong with her.

Tea looked around when she went through the shining, white ironing room. It smelled of cleanliness, and a girl was standing in a long smock and guided the hot iron with calm movements. So think about your daughter, Mrs. Mogensen said.

She went up to the back of the Fabians' house and knocked on the kitchen door. Tabita was alone in the kitchen and opened the door. Her face beamed with a smile, and Tea got tears in her eyes.

Are you here to visit, mother, she shouted with joy, but she became anxious and asked: Nothing bad happened at home, did it?

No, of course not, Tea said and kissed her daughter. I just thought I wanted to talk a bit with your master and mistress. I don't think you should be here any more. Tabita's room was very small with moist spots on the wallpaper and tattered curtains. A framed sign hung over the bed with the words: "God sees everything." It would surely have been better if the mistress had hung it up over her own bed, Tea thought. The furniture consisted of a wooden chair and chest of drawers, but on the chest was a picture of Jens Røn and her in a gold frame, which Tabita had bought with her wages. Next to it lay a piece of amber she had found by the sea when she was a child, some stones from the shore, and a sewing box of shining little shells—a gift from Anton Knopper.

Are they bad to you? Tea asked.

Tabita's face twitched: I really miss home, she said. All day long I go around and think about how you all are. At night I often dream something has happened to father in the fjord; I know it's just a dream, but still I'm afraid it's got to be a warning.

Sobbing, Tabita threw herself on the bed, and Tea sat down beside her and gently stroked her hair.

You know, you *have to* go out into the world, little Tabita, she said.

But not here, Tabita cried. I'll go anywhere else, and I'll never complain—just let me get away from here.

Tea raised her up and dried her eyes with her handkerchief. It was hard when your children had grief. Tea felt poor and insignificant. She wouldn't be able to have Tabita at home forever. It would look bad if poor people had a grown daughter staying home and doing nothing.

Now don't cry, Tabita, she said. I'm going in and giving notice for you. Then in November you'll have another job where you'll be happy. Tabita went with her mother through the dining room and knocked on the mistress's door, but Tea went in alone. Mrs. Fabian was lying on a divan and reading. She looked at Tea with surprise without immediately recognizing her.

I'm Tabita's mother, Tea said.

Oh, it's you—I thought so—Mrs. Fabian nodded and got up. Yes, I expected you'd want to come. You know, the child has given notice because she thinks it's too lonely here, and as I wrote to you, she's unfortunately a difficult person and lacks the ability to subordinate herself. Oh, won't you sit down, please. But, to be candid, I think you should let her stay here. I've tried to do as well by her and to protect her as if it were my charitable duty to a heedless child.

Tea sat there embarrassed and stared at the mistress's ring-bedecked hands. That she had ever trusted her and put Tabita under her power! She looked at the Christ figure. It should be forbidden to put a sacred statue in a defiled house.

We feel it's better to place her with people we know better, she said.

Now I'm going to tell you, she's difficult, the mistress answered with irritation. She's obstinate and unsociable—and she has no notion of cleanliness.

That startled Tea: that was too much. If someone was going to say she hadn't taught Tabita to be tidy, that was the last straw. And she had to hear it from a woman who seduced her husband's salesman into fornication.

I hate to say anything bad, she said in the gentlest voice. But it's not good for a child to become acquainted with everything, especially when she's with people who call themselves pious and God's children.

The mistress jumped to her feet: What are you getting at? she asked sharply.

I mean you're leading a lewd life, Tea answered.

Mrs. Fabian grabbed a pillow, and it looked as if she wanted to fling it at Tea. But suddenly she fell back screaming onto the divan. She kicked her legs convulsively, and saliva formed around her mouth. Terrified, Tea stared at her. Fabian and Tabita came rushing in at the same time.

Get some water! the dry-goods merchant shouted while making violent arm gestures. Cold water!

He kneeled down at his wife's side and unbuttoned her dress. Tabita came running with a can of water, and he moistened her face and breast. Gradually the screaming turned into convulsive crying, which called to mind a dog howling.

Little kitty, Fabian said. Pull yourself together, little kitty, little kitty.

He patted her reassuringly on the arm, and his thin hair bristled as if in the wind. Tea stood there lost and didn't know what to do. She couldn't go and leave Tabita behind alone. Mrs. Fabian's crying calmed down and ended finally in sniffling.

What's wrong, little kitty? Fabian asked. Something must have happened that your nerves couldn't bear.

Mrs. Fabian lifted her face from the pillows on the divan and pointed at Tea: Get her out of here, she wailed. She's got to get out of here immediately, and her daughter with her. I don't ever want to see them again. Oh, get them out, Fabian!

The dry-goods merchant turned toward Tea: You have to go, he said, and when Tea hesitated: Can't you understand—You must go. Do you hear! She can't bear it!

Down in the servant-girl's room Tea helped pack up her stuff. Tabita looked at her mother with astonished eyes.

What did you say to her? she asked.

I said the truth, just as it is, Tea answered. But she's really a terrible person, and I'm glad you don't have to work here any more.

Won't I get the wages they owe me? Tabita asked, and Tea dropped what she was holding. She had totally forgotten the wages.

I haven't gotten anything in three months. Tabita said.

Of course you'll get your wages, Tea said. That's the last straw. The rich people won't trick you out of it. I don't think even they're that bad.

They stole down the kitchen stairs, and Tabita remained standing outside on the street with her suitcase, while Tea was inside in the store. She explained to the store clerk that she had to talk to Fabian. The clerk pressed a button, and a moment later Fabian came down the stairs in the corner.

What! he said ill-temperedly. You again? What do you want now? What do you want? Haven't you caused enough misfortune today? He stamped on the floor heatedly.

I want to talk you about the wages you owe Tabita, she said anxiously.

Wages! the dry-goods merchant said. She's going to get wages to boot? After you and your daughter abused my wife with swear words she wouldn't utter? I should truly go to the police, I should.

Tea got angry. I can't talk to you any further about the thing, she said. But the girl has to have her wages for the time she was here. I won't demand the rest. I thought you were an upright man, but I understand alright that neither you nor your wife are what you pass yourselves off as.

What aren't we? What are you accusing me of? Fabian said trembling with rage. But you, *you* are a devout and pious person, who sneaks into a home with evil slander, and afterwards you want to get your wages! Never! You won't get a penny! Nothing doing! Not a penny! Fabian pounded his hand on the counter, but turned immediately toward the stairs and listened.

Fabian! the plaintive call could be heard. Fabian! Come up here a second.

I'm coming, little kitty, he shouted and rushed up the steps in quick bounds.

He returned out of breath.

You'll get the wages for the three months, he said. My wife wants to repay evil with good, although you haven't earned it. But you'll have to take the money in goods. It's no use protesting—there's no other way.

Tea thought twice about it, but hesitatingly said yes. There was obviously no talking to the man, and she didn't want to reveal what had happened between her and Mrs. Fabian.

You can choose your goods, Fabian said. I'm going upstairs again. But first I'm going to give you the word from Paul: Let no corrupt communication proceed out of your mouth, but that which is good to the use of edifying. Let that be a lesson to you.

With dignified, mincing steps Fabian went his way, and the clerk began to take goods down from the shelf. Tea wanted linen cloth and cotton clothing. There was good quality here. Expertly he took the material between his fingers and praised it. But Tea was smarter.

I want to choose from the goods that are in the window, she said. There are price tags. I think what's on the shelf has surely been lying there a long time.

— Tea and Tabita dragged the suitcase and the heavy packages down to the harbor.

That you dared do it! Tabita said. I was just about to run off, when she began to scream.

I'll tell you, Tabita, Tea answered. I thought it was something I had to say, and maybe the admonition can lead her on to the right path. But you must never trust those who mouth pious words and secretly live a scandalous life. They are much worse than the undisguised sinners.


Tea had proved herself a witness to the truth and harvested honor for her frankness. Even Mariane was impressed. Did you say it to her point blank? she asked. I said it right to her face, Tea assured her. I said: You're leading a lewd life, and she went into convulsions and fell down—it was probably her conscience. But we children of God must speak the truth without taking into account who we're talking to. If only you people always did that, Mariane said. Well, we're only human beings, Tea said. And there are many hypocrites in addition. But I did in fact say to her: You're leading a lewd life.

Jens Røn listened to Tea's story silently. Deep down he was proud of her; he himself would never have dared oppose sin so adamantly. But he said: Still, your words were rather harsh. You know, we mustn't condemn. Tea had an answer ready. I wasn't condemning, she said. I just spoke the truth straight out. But when people who call themselves believers lead such a life, I think it'd be better for us to let Tabita be an apprentice with Mogensen. Maybe that was right, Jens Røn said. In any case we can't have her staying at home.

Jens Røn thought the matter over for a long time; it was as if there were no hurry in getting Tabita off. Tabita had become so mild-mannered and compliant: she helped Tea in the house and cooked, and Tea had time to go outside and look around. Povl Vrist was to build a house. The site was already dug, and it promised to be big.

You two have been lucky, Tea said, but then Povl Vrist is also a capable fisherman.

Yes, we have nothing to complain about, Mariane admitted. But we've also worked a lot. I can recall when we were just married, often I went to the fjord with Povl and gave him a hand with the work even though people talked. We had no hired helper and were strangers here in the area who couldn't expect help. And I've surely mended just as many traps as other wives have knitted stockings.

Tea sighed a bit uneasily. She'd never be such a capable wife as Mariane, and she'd probably never get her own house. It was impossible to understand the success Povl Vrist had despite the fact that he was almost an unbeliever. Povl and Mariane were lucky in everything. Even their children were smarter than other peoples'. Aaby often talked about the oldest boy—he was gifted, and Povl Vrist had to make him stick to his books when the time came. Povl Vrist shook his head with a little smile: What should he be when he grows up? Well, he could for example go to the seminary or take the schoolteacher exam, Aaby answered. Schoolteacher, Povl Vrist said, I think it would be hard to sit all day long and read with the children, and the boy is physically healthy and can work hard—Yes, well, I know it's important work, but I don't believe we're going to consider it.

Aaby didn't answer, but shook his head. He didn't talk much any more and could barely control the children in school. It would soon be time for him to retire. He didn't have much to do with the youth association, and he didn't send for speakers even though he was chairman. He presumably felt it did more harm than good. But every day he took long walks with the Bible in his pocket, sat down on a stone in the sunshine and read and walked a bit again and stopped and banged his cane on the ground. In the evenings, too, he had begun to wander out and be restless. Often he met Malene down by the fjord; she barely saw him and they didn't talk to each other.

Malene had become strange and no longer looked like herself. When someone talked to her, she responded absent-mindedly, and in the house things went as well as could be expected. She thought about the boys who were lying in the fjord. Many times she got up at night and went down to the wharf and stared out over the water with a heart turned cold by horror. They were lying someplace out there with their pale faces turned toward the yellow moon. Lars Bundgaard and she didn't talk much to each other and avoided looking at each other. They had become stooped and associated very little with other people.

— Far to the west the children's corpses were found in the fjord. The parish constable came and told them in cautious words and said Lars Bundgaard himself should go down there to get the corpses. Lars Bundgaard went out into the kitchen.

So they found them, Malene, he said.

Malene propped herself up against the wall and breathed heavily, but a glimmer of joy flickered across her ravaged face.

Oh, thanks be to Jesus, she said. Now we'll take them home.

Early the next morning Lars Bundgaard left, and the day after he brought two children's coffins home in the motorboat. The boys were buried. Malene went up to the churchyard and sat for hours, but she got her own spirit back. Now that the children were in the earth, she had a grave to look after and she could take care of the other lives that were entrusted to her.

— One day right during lunchtime Andrea got labor pains and felt the birth would be any minute. Anton Knopper rushed off for the midwife, and people stared at him; he was wearing stockings—he hadn't had time to put on his wooden shoes. Out of breath he knocked on the door; the midwife wasn't there, and he dashed through the house like lightning. The sweat was pouring from his forehead: now everything was going wrong. He ran out into the yard, saw a key in a door and ripped open the door. The woman was sitting there and stared at him.

You have to come immediately, Anton Knopper said. There's not a moment to lose—it's all going down the drain.

Close the door, man! the midwife shouted angrily. Have you completely lost your mind?

Anton Knopper paced the parlor, while the screams of childbirth resounded through the house. If it went wrong now, he'd be responsible forever. Finally Andrea gave birth. When he came into the bedroom, she was lying in bed tired, while the midwife was swaddling the child. It was a big boy. So, it was a boy, Anton Knopper said and acted calm. Yes, it's not hard to see for someone who knows the difference, the midwife said. And he's healthy and alright? Anton Knopper asked. He couldn't be better if I had made him myself, the midwife answered. Yes, yes, Anton Knopper said. He's welcome—that's for sure.

Anton Knopper became sedate and calm. He was far beyond his youthful years when the boy began to be formed, but it went by in no time and wasn't so hard as he had imagined. Every moment he could take from work, he sat by the cradle and looked at the boy. I almost believe he recognizes me, he said, and it's amazing how he looks at me. Anton Knopper was a newly married man and his nest wasn't full.

After the date the interest payment fell due, the hotel was reopened. Kock had bought it for a song and wanted to be an innkeeper. Kock stood on the steps and filled in anyone who asked. Did he believe he could make a go of it? Oh, yes, Kock said, he wouldn't have to be paying a lot of money in interest and would have his wages on the side as a customs official. That would surely be as good as repairing shoes. So is there going to be dancing here? Anton Knopper asked. I don't dance myself, Kock said. And I don't understand what use it is, but I'll never be opposed to others' doing it. But in particular I could imagine organizing meetings with discussions for the fall. Is it going to be about the Jews? Anton Knopper asked. We're going to drop the Jews for the time being, Kock replied, there are other important problems—for example, limiting births. We're not going to be allowed to have any more children? Anton Knopper asked, appalled. How is that possible? Of course, Kock instructed him. There'll be more children, but it will have to happen in moderation and according to a prearranged plan. It's my view the world is in need of more reason and deliberation. You're not married, Anton Knopper said, otherwise you wouldn't speak that way.

Kock hired Katrine, and she was at the inn again. She had become more voluptuous, and her bosom was on the verge of bursting her bodice. The fellows had their eye on her. When there was dancing, Katrine didn't leave the dance floor; she rushed from arm to arm, and the silver cross hopped on her breast. Anders Kjøng was melancholy: he couldn't find favor with the girl. He became bitter and decided not to look over at the side where Katrine was. She was surely in great demand—she could get ten if she could get one—but she was a sensible girl and wanted a ring.

The grain was taken into the barn. Thundershowers drifted over the fjord; on the horizon you could see the glimmering of distant fires. The seaweed sparkled in various colors like a flower bed at the bottom of the water. The summer was soon over. Tabita went to town and got a job with Mogensen, and old

Martinus died and was laid in the earth. He left a little money when he died, and Anton tithed it to the Mission. God had given to him, and he gave back. Once in a while a letter came from kin and friends, but the old country had become so distant. They had come to feel at home here and they were no longer strangers.

Pastor Brink looked for a post, and emissaries from distant parishes attended church to hear his preaching. He was reserved, almost a bit shy of people, and when he discovered a strange face in church, he became uncertain and stopped short. In the evening he paced in his parlor, back and forth across the carpet's flower pattern and was always careful to step on the same spots. It turned into a mania. Even when he walked on the church floor, he made sure to put his foot exactly where the tiles met. He gave long speeches to his wife while he walked back and forth, right foot there, left there: I've been knocked out, simply, squeezed to death by a stubborn invisible resistance. The great Boyg, he said, the great Boyg, I didn't want to go around, you see. They sit cold and stiff in church; lying in wait, they watch me. And I can't exist without spiritual warmth, I *must* have confidence and spiritual authority. I don't want to be in a straight-jacket, I *don't want* it, Sofie. — —

His wife followed his endless wandering with eyes red from weeping: when he was transferred, everything would be better. Yes, it will, he replied, if it would only happen; I have to go somewhere where I can keep my spiritual freedom. — Right foot there, left foot there—I can't talk to these people; you know, actually they're living in the middle ages with persecution of heretics and witch-burning. Humanism—what do they know about it?

Finally he was chosen for a Grundtvigian parish on the islands. It took several months before the new pastor came. He was young and zealous, and the Pious liked him.

— By the time the eel-traps were to be set out, the North Sea fishermen were uneasy and didn't know what fate awaited them. The people to the south had threatened to put nets in their fishing spots. It could easily come to a collision and litigation, and it wasn't easy to know how that might end. But nothing happened;

the nets were tarred and set out. The wharf was alive: people stood in clusters, fishermen ran back and forth, and farmers and day laborers came rushing over with traps. But in the evening, when the work was over, the talking began, and Anton Knopper was the subject of teasing inquiries and got strange advice. He took it calmly and neither engaged in quarreling nor got hotheaded. No, he was a different man. So will the boy soon be able to read? Povl Vrist asked. No, Anton Knopper said, that's demanding too much, but he is smart—that's for sure; I don't think it'll be long before he begins speaking. He's probably good at sucking, Jens Røn teased. He's taking care of that, he has to take care of that, and we can't ask for more, Anton Knopper said a bit offended. If the rest of us would only do that too.

On the southern side of the fjord the green and yellow fields on the hills shone in the evening sun. The wind blew a little, and the boats at the wharf swayed in their moorings, drifted a little way, stopped with a jerk, and drifted back in a half-circle.

People came, people went; one day the weather was good, the next day it was windy. But the rows of posts grew under the mallets' hollow droning. Kock came sauntering whenever people were standing gathered in groups; he liked company, but didn't demand that people patronize his hotel. It was open to everyone, but everything was voluntary, and Kock was a man of freedom. He had become an innkeeper for idealistic reasons, and because the inn could be had for a trifle. So, you're all standing and chatting, he said and greeted them lightly with a finger to his hat. Well, the time has to be filled in with something, as they say, but don't let me disturb you—Oh, you're discussing eel migrations; yes that's a curious problem that gives scientists gray hair. And Kock developed science's view of the matter and his own theory: The eel are formed deep in the mud like the earthworm in the bowels of the earth.

But I've never seen an eel with offspring or roe, Povl Vrist said.

To that extent that's a correct objection, Kock said. But have you seen a caterpillar with eggs? It's conceivable that the eel went through a metamophor, like, for example, the butterfly.

Maybe it digs its way down into the mud, and that's where the fructification takes place, to call the thing bluntly by its name. The female eel remains deep in the mud until the offspring are born—and the offspring pass into the chrysalis state or sit like lugs deep down and make their first appearance as fully developed eel —

I've heard smart people say things like that, Anton Knopper said.

Perhaps you don't regard me as smart, Anton Knopper? Kock said ironically.

Oh yes I do, Anton Knopper answered, frightened. Please don't misunderstand me. I just wanted to say that others have said the same thing, even if they didn't know how to express themselves in learned words.

The proof is lacking, Povl Vrist said. I read something about it, and —

Yes, it's a scientific hypothesis, Kock interrupted.

In the old days, there were many who thought blenny were eels' offspring, but there can't really be anything to it, can there? Anton Knopper asked. No, Kock answered. That's only common superstition. — That's what I thought, Anton Knopper said. That just couldn't be right.

One day the new pastor came down the wharf with wife and daughter. He was a lanky, gaunt man, who limped on one leg. His facial features were flabby: when someone talked to him, they tightened up, as if you were pulling a string. The wife and the little girls were pale like potato sprouts in a cellar. Hello, Pastor Terndrup said. So, the fishing is taking its course, yes, yes — Yes it can, Thomas Jensen said, if the weather would let us put out the nets. Of course, the pastor nodded. By the way, I just got a letter from a pastor who'd like to talk to us in the Mission house—if the Lord will. That's nice, Thomas Jensen replied. We always need good words.—Yes, certainly, the pastor said. Well, blessed be your work, brothers and friends.

The eel-traps were out, and the fjord foamed cold as the winter approached. The summer was over. In gardens and the fields birds of passage gathered in flocks. The singing of hymns resounded from the Mission house, and the pastor preached God's word from the church's pulpit. He was a believing man, an intrepid soul. He stood pale and calm with a cold luster in his eyes and pricked people with nails that were made red hot in a fire. You are such and such. You cheat in trade, and you eat yourself into perdition. Without fear of man he fought against evil and named things by their name. He talked to the old people about hell. And he reproached lewd girls for their lives when they came to church and were to have their children baptized. His words had bite and sting.

Povl Vrist's new house was one of the biggest in the village. There were spacious rooms and a veranda with colored windowpanes, and in the kitchen the wall near the range was covered with shiny tiles.

I've never known the likes of it, Tea said, impressed. You'd think it was a palace.

Mariane felt flattered: Now you're mocking. Really, we're not doing that well. But a wall like that is easier to keep clean.

If only you're blessed in your new abode, Tea said and thought sadly that such splendor would doubtless never be her lot. If she and her family just got their daily bread, that was a big thing. But there were others who had it worse, Tea sighed; it looked bad for Kjeld and his family.

Kjeld had had work all through the summer, but later in the fall it ran out. He managed as best he could; he did a day's work here and there and caught eel with a hook or with a purse-net. The furrows around his mouth had become deeper, and his temperament became more and more quarrelsome. When he discovered that someone or other had come with gifts, fish or groceries, he got angry, and Thora had trouble explaining there was no shame in accepting them. During the time he wasn't at work, he'd mostly lie on the sofa and gloomily stare up at the ceiling. Andrea often came to visit and whispered with Thora in the kitchen. The two women liked each other, and Anton Knopper was glad to see Andrea give the help she could. He was sorry for the man, who couldn't get on with people.

The day before Christmas Tabita came home. Tea clapped her hands with joy when she saw her. Tabita had gotten city-style clothes, and short dresses and silk stockings, and her hair was shorter than ever.

But Tabita, she said and let her hands sink.

Well, I have to dress like other people, Tabita said and the welcome brought tears to her eyes.

I thought I heard you say *I* differently than we do, Jens Røn said, and could scarcely believe his ears

Yes I did, Tabita declared. If I'm going to be in town, I'm going to have to use the language they speak there.

Jens Røn didn't answer; in a way, Tabita was doubtless right. But it was as if she had become a stranger. He stole a glance at her. Was that his little girl, who was refined like a city lady and spoke a foreign language? But Tea wasn't calm. Just as long as nothing bad happens to you, she said. I hope you're watching out with the men—they don't want to do well by you. Tabita blushed and said there was no danger of that. Well, just take care of yourself, Tea warned. I certainly know about these things. There may be danger afoot before you yourself know about it. And I'll be blunt: you could really make your dresses a little longer, Tabita.

But deep down Tea was proud. Tabita had gotten prettier, slim, and lively and had delicate, regular features. Her reddish-brown hair curled up so prettily on her neck, and her skin was white and delicate. Tea found some pretext to go up to Mariane's and took Tabita along. Mariane had a house that Tea would never have the likes of, but Tea had her children, and they were worth showing off. Mariane was full of astonishment over Tabita's splendid appearance, and Tea thought it right to contradict her a bit. Now I don't imagine you ever go dancing, she said. No, Tabita answered and blushed. Because then I'd never stop worrying for a minute, Tea said. I think that's the worst thing in the world when children mock what's true and right.

And finally, Tabita, remember what we taught you here at home. Tea was like a hen, who constantly had to have the chicks under her wing. But still it was nice that Tabita had gotten her magnificent feathers.

Tabita was glad to be at the Mogensens. How is she treating you? Tea asked. Oh, she can get angry, but it doesn't mean anything: ten minutes later she's forgotten the whole thing. And Mogensen—can he manage in town? Jens Røn asked. Tabita explained that things weren't so good with Mogensen. He drank a bit and went a lot to bars. But there wasn't anything evil about him—he just talked nonsense and boasted how much he accomplished, though it was his wife who put the food on the table.

Jens Røn and Tea were in church New Year's day, and while singing hymns Tea sneaked a look around. On one of the rear benches she discovered Kjeld and Thora. She was startled to see that Thora's father was also there. She nudged Jens Røn in the side and whispered: Mogens Koldkjær's here.

In the afternoon Tea stole down to Kjeld's and found Thora alone in the kitchen. Has he come? she asked out of breath. Yes, Thora smiled. He's finally given in, and the plan is for us to move home immediately. But come on, please go into the parlor. Tea refused, but without further ado Thora took her by the arm and led her in. Mogens Koldkjær was sitting on the sofa between the children, and he and Kjeld seemed completely satisfied with each other's company.

Well, that's her, Mogens Koldkjær said. Yes, we're acquaintances, hello. You're the one who's Kjeld's sister.

Yes, Tea answered. You came to visit at Christmas.

I certainly did, the small farmer said. And there's no hiding that I came to take these foolish people home.

Oh, really, Tea said and her voice turned meek. Mogens Koldkjær didn't like her tone and looked at her grumpily.

If it's permitted, I'd be tempted to say womenfolk are the most damnable rabble I know of.

What did you say? Tea burst out appalled.

What I said I'll certainly stand by, Mogens Koldkjær said and wrinkled his brows. Womenfolk are the most damnable rabble. I can't keep them from my bed.

What in the world women are you talking about! Tea asked with annoyance.

It's these housekeepers, Mogens Koldkjær explained. They were just about to chase me out of my house. First I had one—she was tall and gaunt like a bag of bones. She went around and fawned over me for a time, but I acted as if I didn't notice and gave her no encouragement. Then one evening when I was going to bed, she crept into it.

I never heard the likes of it! Tea burst out. How could anyone do such a thing?

I said to her: Don't inconvenience yourself—I can keep the bed warm by myself. And then I asked her to leave as soon as possible. The next one I got, by the way, was a big, beautiful womanfolk, fat as a smelt she was and a capable worker. So if I hadn't been up in years, things could easily have gone haywire. With her I was satisfied. — But one evening I also find her in my bed. I chased her away, but I thought: it's bad to have to deal with Kjeld, but womenfolk are still worse. They can't control themselves when they have to be alone around a manfolk, no matter how old he is.

The children don't need to hear that, Tea said softly.

Come on, they benefit from being warned in time, Mogens Koldkjær answered. Can you remember, little Kristiane, watch out so you don't let anyone talk you into anything, because then it'll all go downhill. — And keep away from womenfolk, as far as you can, little Mogens. You'll wind up stuck with them like a fly in syrup.

That's a lovely doctrine, Tea objected.

It's a very smart doctrine, the small farmer said and patted the children on the head. Now let me see: you watch out so things will go your way in the world.

Tea felt like saying that Mogens Koldkjær should rather have given advice to Thora while there was still time. But that would have been rude.

So Kjeld perhaps is going to manage your farm? she asked.

The old man looked as though he had swallowed an awful

bite of something.

You're probably the kind that wants to know how the devil buys iron for his hoofs, he said ill-temperedly. But I'll gladly give you a full report. You see, back then when Kjeld wanted to put pressure on me, I resisted, because his demands weren't reasonable. But no one can say I'm obstinate. And that's why I've decided of my own free will that Kjeld will get title because now I want to go into retirement. That's what I want.

Tea sighed with relief. Now Kjeld would become his own man and escape his wretchedness. She asked repeatedly whether Mogens Koldkjær would visit them while he was here.

But the small farmer shook his head.

Thank you, he said. But you know we have to leave as quickly as possible. I can't easily be away from the farm very long. But maybe sometime you'll come visit Kjeld. You'd be welcome.

— Several days later Kjeld and his family moved away with their furniture. Tea felt as if it were a deliverance. Things were tight with money until the spring fishing began, and it hadn't been easy to give her brother some help. There was biting frost, the fjord was frozen over, and Jens Røn went on the ice with his eel-spear. When he came home late, he heard the noise from the hotel.

Yes, they're dancing, he said morosely.

I never believed it would get better when Kock bought it, Tea replied. He's a hideous person, I don't trust Katrine either. She goes about with a cross around her neck, but I think it's almost blasphemous to see the Lord's cross on a girl who's so loose.

The nickelodeon was repaired, it made noise and howled, the clown came forward and bowed and thrust out its arms, and the dancing thundered in the hall. Katrine flew from arm to arm. Anders Kjøng had again begun courting her. At some point she'd probably give in. May I sleep with you tonight? he asked her so loudly that others could hear it and notice he was a daredevil guy. Go home and suck your mother's breast, Katrine said contemptuously and put her tray in front of him.

The dance went on, the cups and glasses rattled on the shelves behind the bar, and the green lamp with the wide shade jingled under the ceiling. The men stomped with their feet and sang, smacked their hands, and whistled the melody or simply roared at the top of their lungs. The girls shrieked and laughed. The light flickered above them, and the shadows whirled away on the white wall. Spring was approaching, and the young people wanted to have fun. Anders Kjøng tried to seduce Katrine with gentle words, and his voice took on a deep guttural sound; he took her tenderly around the waist and got a hard elbow in his side. Kock kept an eye on them from his seat, though he acted as if he were reading. His cheeks got a darker color.

Anders Kjøng! he shouted. Come here for just a second..

Anders Kjøng let Katrine go and went over to the bar. Is there something you want, Kock? he asked.

Indeed there is, Kock said and closed his book with a smack. I want to say a word to you as an experienced man. It seems to me you're a bit fresh with Katrine. I won't have it.

I don't think there's any harm in it, Anders Kjøng said. And Katrine definitely looks as though she's able to take care of herself.

That may be a very good consideration, Kock said calmly. But the matter has to be viewed otherwise. Here in my hotel fun and zest for life are allowed, but the waitress must be permitted to go in peace while she's doing her work. If you won't conform to it, then it would be better for you to stay away.

Anders Kjøng got angry and replied: I'm not your employee.

Of course not, Kock said and took it calmly. I certainly understand that: You're a young man, all of us raged in our youth and smooched with the girls. — Yes, passion has its rightful place: I know that as well as anyone.

Anders Kjøng noticed that Kock was speaking to him in an almost chummy way, and he wanted to admit that maybe he had been too violent. He said apologetically:

She's a good girl, that Katrine!

Certainly, Kock replied and felt like showing he could express himself freely, even if in a different way about intimate relations. But eroticism has its own laws, and you're going about it all wrong. Look: the point is to find the right manner of proceeding in each individual case, and Katrine isn't the kind it pays to fawn over. She has to be taken in an instant.

Can that really be the case? Anders Kjøng asked.

It is, Kock nodded.

I also tried it that way, Anders Kjøng said hesitantly. But that didn't lead anywhere either.

Then you weren't determined enough in your approach. If you, Anders Kjøng, had occupied yourself with the philosophy called ethics or the doctrine of morals, then you'd know there's something that's called the categorical imperative, that is, you know, the imperative mood, as, for example, when I say to you: You shall! Look, Katrine has to be treated with a categorical imperative—that's the kind she is.

Kock plunged back into his book, but he stole glances at the girl more often. Actually Katrine wasn't beautiful, but there was something about her that wouldn't leave him in peace. He lit a cigar and looked thoughtfully up at the smoke. The categorical imperative!

After everything was closed and turned off, Kock stole across the attic in his stocking feet. He stood for a moment outside Katrine's door and listened to her calm breathing. She turned heavily in bed, and Kock scratched on the door.

Katrine! he called gently.

Who is it? the girl asked drowsily. Kock was just about to open the door, but was gripped by fear and sneaked down the stairs again.

The next day Katrine looked at him questioningly; Kock stroked his mustache and acted as if nothing had happened. But he became increasingly absentminded and smoked cigars all day long. One evening—the customers had already gone—he called the girl, who was gathering up the cups and glasses on the tray.

It seems to me the fellows are a bit fresh, he said. If it gets really bad, just tell me.

Oh, pfff, Katrine answered. I don't take that seriously.

Kock took a bottle down from the shelf and poured a shining, red liquid.

I think we should have us a glass, he said a bit embarrassed. It's not alcohol, but a tasty fruit liqueur.

Katrine looked at him with astonishment. Thanks, I don't want anything.

Certainly, Kock said and patted her brown arm. Sit down, there's something I'd like to talk to you about. You see, Katrine, marriage has many advantages, and I've often thought about making a change. Actually, marriage is the most rational connection between the sexes, and I'm a liberal-minded man, who doesn't care about the external things so many people are fixated on and that we call position and wealth. I look at the matter this way: Eroticism has to conform to the erotic laws—there aren't any other considerations. Now, Katrine, do you perhaps understand what I'm leading up to?

No, the girl whispered.

Kock got up: I want to ask you whether you feel any inclination—whether you want to marry me, Katrine?

Get married! the girl burst out flabbergasted.

Yes, precisely, Kock replied.

Yes, Katrine said and cast down her eyes. I'd like to do that.

Several days later Kock and Katrine went to town and bought rings. Everyone could see how things stood, and Katrine wasn't easy to look in the eye. You surely know I've gotten engaged, she said to Anders Kjøng and displayed her gold ring. Now you'll please keep your hands to yourself. Once again Anders Kjøng felt shamefully deceived by fate. Yes, there you're surely getting a man who's good for something, he said. I'm better off with him than with ten of your kind, Katrine replied, but, by the way, you can keep your mouth shut until you're asked.

Esben came trudging from the meadows and greeted Kock and repeatedly congratulated him and offered his blessings.

That was good news, he smiled humbly. To have your daughter engaged to a solid man! But might I now ask when will the wedding take place?

Marriage? Kock said. We're not going to have that kind of

actual wedding.

What? Esben asked horrified.

No, we'll go to the parish constable, Kock explained, and be married in what they call a civil ceremony. I go to church only when there's a funeral.

Esben shuffled his feet uneasily: But this civil ceremony, or whatever it's called, is valid, isn't it? he asked.

It is, Kock answered. It's a completely valid marriage ceremony, which was introduced out of regard for the enlightened people, who haven't joined any religious community, but instead use their reason. That's what it's about.

Yes, okay, Esben nodded. We can't know all of that stuff they think up. But if it's valid, then there surely can't be anything to object to. And once again I want to congratulate and bless you. I wasn't able to give Katrine any training, but she's a clever and industrious girl.

Esben was deferential to his daughter and spoke to her as if she were already a woman with a prominent station in life. There are three chimneys on the hotel, he said. You're going to be a lady, Katrine. — Before he left, Kock and Katrine had to promise to visit him soon. And thanks for the coffee, he said. You know, I can see there are finer things than I'm used to.—


One spring day Martin came home in the cold rain from the farm where he was working. Tea saw his wet face against the parlor window, and she put down the plate she had in her hand. She opened the door and called out softly: Martin! Jens Røn kept eating and hadn't a clue before the boy was standing in the parlor with the rain dripping from his soaking clothes.

Did you get the day off today? Tea asked anxiously.

I ran away from the place, the boy said and threw himself down across the table in tears. I don't want to be with the farmers any more.

Finally it dawned on Jens Røn what was going on. He

straightened himself out in his seat:

What! Did you run away from your job? he asked.

Tea sank down on the bench next to her son who was crying. What did they do to you, dear Martin? she asked.

Can't I go out to sea? the boy cried. Those people are impossible.

Tea stroked his hair and consoled him: Just compose yourself a bit, she said. You'll see—we'll find a way out if we just think hard enough.

Jens Røn got up.

You doubtless side with the boy, he said.

No, no, Tea said almost wailing. I don't, you know that Jens, but—I can't just chase him out in the rain.

Well, he's to go back to his job, and I mean immediately, Jens Røn said. He had no reason to run off.

Sit down and get something to eat, Martin, Tea consoled him. Then your father will go back with you and talk to your master. I mean, you don't want to shame us, my son; I can't believe you'd do that.

The boy swallowed his tears, and Tea got him some food, while Jens Røn went in to shave. A half-hour later father and son walked out of town. The road was slush, the fields wet with cold puddles. The rain was quiet and dense.

Jens Røn was silent while they walked through town. But when they got out on to the open road, he said:

Now we'll have to ask the man for forgiveness. It wasn't right of you to go off, even if you were tired of being there.

Yes, the boy said and scrunched even deeper into his wet clothes.

And remember now once and for all that you must honor and obey your master, his father admonished him. We have to be humble—otherwise everything will go downhill. Always think about this, dear Martin, when you believe you've been wronged—it's not for us to talk back, but we must let Our Lord do that. And you must also remember you're a poor child, and the only property poor folk have is their good name, and that's why we have to go about things cautiously in the world. . .

Now that no one could see them, Jens Røn had taken the boy by the hand. He walked a bit bowed and spoke in a subdued voice.

You have to remember the rich, too, are servants, and we don't know what things will be like in the next world. Maybe he who has been faithful in small things will be seated closer to Jesus than many big people.

You have to come in, too, father, Martin said, when they were standing outside the farm. I don't dare go in alone.

The farmer was a tall, lanky man with sullen facial features. We aren't used to having people run off, and I can't see that the boy has anything to complain about.

It won't happen again—Martin has promised me, Jens Røn answered. And he'd like to ask you profusely for forgiveness.

Yes, I won't keep him here if he wants to leave, the farmer said sulkily. So it would be best if he left in November. But I think it would have been smart of you people to bring up your children to be among strangers.

Jens Røn bowed his head without answering. When he got home, he said to Tea: We certainly didn't discipline the children enough. Now people will say he can't stay at his job.

I'll never have peace of mind if he goes to sea, Tea cried. But it may be that I'm not allowed to think of myself. I know, too, that only God's will happens at sea.

The herring nets had been out for a long time, and the air was warm. The sheep had lambs, and the birds had their chicks in their nests. The days got longer and longer, the sun was warming things up, and before anyone really realized it, it was time to take in the seine nets, and it was the middle of summer. A man came riding on a rattling bicycle and put it outside Thomas Jensen's door. It was Peder Hygum in a nice blue jacket and with his hair slicked down. I'm not disturbing you, am I? he asked with a smile. No, Thomas Jensen said, come in, Peder Hygum, and take a rest.

Peder Hygum had had success: he was calm and solid in his character and had fine words on his lips. And how are things? Thomas Jensen asked. Your wife and child—they're thriving?

Yes, the hawker thanked him; they were still with his father-in-law, but now it looked as though he would soon have his chance to set up his own home. Thanks to God's grace, he added, and looked up at the white-calked ceiling. And you're still selling books? Thomas Jensen asked. To some extent, the hawker answered. But I have prospects of a richer enterprise in the vineyard — — Thomas Jensen was silent and didn't want to ask more, but he was glad that Peder was getting ahead.

Peder Hygum was in no hurry to get on. He was popular where he made his visits. On the hot days it was refreshing to have strangers who could tell about the world outside. Many was the hour he conversed with Anton Knopper, who was mending traps in his out-building. Little Martinus was sleeping in his baby carriage under the elderberry bush just outside, and Anton Knopper instinctively muffled his voice so as not to wake him.

He's a splendid boy, Peder Hygum said, so big and healthy I've virtually never seen his match. I'm really satisfied with him, Anton Knopper said proudly. But there are many difficulties with children, and the worst don't even come until they're growing up. Anton Knopper was silent for a moment, then he said: Many's the time I've thought about how terrible it must be if such a little, innocent child grows up to be a sinner and ends in hell. It's a horrible thought that I could possibly be sitting in heaven while he was burning in eternal torment.

That's nothing for humans to ponder, Peder Hygum said. But, you know, we must have hope that God will let us forget the kin who have ended up in the wrong place so we aren't reminded at all they ever existed.

I think that would be much worse, Anton Knopper said. Am I to forget those I loved here on earth? I wouldn't like to think so.

That might well be really hard, Peder Hygum answered. But, after all, we know God's infinite mercy, and we can rely on it and guard against temptations and doubt.

Anton Knopper conceded that: you know, we humans ultimately don't know anything about what God wants to do with us. We have to surrender ourselves to faith. We have to. —

Peder Hygum drank coffee many times at Tea's and didn't make a secret of how much she had meant for his salvation. Those were good words you gave me to take along, he said and smiled sadly. They have given much support to me ever since. — In any case, they were meant honestly, Tea answered proudly. And maybe the Lord was using me as his instrument, though he could hardly have found someone less significant. The last days of his stay he went around and talked to the fishermen about the matter he had actually come for. He wanted to get a bank loan to begin his own little business with books and paper. Other friends were willing to help and support him, but it was absolutely necessary for him to get five hundred crowns if it was to be really serious. He asked whether collectively they would stand surety for him. That's a lot of money, Thomas Jensen said. Yes, Peder Hygum sighed. And it's with dread and shame I'm asking you all for this act of friendship. I know you haven't much reason to trust me.

It wasn't easy to say no, and when Peder Hygum left, he had the signatures on his piece of paper.

— It was a quiet, peaceful time in the middle of the summer. The work was going smoothly on the farms; once in a while cars drove in from the country with people who were on an outing to the fjord. Or a sailboat from town docked at the wharf, and the party drank coffee in the inn garden. Katrine waited tables, but she was dignified in character and didn't put up with anything from either rich or poor. But she also didn't slam the doors the way she used to or use rude expressions. Katrine was gentle as a dove and sat every evening and read books. Kock wanted it that way, and she accommodated his will. At night Kock stole in his stocking feet across the attic and stopped every time a floor board creaked.

Tea didn't know what to believe. Was Kock an honest man and did he want to marry the girl, or was he using tricks to seduce her? Kock's housekeeper didn't keep many secrets, and Tea was short of breath when she considered what was happening in Katrine's room. The women whispered about it in private and turned silent and blushed when a man entered the room.

Mariane took the matter lightheartedly: They sleep together; yeah, so what—she said. We've seen a fat girl in church before. How can you take it that way! Tea said with irritation. Malene and Alma joined Tea and condemned it. After all, we're not supposed to do it for lust's sake, Malene said. The point is we have to put children in the world in a decent way.

Mariane just laughed and ran her hand through her hair. Let's not make ourselves better than we are, she said. There's really no one who doesn't think about the children until afterwards.

— Kock and Katrine hadn't visited Esben. I'm not a family person, Kock said, but if you'd absolutely like to, we can go there Sunday. Katrine nodded, and Sunday they walked out to Dead Man's House. It was oppressively warm, and Kock regretted it before they were halfway. Dead Man's House stood among wind-blown poplars, whose leaves were already yellowed by the heat of the sun. Currant bushes with red berries stood in the little garden, and the walks were gracefully raked. Grass, green and luxuriant, was growing on the roof of the low, tumbledown house. Esben came rushing out of the cow stable.

Oh, bless me! he shouted. Am I getting such prominent guests? Welcome, and please come into the parlor. Hello, Kock. Hello, Katrine! His face radiated friendliness and joy. Company was an infrequent thing.

The parlor was smart-looking with the old furniture, which was painted brown. But it was noticeable that Esben probably for the most part was content with sweeping the floor. Kock went over and opened up a window. — You know, it's warm today, he apologized.

Yes, yes, Esben nodded, we're really roasting, but the coffee, dear children, I completely forgot to get for you.

I'll make it, Katrine declared, and went out into the kitchen.

Esben watched her. It was a challenge to be alone in the parlor with a man like Kock. As long as she doesn't economize on the coffee beans! he said. Of course she won't, Kock said. She definitely knows how to make it the way it's supposed to be.

Still, it was nice of you to want to come and look in on me,

Esben said, when Katrine came in with the coffee. It's very seldom that strangers come here. How are things down in town?

Yes, how are things, Kock said and offered a cigar with the coffee. The Pious go to the Mission house and sing hymns. That's the way time passes.

Yes, you're right about that, Esben said. They're fine people, the Pious; I myself am also converted, as they call it, because we're all sinners—that's for sure. Every time I go to the Mission house, they talk in such a friendly way to me. Yes, old teacher Aaby, he said a while back: You cackle like a goose, dear Esben. He said it with a friendly smile, and it must surely be right. He's got something in his brain, that Aaby, there's no way around it. I talk all too much, that's true, when I get the chance, but it's seldom I see people.

No, Kock said, you're alone alright here —

I am, Esben replied. Katrine's been out working since she was confirmed. I probably shouldn't say it, but she's a capable girl. She has that from her mother, because the other one of us never amounted to very much—no, I've really got to be glad if I can just keep the farm going. But you've got to have your brain working if you're going to run an inn and manage it.

Esben jabbered away like a friendly old bird, and he couldn't stay seated on his chair; once in a while he had to go out on the floor, where he stood and waved his arms. But every time Kock opened his mouth, he was as silent as a mouse and strained to listen.

It looks like there's going to be a storm, Katrine said.

Out to the west the blue-black storm clouds were menacing. The birds in the garden had stopped chirping, and the trees stood with hanging branches and waited. The distant boom was audible, and pale lightning flickered on the horizon.

We also really need rain, Esben said. The fishermen will soon have to set out their traps. They're capable people, and they earn a lot of money. Last time I was in the Mission house, I chatted with Lars Bundgaard; he's a very sensible man. — Well, you came to the meeting tonight, Esben, he said, and shook my hand. — Yes, he's a man it's a pure pleasure to exchange words with.

Malene is going to have a child again, Katrine informed them.

She's a whole factory, Kock said.

Oh no, Esben laughed. What do you call her? A factory! Boy, the way you can make jokes. But otherwise she's quite a woman for taking care of her house and accomplishing things as far as I can understand. A whole factory—Esben was about to die laughing.

Esben was a simple-hearted soul, but hardly appropriate company for a smart man like Kock. They didn't have much to talk about, and Kock sat silently and smoked his cigar.

The stormy weather was directly overhead. Lightning crackled in the black sky from east to west, as if the celestial globe were about to be dashed into shards, and the rain showers splashed against the windowpanes. Katrine barely dared to look out.

It must have touched down, Esben said after a resounding boom.

Possibly, Kock said. But, you know, people buy insurance nowadays.

They went out into the fresh, clear evening. The fjord lay like a deep blue stripe, and over the hills to the south a rainbow stretched its slender bridge. Far off you could see a streak of smoke, which twisted half-transparently toward the sky. It was a farm that was burning. In the garden the yellow summer apples shone with a firm and hard luster, and the bunches of currants sparkled among the bush's green leaves.

That was a blessing, Esben said. The rain was really needed — As long as no disasters took place elsewhere.

While Kock and Katrine walked home, the customs official was silent. He stole glances at Katrine. Yes, she was big and shapely, but it was doubtful how far her intellectual abilities reached. In any case, her father was a man of minuscule talents.

They followed a path across the field, and Kock went first. He turned around.

You know you could take that cross off.

Why? Katrine asked.

Yes, why, why, Kock said acerbically. I should rather think you should be asking yourself why you go around with it. It betrays a tedious lack of fantasy that you've let it hang on your breast since you were confirmed. Oh God, you know the cross is a symbol—a Christian symbol. And if we're to get married, I wouldn't like you wearing it on your body. Please take the cross off, Katrine, and hide it in your bureau drawer.

The girl undid the velvet ribbon and obediently stuck the silver cross in her pocket.

— Kock married Katrine without priest or church ceremony. The parish constable read out an exhortation, and bride and bridegroom wrote their names in a book.

So now it's taken care of? asked Esben, who had listened attentively.

Yes, it will stand up, the parish constable said. A deacon couldn't have done it better.

Esben took a savings book from his coat pocket and gave it to Kock.

There are five hundred crowns, which I've saved up through the years for the time Katrine got married. And when I die, you two will of course get the farm even if it's not worth anything. And so once again I want to heartily wish you happiness and blessings, every day for many years.

Jens Røn and Anton Knopper were at work tarring in the gravel pit when Tea came running. Her cheeks were all red from the heat and excitement, and it took a while before she caught her breath.

You have to come down to Povl Vrist's immediately, she said. As far as I could understand, there's something wrong with the water rights.

With the water rights! Anton Knopper burst out terrified.

Yes, Tea said. I didn't really get the whole story. There was no time to lose—come on, you have to hurry up. The rest of them are sitting and waiting.—

Jens Røn lifted the last trap out of the pot, and they quickly spread it out to dry on the grass.

Let's go, Jens Røn said. And don't say anything, Tea, it's not worth giving others too much to talk about.

They rushed through town, where there were only children playing in the sun. There had long been warnings that the fishermen from the south had been looking askance at the waters they had bought rights to from the landed estates and didn't want to respect their monopoly rights to the eel grounds. Now things had gone haywire, and—who knows?—there might be strife and litigation.

Thomas Jensen and Lars Bundgaard were already sitting in Povl Vrist's parlor.

It's good you people came, Povl Vrist said. I better explain the thing from the beginning. Please sit down. Mariane will come in a second with coffee. — You see, I was in the fjord this morning hammering down some posts. While I was in the middle of my work, a little row boat comes over—it was a man you probably also know of. Jørgen Spliid is his name and he lives on the other side —

Yes, I've met him, Thomas Jensen interrupted. He's a believing man, as far as I can judge.

He had been out to empty a cod net, Povl Vrist continued. He laid his boat up beside mine and asked for tobacco for his pipe—his tobacco had run out. Then he says: They're good fishing waters you folks have; there are probably many people who have an eye on it. — Oh yes, there may well be, I answer, but they'll restrain themselves because, you know, we've both bought and paid for them. You surely have, he says, but it might well be hard to judge how far your rights go. There's been no doubt about it before, I say, but I was beginning to get a little uneasy.

Oh no, that's true, he answers, but there are certainly those who feel you folks only have a right to the seine nets and not to the eel grounds.

Povl Vrist paused for a bit while the others waited breathlessly. A lot was at stake here.

It seemed to me it was smart to get a little more precise information, Povl Vrist said. And I asked him bluntly. Is that the way you feel, too? If you ask me, he said—believe you me, he was a sly dog—let me answer you bluntly that I feel it's hard to get a real sense of it. And ultimately, it's none of my business: I have room enough in the fjord for my nets. But there are folks who are quite sure. So who are they? I asked. But he didn't want to name names, and I couldn't get any more out of him. — Then when I was sailing home, I discovered that markers had been set on the Blue Ground.

What did you say! Anton Knopper burst out.

They've marked off the fishing spots—but I took the markers away.

I wonder if that's lawful, Jens Røn asked a bit anxiously.

I can't imagine it could be anything else, Povl Vrist replied calmly. We have the rights according to the title deed. And if it comes to litigation, I'm the one who bears the responsibility for the work. But if you aren't straight out asked about it, don't talk too loudly about it. One way or the other I can of course understand that they have designs on our waters.

We're not going to put up with it, Anton Knopper said. Back then, when we bought it, they laughed at us and thought we paid way too much. Now they've gotten envious because they feel we catch too much. Most of the fjord fishermen have wretched equipment. But I'm telling you: if they come into my water, I'll pull their posts up.

No, no, Anton, Thomas Jensen burst out appalled. Let's go easy there—we're believers.

That's true, Anton Knopper admitted. I know I have a hard time controlling myself.

Povl Vrist got out the title deed and read it aloud. The words were old and strange, and the meaning wasn't easy to understand.

Wouldn't it be best to turn to a lawyer? Lars Bundgaard

asked. But the others didn't think that was an alternative. Once you wound up in those people's pockets, it was worse than what could happen without them. No, the smartest thing was to stay away from lawyers.

Look, the seine nets, we have a right to that—that can't ever be taken from us, Povl Vrist said, as far as I can understand this piece of paper. When we bought it, it was, you know, also said we had the rights to the eel grounds. But now I can tell you what I've heard. In the western fjord they recently sued over some landed estates' water rights, and the people there got support for their claim that the rights applied only to the seine nets. So we have to be clear about the fact that our position is dubious if the people over there insist on theirs. So we've been tricked by the people who sold it to us—but we'll never get them because we don't have anything in writing.

Yes, but what are we going to do? Anton Knopper asked. We can't just stand there with our hands in our pockets and watch while they set their nets in our waters.

All four of them looked at Thomas Jensen, who hadn't yet expressed his opinion. I think we should drag this business out a little, he said. I'm very doubtful, just like Povl Vrist, that we can win our case. I think the smartest thing we can do is to go over to these folks and talk with them about the matter. It may be that we can avoid quarreling and a hubbub for this year, and then some time will have passed.

Then you want to go over there? Lars Bundgaard asked. I do, Thomas Jensen answered. But I'd really like Povl Vrist to come along. Two are better than one in this kind of business.

It was agreed the two fishermen would sail across the fjord the next day. There surely must be some believers among them who can see what's just, Anton Knopper said. Yes, there must be, Thomas Jensen nodded; we'd also hate to wrong anyone—it's best if we come to an agreement.

Early in the morning the two fishermen left in Povl Vrist's motorboat. The water was still sparkling in the colors of the sunrise, and the air was cool and pure. Povl Vrist was sitting at the rudder and smoking his pipe.

Let's just hope we're lucky, Thomas Jensen said when they were out a ways in the fjord. I know one of the biggest fishermen over there, he's Pious, and I thought we'd turn to him—he probably has influence among the others.

It's really strange that we have to go out and arrange a compromise, Povl Vrist replied. I can remember what my father told me about the North Sea fishermen in the old days. They were totally unruly people. Out in the western part of the fjord there was a farm situated on a headland, and when fishermen were out on an expedition in the fjord, it frequently happened that they went on land and pitched the people out of their beds so they could lie down and sleep. They complained, but it was no use—it was too far to the next village. My grandfather was involved in it. —

Yes, those were bad times, Thomas Jensen replied. It was whiskey that led them into misfortune. They were like wild animals when they drank.

They really were, Povl Vrist said. My uncle emptied a pint every day of the year. And he wasn't even considered alcoholic. It's just odd they were able to live so long, those people. Because the temperance people, you know, they show with statistics that people who drink don't get to be nearly as old as the temperate people, and he lived to be 93—

It seems to me people think much too much about *how long* they can live, Thomas Jensen said. It would be much better if they thought some about *how* they live.

Now the boat was in the broad waters, and the sun was strong. The farms' wind motors were shining like shiny flowers in the flat, green land to the north. A schooner came gliding toward them with all sails set. Out here in the deep course the current was hard, and the boat thumped its way forward. At times a wave splashed in over the railing.

Listen, Thomas Jensen said.

From both sides of the fjord the church bells were ringing up the sun.

That's a beautiful sound, he said.

—The fishing settlement was situated in a hollow between

the hills, and they moored the boat to a post and rowed in in a yawl. Two fishermen were standing on the shore and tarring a fish-chest. Thomas Jensen went over to them. You couldn't tell me where Karl Povlsen's house is, could you? he asked.

The men explained it in detail, and they walked up through the little village. It was a small, thatched framework house with hollyhock up the wall. There was no one in the parlor, but out from the kitchen a voice could be heard scolding. It'll be just as I said—it resounded through the house—I don't want to hear all your nonsense; when I said that I don't want womenfolk hanging around here for coffee, I mean it. A deep woman's voice growled an answer. It almost sounds as if the people were having a disagreement, Povl Vrist said with a smile. We better let them know we're here. He knocked on the kitchen door; there was a brief silence, then a small man with a pointy nose stuck his head in.

So, there are strangers in the parlor, he said, and came all the way in. I think I've seen this man before. Please, sit down. But, of course, it's Thomas Jensen from up north—we know each other from the meetings. And who's the other man?—I don't know him.

Povl Vrist said his name, and Karl Povlsen greeted him with a series of small smiles, which came and went like fast flashes across his whole face.

Please, sit down, sit down, he said. Yes, I better say it straight out, just the way it is: I set my house in order the way the Scriptures command. You could probably hear it, and it has to be, yes, it has to be. So, you've come across the fjord today.

His speech came from his lips like a monotonous song, and he didn't give the others a chance to say a word. There was something soporific about him, like a bumble-bee buzzing against the windowpanes with small, hard smacks. But suddenly he rushed over to the door and roared: Coffee! Povl Vrist gave Thomas Jensen a look: Was the man all there mentally? Thomas Jensen answered with a blink that meant that he had all his faculties. Karl Povlsen turned quickly and kept talking. If the good weather would just hold until the traps are out; then it would be best if a little turbulent weather came—that would be best, that would be best. — Finally his wife came in with the coffee on a tray. Her shapeless legs carried a huge body, and her face was dull and bloated. She had elephantiasis.

Please, go ahead and drink, Karl Povlsen said. Help yourselves. That's my wife. Can you greet them, say hello, say hello, shake the strangers' hands.

The wife extended her hand sluggishly. It was spongy and unpleasant to touch, as if it had no bones. While they drank coffee, the host talked nonstop. But now Thomas Jensen felt the time had come to discuss the matter that was on their hearts. As soon as he opened his mouth, Karl Povlsen's face became rigid and immovable, and his eyes turned into two narrow cracks beneath his colorless brows.

We've come to you because I know you best, Thomas Jensen said. I know you're a believing man and an able fisherman, and I'd very much like to ask you if you could give us some advice. As you know, we have some fishing waters in the fjord, and we've heard you fishermen over here feel our rights don't reach beyond the seine nets. I'd very much like to know how you look at it.

Karl Povlsen rocked a little back and forth in the chair. Oh, what do I think? he said. I think it would be nice, it would be nice, if everyone could live in peace and tolerance with everyone else. That's of course the way we look at, we children of God, we children of God.

Yes, I'd never deny that, Thomas Jensen said a bit impatiently. But it's a serious matter for us if we aren't permitted to use the rights we've acquired.

Yes, that's true, that's true, Karl Povlsen sang. But maybe we can say that people over here are also in tight straits; it's not easy to give everyone his due, the way we should, the way we should. But you have to stay here and eat lunch; then I'll send for some of the others. He got up with a bound and darted out into the kitchen, where he shouted the orders to his wife. While the wife cooked, they sat for an hour and talked about other things. They could hear her heavy, trudging steps, and at times she grumbled to herself. Finally the food came to the table: pearl barley soup and roast pork, and Karl Povlsen read a long grace. Thanks, good friends, he said, when he was finally finished. You're welcome, yes welcome. But as soon as he had put the spoon in the pearl barley soup, he darted up from his chair. The raisins! he shouted. The raisins. You ate them yourself, you sow. The wife turned sluggishly at the kitchen door where she was standing. That really doesn't matter as far as we're concerned, Thomas Jensen said reassuringly. You absolutely mustn't make your wife feel bad; we all know that people with this sickness can't stop eating.

Oh, thanks, Karl Povlsen said. Yes, I have to bear with it, though it's a cross, believe you me, it's a cross.

After the meal Karl Povlsen said grace fussily and went to fetch a few other fishermen, who knew something about the matter of the landed-estate waters.

I'm almost completely sick of being in this house, Povl Vrist said as soon as he was out of the parlor. Do you really think he's all there?

Yeah, now I almost don't know what to believe, Thomas Jensen answered irresolutely. I heard him at a big joint meeting, and there it was a joy to hear him talk. But here at home his behavior is somewhat odd.

That poor woman—she's in bad straits, Povl Vrist said sympathetically. But she probably doesn't notice it so much in her condition.

Karl Povlsen returned with two fishermen. The one was a tall, strong man with a sulky face and a drawl in his voice. His name was Lars Toft. The other, Jens Kolby, was a young, smiling fellow with quick movements like a pole-cat.

We'd like to reach an understanding with you about the landed-estate waters we bought, Thomas Jensen said.

So, you people have realized you don't have rights to the eel grounds? Jens Kolby said bluntly.

That startled Thomas Jensen, and he blushed in his temples.

If we'd realized that, there'd be nothing to talk about, he said. We feel we have the rights, and they've never been contested before. We'd like to talk to you and explain to you how we look at it to avoid strife and litigation, but we didn't think you people would take it that way.

No, no, Karl Povlsen said. You have to be tolerant, dear Jens, you have to be tolerant and can't get all fired up; so let's talk about the things like good friends and God's children, yes, God's children.

Lars Toft began a long lecture on the way the situation, as far as he knew, was historically. The waters had belonged to this farm or that farm originally, and at that time people probably cared most about herring. That was what produced the money. Yes, the fishermen did earn something: it was said they drank beer from a silver mug, and their wives were dressed in silks and had gold chains around their necks. —

Hot headed, Jens Kolby broke into his long speech. I'll be blunt, he said. I don't care what happened before, but I don't feel you have rights to the eel grounds, and I intend to put my nets there in the fall.

So, that's what you want, Thomas Jensen said calmly. But I'd like to bring to your attention that if the courts think we do have the rights, it will be expensive for you. I can tell you ahead of time if there's litigation, it will be carried straight on up to the supreme court even if all of us have to lose house and home. That's for certain.

You want a fight, let's do it, Jens Kolby said. I've thought about putting up nets in Blue Ground. It doesn't seem right to me to hide that from you since you've come over here to get information.

No, we'd also like to thank you because you're not tricking us, Thomas Jensen replied. But maybe you'd also tell us if there are others who have the same intention.

I don't know exactly, the fisherman smiled. But it may very well happen that more will feel like doing it once I've begun.

So finally there was nothing more to talk about, and Thomas Jensen and Povl Vrist went down to the boat. They didn't have any good news to bring back.

Big things were at stake. The point was to be first and get their nets out, but not all the traps had been tarred yet. Anton Knopper felt they had to help one another and keep the tar-pots boiling all night long. If there were just calm weather the next day, they could begin to set them.

We have to stand by one another, Anton Knopper said. If we don't stick together, they'll overpower us. And I'd hate it if people started saying those folks over there made fools of us.

The moon was like a yellow horn in the sky among white star-dots. The cement pot shone with a fire-red tongue of flame, and the shadows flickered on the sand pit's steep slopes. The men dragged the nets and shouted to one another in hoarse voices, half choked by smoke and tar vapor, wet from night-dew and sweat, and dizzy from the heat of the oven. Insects whirled in the light; at times a bird shrieked in the field. Once in a while one of the wives came with a can of coffee and poured it into a cup with no handle. Then they begrudged themselves a moment's rest and poured the coffee down their throats in front of the cement pot, while the darkness closed in on them like a wall. And then they staggered back to work. Povl Vrist and Thomas Jensen hoisted the traps down into the tar and up again on the whistling tackle. Lars Bundgaard and Anders Kjøng had lanterns and made sure the traps were laid on the grass properly. They were smeared with tar from head to toe. Jens Røn, Anton Knopper, and Povl Vrist's laborer, Laurids, brought fresh piles to the pot on a wagon. The wheels thumped against the road, and the iron made sparks fly. Anton Knopper shouted and screamed for them to work faster. Night wanderers came by and watched the work and shook their heads: they were crazy.

It began to get light, and the sun was rising among the red clouds in the east. The whole world appeared in unreal tints: the green grass shone brightly with cobwebs in the blades, young cattle bellowed in the pens, trees and houses sprouted up out of the morning fog. The last nets had been laid out to dry, and the men stood for a while and looked at one another.

Now what? Lars Bundgaard asked. Can we begrudge ourselves a few hours rest?

Rest! Anton Knopper said. We're not getting any rest until the traps are set even if three suns rise in the sky.

Anton Knopper was reeling from fatigue, but he was in high spirits. Menacingly he clenched his black hand: The fools over there will see who they're dealing with! Fishermen who are accustomed to traveling on the sea, men from the great sea! We are of course pious folk, he said. But they shouldn't think we'll put up with everything. No, they're totally mistaken if they think that. His enthusiasm for fighting was infectious. The rest of them nodded cockily toward the traps, which were lying newly tarred in rank and file, and Jens Røn lowered his head like a bull that was ready to gore. No, just let them come, he said—we'll teach them a thing or two. But they don't think we're so fast on our feet.

Come to my house, Povl Vrist said. Mariane doubtless has everything ready. The wives have to come along too—they also had an anxious night. And then we can talk over what has to be done so this business can have a successful outcome.

Mariane was as fresh as a blade of grass in the morning sun even though she hadn't been out of her clothes all night. Come in, she said, don't bother about the tar—you can't wash it off anyway; it'll wear off. Malene, Tea, Alma, and Andrea came a bit later, and after Thomas Jensen had said grace, Mariane poured coffee. There was excellent, freshly baked rye bread to go with it and all kinds of spreads. Afterwards Povl Vrist passed around cigars.

That's quite a big to-do, Jens Røn said almost disapprovingly.

Oh, by pure chance I have a box in the house, Povl Vrist replied. There was a salesman who foisted it on me. I don't even know if it's decent goods. But probably they can be smoked.

They talked about what was to be done. Posts and traps had to be loaded on the prams, little by little as the nets became dry, and sailed out to the fishing spots.

I suggest we take what's finished and immediately begin to set them, Thomas Jensen said. We can't be too precise about where each individual net winds up. Later we can take care of it. And even if some of the traps aren't so dry, there'll probably be time to take them out of the water before it's dark again. The point is to finish before they come.

So who's going out to the fjord? Lars Bundgaard asked.

Practically the most important work is getting the equipment out there, Povl Vrist said. I feel two of us should start hammering in the posts, and the rest should restock the prams and sail them out. But I have to go out with the first crew because it's important for us to set one of the traps where the markers stood when I took them out.

And what if they come? Anton Knopper asked.

Then we'll have to try once again to reason with them, Thomas Jensen said. But I used my eyes as best I could when we were over there. And I'd be very much mistaken if they're ready to set out the nets.

Mariane was standing and shuffling her feet—she had a suggestion.

I think you should all go to the fjord together, she said.

But then who'll take care of everything else? Thomas Jensen asked.

Oh, come on, that's not a problem, Mariane said. We women can easily manage it. Don't you men believe we're smart enough?

Annoyed, Tea looked at her with her eyes wide open—how she puts on airs and thinks she's so smart. And even Povl Vrist felt she should behave more cautiously and not take things so lightly. But Anton Knopper shouted out:

I say you're terrific, Mariane!

They decided to do what Mariane wanted. Malene was to gather all the children at home with her and take care of them, while the four women helped Anders Kjøng and Laurids.

So we better start right now, Thomas Jensen said. But let's pray together before we move out. Because after all it's a matter of our daily bread.

They bowed their heads, and Thomas Jensen heartily prayed for help in this difficult undertaking.

The men loaded two prams with posts and nets and attached the motorboats in front. Slowly they moved out toward the broad waters, but soon they appeared only as black spots in the fjord. Then the women got to work.

Mariane, with a big mouth and her hair in a crow's nest, was the leader. She borrowed horses from one of the farmers and was herself the driver. She stood up in the wagon with the reins in her hand and shouted to the horses so loudly it resounded in the street: Can't you stand, you foolish ass! Sleepy, people appeared at their doorsteps and wondered what was going on.

Tea didn't feel like witnessing this. I just hope we're not made fools of, she whispered to Alma. But Alma replied: We'll be much bigger fools if the men don't get the traps in the water before the other fishermen.

It was unfamiliar work, but it went quickly. The women carried seine net after seine net to the wagon, and the laborers threw the posts into the boats with a heave-ho. They could already hear the mallets booming and the men shouting out in the broad waters. The whole town was on the move, and people gave a helping hand. An old fisherman came trudging over and recalled the time when the women used to help the men in the fjord. Yes, you can really do it, you West Coasters, he nodded. The farmers' wives watched in amazement. Tea doubtless noticed it and felt ashamed. After all, they were wearing their oldest clothes. But Mariane thundered away with the wagon way out on the wharf. You've surely driven a couple of horses before today, the old man said. You bet your life I have, Mariane said. Yeah, if there were many of your kind, most of the menfolk could surely retire.

It was a warm day. The sun stood in the sky like a catherine wheel, and the heat rose from the tarred nets. The women were about to faint from exertion. But by evening the work was over. Only the last tarred traps were still lying there to be dried.

It took a long time before the boats returned, and when they finally approached, people were standing on the wharf and waiting.

Did you see anything of them? one person shouted.

No, they stayed home, Anton Knopper shouted back.

As soon as they came on land, they were surrounded by fishermen who wanted a report. But there was nothing to report.

They'll come tomorrow, one person said. They doubtless noticed you people had begun.

I just hope you were able to dry them out decently, another person said. We've always had trouble with them. They're a quarrelsome folk, and they'd prefer to rule over the whole fjord.

The others agreed: the fishermen from the south were rough customers, and there was no harm if they met their match.

But Lars Bundgaard swayed back and forth from fatigue, barely able to hold himself upright.

We have to go out again early tomorrow, he said. The smartest thing is for us to go home and catch whatever sleep we can get.

They trudged home, stiff in their limbs and with burning eyes. After they had gotten something to eat, they threw themselves into bed without taking their clothes off.

At the crack of dawn Povl Vrist knocked on the others' windows. It was time to begin again. Drowsy, they staggered down to the wharf and sat and half-slept in the boats on the way out. The work moved along, the posts were hammered in, and the traps set in place. The sun glistened in the water—it cut your eyes like a knife. They switched over to using the heavy mallets, but once in a while they peered out across the fjord to the south.

They're probably making fools of us, Anton Knopper said. But Thomas Jensen had a different opinion. Jens Kolby was a man who didn't make jokes.

Toward afternoon Povl Vrist shouted: there they are! Three motorboats came chugging along with prams from the south. That was the enemy. Let's keep working and act as if nothing happened, Thomas Jensen shouted back. The fishermen swung the mallets, but kept a constant watch. When the little flotilla had come close, a motorboat chugged forward. Jens Kolby and another man were sitting in it.

What are you people doing here in Blue Ground? Jens Kolby shouted. Maybe you didn't see there are markers set out.

We've no reason to respect the markers in our own waters, Thomas Jensen answered.

You have to understand this is illegal, Jens Kolby threatened. And now you'll have to accept the fact that we're going to take the law into our own hands.

He was red in the face from excitement, and his voice misfired. He turned the rudder around hard, and the boat swung back to the prams.

Do you suppose they're going to sail away? Anton Knopper said to Thomas Jensen. But Thomas Jensen shook his head. I don't think this is all going to end well, he answered.

The other fishermen cast the moorings from the prams and anchored them to the bottom. There were three motorboats with two men in each boat. Thomas Jensen knew one of them—that was Karl Povlsen. He felt strange—it wasn't nice to discover that one of God's children could be so dishonest in his conduct. Once again Jens Kolby steered his boat closer.

So the first thing we want to know is if you people will voluntarily remove your equipment from the places where our markers were standing, he shouted.

No, Thomas Jensen shouted back. The markers weren't lawfully set out.

Again the boat swung back, the two others followed suit, and a whole wake foamed up after them. They headed toward the south side of Blue Ground, where a row of traps had been set.

Now they're going to rip down ours, Anton Knopper shouted.

Oh, surely they're not going to do that, Thomas Jensen said doubtfully.

But Anton Knopper was right. Jens Kolby laid his boat on the side of one seine net and began to untie the rope from the main post. It was clear he intended to destroy their work.

We have to get over there, Anton Knopper said, and they quickly jumped from the pram over into the blue cutter. From a distance the other fishermen had been following what was going on, and while Anton Knopper struggled with getting the motor started, Povl Vrist's boat swept by them full speed ahead. Behind him came Jens Røn and Anders Kjøng rowing with all their might. Finally the motor obeyed. The boat bounded ahead with a jerk—Anton Knopper was moving full speed ahead.

Stop, you devils, Anton Knopper blurted out. He regretted it immediately and smacked himself hard on the mouth, but Thomas Jensen didn't notice his swearing. He sped toward Jens Kolby's boat and came up on the side of Povl Vrist, who had Lars Bundgaard on board. The south fjord fishermen had already gotten two traps overturned.

Stop—otherwise we'll sink you, Thomas Jensen shouted, beside himself.

Come on, if you dare, someone from the enemy boats roared back.

Thomas Jensen's face was white and he clenched his teeth. Ready with the boat hook, Anton, he shouted. Anton Knopper jumped into the bow and was ready for the collision. The seaboat snaked toward the other boat's side, and Anton Knopper was over there in a bound. With one punch he felled Karl Povlsen, who fell backwards over the thwart. Then Jens Kolby rushed at him. They rolled around in the boat, any moment about to fall into the water. The other boats laid up on the side—everything was chaotic. The men staggered toward one another. Thomas Jensen swung a bottom board and hit a man in the head so hard he dropped. Povl Vrist defended himself with the tiller; he had jumped over into one of the strangers' boats, and two men tried to overpower him. Lars Bundgaard used a boat hook as a lance, and in a violent sortie managed to throw his opponent overboard, and hurried to Povl Vrist's aid. The man clung to the railing—you could see just his pale, terrified face. The fjord resounded with shouts and tumult, the racket of motors and noise. Jens Røn and Anders Kjøng came rowing so hard the oars lashed the water.

Lars Bundgaard flung one of the people Povl Vrist was occupied with around in the boat and hit the other one in the head so hard he remained lying semi-unconscious and clinging to his opponent. But the battle was over and the North Sea fishermen had gained the upper hand when Jens Røn and Anders Kjøng boarded the sea boat. A roar could be heard from Anton Knopper, who was still fighting with Jens Kolby.

He's got a knife!

The others quickly jumped in, but Anton Knopper had sunk back onto one of the thwarts, and Jens Kolby's knife gleamed hideously in the air. Three men rushed him, took the knife from him, and threw him down, while Thomas Jensen tied his hands with a piece of rope. Quickly Jens Røn tore Anton Knopper's jacket out of the way.

He got me, he said. I could feel it.

His shirt was already oozing with blood, but the wound was only a long slash across his chest. Lars Bundgaard came tottering over in the boat; he was pale, but hadn't suffered any major injury. Both sides had taken a drubbing, and one man was dripping wet and exhausted.

So, you're that kind of guy, Thomas Jensen said and turned toward Jens Kolby. You're a bandit who wants to kill people. And I scarcely expected to meet you like this, Karl Povlsen.

Oh no, Karl Povlsen sighed and dried the blood from his mouth. What can I say, what can I say. It's terrible that we got into such a scrape. I got two teeth knocked out of my new set of teeth. That'll be expensive, that'll be expensive.

There may be something else that'll be more expensive, Thomas Jensen said and nodded toward Jens Kolby, who was sitting and staring into space. But now you strangers better see about getting back home to your place.

And thanks for the visit, Anton Knopper shouted. Be absolutely sure to come again soon.

Oh, shut your trap, you big devil, one of the enemies roared. But they had gotten the motor started and sailed over to the prams.

We have to stay and see what they're up to, Lars Bundgaard said. Otherwise they'll overturn our posts again.

The troublemakers were busy raising the prams' anchor

stone, and a little later they sailed away.

Let's just get home, Thomas Jensen said. It's already afternoon, and after this round we can surely stand some rest. My head is spinning. —

They looked like savages when they came on land. Anton Knopper's shirt was red with blood, and he couldn't put on his sweater without irritating the wound. Lars Bundgaard had a head wound, and the blood had run down across his face. They were frightening to look at. Scratched and covered with blood, tar, and mud, they tottered up the road in their heavy boots. Tea came running as soon as she saw them coming.

But Jesus Christ, what happened? she screamed.

People flocked over to them. Women and children looked at the combatants with eyes wide open. Dangerous things had happened! God's children had been in combat. Anton Knopper declaimed left and right while he strode on.

We've fought for our fishing waters! he shouted. He laughed and shouted out and roared like a bull. The blood was flowing in streams; blood and dry thrashing! Anton Knopper said blood in a tone deep down in his throat. He was wild. Jens Røn's voice was high-pitched and whimpering. Oh, Our Lord! those people, they used knives, and it almost came to a terrible end. It's horrible that kind of person exists. Lars Bundgaard had quietly stolen home so Malene wouldn't hear exaggerated rumors and nothing bad would happen to her. But we beat them, Anton Knopper shouted; they took a thrashing, and I think they'll stay away from our waters—otherwise they can get more of the same. Oh, did the blood flow! Anton Knopper's eyes rolled in his black face—he resembled a dangerous man. Now Andrea came running: Anton, she shouted, Anton! did anything happen to you? And without paying attention to the people standing around densely packed, she threw herself on him sobbing. Anton Knopper was standing there in a public place with a woman in his arms.

— The fjord's peace had been broken, and whose fault was it? Povl Vrist had, to be sure, removed Jens Kolby's markers—that was illegal; but the waters were theirs—they had acquired them honestly. Most people sided with Thomas Jensen and his people. To knock down the traps was a capital offense.

The next day the last traps were set out without incident. Jens Kolby and his associates had sailed further west out into the fjord. They didn't talk much while working, and it was as if they avoided looking at one another.

While sailing home, Thomas Jensen said: I'm not totally free from doubt. I wonder whether we didn't act a little violently.

I scarcely know what to think, Anton Knopper answered.

It's not good for us children of God to get into an altercation with others, Thomas Jensen said. The Bible says: And unto him that smiteth thee on the one cheek offer also the other. I'm afraid the savagery ran away with us. And we didn't set a good example for other people.

But what should we do? Anton Knopper asked. We couldn't very well let them take our property away from us.

We certainly would have done that if we were really saved, Thomas Jensen answered. If we erred, we'll surely be forgiven, Anton Knopper said. We're nothing but simple people.

Thomas Jensen didn't answer. He, too, was confused as to what their duty was. Lars Bundgaard felt the same way.

All the impious young people look up to us for our action, he said. And it's not a good sign when worldly children honor someone. I'm very fearful we hardly acted the way we should have. But if we blundered, we'll surely find out.—

— A week later, after all the traps were out, people sailed over from the south. It was Jens Kolby and Karl Povlsen. They found Thomas Jensen at home, and Povl Vrist was sent for.

Karl Povlsen spoke up. He wept and wailed profusely and wanted peace.

We've come, we've come, he said, to find reconciliation with you. That was a terrible business out there in the fjord; I can't understand at all how that came to pass.

You people wanted to pull our traps out, Povl Vrist replied. Surely you can remember that.

Yes, that's what we wanted, that's what we wanted, Karl Povlsen said weepily. You know, we went crazy when we discovered you hadn't respected our markers. But I've prayed and talked to Jesus, to Jesus in his mercy. And now we want to say: Let there be peace among brothers.

So, you want peace, Thomas Jensen said and pondered what might be at the bottom of it. Karl Povlsen was a hypocritical man—he understood that. But Jens Kolby said bluntly what was tormenting him.

I happened to make a mistake with a knife out there in the fjord—it's incomprehensible how that could happen. Once in a while I get so worked up I can't think straight. But I'd hate to have the law after me saying I outright kill people. Did you report it to the authorities?

No, we didn't, Thomas Jensen said. We felt there might also have been mistakes on our part.

You don't say? Jens Kolby shouted and sat upright in his chair, while Karl Povlsen whimpered: Oh, you don't say, you don't say.

The man wasn't really hurt from what I heard, Jens Kolby said. But that was hardly my fault. If you let this business be forgotten and not talk about it too much, I won't contest your rights to the eel grounds—even though I don't think they extend that far. And I don't think there are others over there among us who feel like getting their fingers pinched.

No, Karl Povlsen assured them. You can rest easy—we'll keep to ourselves for good, for good.

I like the fact that you're not afraid of admitting what went wrong, Thomas Jensen said. We'd also like to ask you and your people over there if you'll forgive us for our offenses. You'll just have to stay for a bite to eat.

The strangers ate lunch at Thomas Jensen's. Afterwards Karl Povlsen wanted to see the Mission house, and Thomas Jensen went with him. Povl Vrist and Jens Kolby sauntered down to the wharf. Suddenly Anton Knopper showed up.

I wanted to say hello to the man, he said and extended his hand. You absolutely have to come home with me and have coffee. And you, too, Povl Vrist. You mustn't think that I bear a grudge—no, I myself was at fault for the slash I got. Anton

Knopper was a frank man and not faint-hearted. He patted Jens Kolby on the shoulder and said: my good old friend!

In the fall the eel fishing didn't go well. A storm one night knocked over half of the staked traps, and many nets were torn to bits. And after the damage was finally repaired, still no eel swam into the traps. Even Anton Knopper was on the verge of losing his sense of humor, and Povl Vrist was a pain to have in the house, Mariane said. He couldn't stand it when his luck turned against him.

But was it bad luck or was there some intention behind it? With the exception of Povl Vrist, who was not one of God's children, they all pondered it. The other fishermen there had good catches as always and no one had any reason to complain. It was odd that they should catch so little precisely this year. One evening when they were at Povl Vrist's the subject came up. Yeah, you can never figure how silver eel will do, Povl said. There can be spots where no fish come, and the traps right next to them are full every single day. And the next day it can be just the other way round. It's the bottom it all depends on.

Yeah, that's for certain, Anton Knopper said. Silver eel like best of all to go to the spots where there's eel grass. But we know there was good grass where we laid the traps.

True, but then there's got to be some other reason the eel migrate on by, Povl Vrist replied. The conditions of the current can also be important. We saw earlier that the current destroyed the fishing spots when, for example, the sailing channel was deepened.

There hasn't been any deepening of the fjord, Anton Knopper said. And I don't believe there's any natural cause to be found.

Povl Vrist impatiently shook his head, but the others sat silently without looking at one another. None of them had any doubt Anton Knopper was right. And one evening on the way home from the Mission house Lars Bundgaard said:

I've thought it over for a long time, and I can't believe anything except that we're now getting punished because we acted rashly toward our enemies. It was wrong for us to insist so stubbornly on our rights and to hurt other people.

Yes, we got too fired up and were no better than brawlers, Thomas Jensen said. I was clear about that as soon as it happened. But when the people came and wanted reconciliation with us, I felt the Lord had softened their hearts and forgiven us.

But what do you think we should do? Lars Bundgaard asked.

Well, what do you yourself think, Lars? Should we give the people over there the right to lay their traps in our waters next fall?

Lars Bundgaard thought about it—they sat for a while in silence. Behind them they heard the women whispering to one another.

I don't believe Jesus will demand that much from us, Lars Bundgaard finally answered. — After all, he knows our conditions and knows we are far from being prosperous people. And if he made such a great demand, he would surely have given us a plain signal to look for. But I believe we should present the matter to the parish in humility and confess how we've sinned.

I agree with you on that, Thomas Jensen said.

At the next meeting in the Mission house Thomas Jensen stepped forward and earnestly asked for forgiveness for their offense. Lars Bundgaard, Anton Knopper, and Jens Røn got up and stood with their heads bowed.

But now it was time to take the traps in. Jens Røn and Tea were in the worst shape. Eel fishing had, so to speak, brought in no income, and now they had to borrow and go into debt again. With a sigh Tea gave up her secret hope that they, too, one day could have their own house—not big houses like Povl Vrist's and Lars Bundgaard's, but a modest, little place. It wasn't to be. They had to be thankful if they could meet their obligations.

In November Martin came home from the farm. He was now almost sixteen years old and a small, compact boy, who resembled Jens Røn in his whole nature. It was their intention that he'd go to sea. Jens Røn had gotten him signed up as a cook on a little schooner that sailed the Baltic trade and laid up in the winter. But Martin had big plans about becoming a mate and captain.

Tea taught him to cook, and Anton Knopper made him a present of a cookbook.

He'll be a good cook, Anton Knopper said. I think he'll beat out most of them, but he probably has that from you, Tea, because you've always been a capable wife in your house.

No, I've never been the way I should, Tea said, delighted by the friendly words. But I hope the children will have it easier than we did.

Martin was a bit cool toward the praise for his cooking and would have preferred to show how to put hitches in a rope. This way and that way—he tied a knot in a piece of twine, and Anton Knopper nodded applause. That's just the way it's supposed to be. You have a talent for it, he said, and Tea was listening with half an ear, but couldn't totally ignore that her children were gifted. It wasn't at all implausible that one day she'd get to see Martin in a lofty position. And that was consolation to think about now that poverty was once again knocking at the door.

— The autumn rain lashed down, and the wind swaddled the low houses. Every evening the bible and hymnbook were taken down from the shelf, and the word resounded. Black-clad, serious people went to the meetings in the Mission house, where the walls were green from dampness. The missionaries and pastors passed like migrating birds through the parish.

Malene went to bed and gave birth to a little girl. Pastor Terndrup came to visit, while Tea and Mariane were sitting by the bed. He patted the newborn on the cheek with one of his long, thin fingers.

You lost two children, he said. So you see God's mercy. Now he's given you a little girl.

Malene was lying with the down quilt drawn up to her throat. Yes, she replied. We're also thankful for it.

It's a beautiful child, the pastor said in his small, cracked voice. It resembles its father more as far as I can see. Yes, it's born facing many temptations, such a small child.

Yet the little one has the advantage of being born in a home where the spirit of God dwells, the pastor said. At times, you know, it can be depressing. Three days ago I visited a girl in West Fens, who had had twins—and she admitted to me she wasn't completely sure who the father was. There were two—two!—it might have been.

So what—then there'd be one for each, Mariane blurted out, and Tea gasped with horror.

Pastor Terndrup looked at her a bit confused, and Mariane blushed. Now she had gone too far.

I mean, each of them will pay for one of the children, she said and put on a simple-minded expression.

I'm thinking not of the economic arrangement, but of the moral responsibility, the pastor explained. One shudders when one considers the life that such a girl has lived. Threw herself into the arms of every fellow who came near her.

Yes, it's terrible, Tea said out of breath. I mean that sort of woman ought to be whipped because they're the ones who lead the men astray.

The pastor shook his head: I scarcely believe you're right about that. In my experience the men are often the worst. I'll go so far that I'll straight out demand of the secular authorities that every man who seduces an untouched woman be punished in a house of correction.

That would be really harsh, Mariane said, shaken.

But not at all too harsh, the pastor replied.

I think that at the very least the girl should be forced to reveal her sin, Tea said.

Perhaps, the pastor said. Perhaps. In any case, lewdness is a terrible danger. It's just like weeds one believes one has gotten control over and weeded them all out by the root, and a month later the flower bed is overgrown again.

Exulting, Tea looked at Mariane. Now she could certainly understand that her views were correct and were endorsed in higher places. But without wincing Mariane put on her most inflexible face.

Then there's the hotel, Tea said cautiously.

You're right about that, Pastor Terndrup said. But do you think it's worth talking to the man?

He's obstinate, that he is, though I absolutely believe the wife is the worst, Tea answered. To put it bluntly, I consider her a sensuous woman. But I think it would be an eye-opener for many people as to what dancing is about if the pastor had a word with Kock.

Perhaps I could try, the pastor said.

— Kock had dismissed his housekeeper, and Katrine managed the hotel. A new girl was hired, who was to wait tables. Dead-Esben came trudging one day for an infrequent visit and patted Katrine on the cheek: You have it really good, Katrine. Now I have no concerns and can think about my salvation—yes, I have to take care of the farm as long as I'm alive.

But when Katrine stood behind the bar, young and full-bosomed, and watched the dancing couples, her heart felt heavy in her breast. When there were no customers, Kock read aloud to her from his books. Katrine nodded over her knitting. You're not sleeping, are you? Kock asked sulkily. No, no, Katrine assured him—I just dropped a stitch.

Kock was often out traveling—he had gotten into so many new things. He had joined a movement, which was called Joint Governance, and he traveled to all the meetings. He spoke and found attentive listeners; it was an association that wanted to organize society on an intellectual and liberal basis and solve every political difficulty.

When he and Katrine went to bed at night, Kock discussed the problems until she dozed off. The parliament was to be abolished, he said, and we'll all take part directly in the public proceedings that interest us.

We will? Katrine replied from her bed. I think that'll be kind of complicated.

Not at all, Kock said, the technical problem has been solved. At the last meeting a picture was shown of a newly invented voting machine; so we can easily begin tomorrow.

Oh, tomorrow, Katrine mumbled drowsily and fell asleep.

Kock became more straight-backed and twirled his mustache upward. If a magazine was started, he had every chance of becoming editor. He could no longer be annoyed by the fact that Aaby had gotten control of the youth association and made it into a bible circle. He regarded his surroundings with mild irony and did what he could to educate his wife. You mustn't eat fish with a knife, he said—nobody does that anywhere. Katrine obediently laid the knife aside. And it would be appropriate if you'd begin to say *I* instead of *a*. — No, I couldn't ever get that past my lips, Katrine replied.

Katrine felt like dancing, and as often as it could be arranged, she herself served the customers. Anders Kjøng was bitter and evil-tempered and treated her with mischievous politeness. Madame, he said and bowed. Excuse me, I didn't shave today. He rubbed his stubbly chin.

You're a fool, Katrine said angrily.

I don't read books, Anders Kjøng said. And imperative, or whatever it's called, I don't know anything about it. But ask your husband. Can the cock do anything but crow? That was surely a bad twaddle-cook you got, Katrine.

Watch yourself, Katrine said and went her way.

Kock had caught a word of the conversation from his seat, and a little later he went out into the kitchen and asked what Anders Kjøng had said.

Nothing, Katrine said sulkily.

Nothing, Kock said didactically. One can't say nothing.

Katrine blushed, her eyes shone angrily, and she gave Kock one on the side of his head so hard it sang.

Now you can learn *that*, she shouted.

Kock tumbled back and held his hand up to his cheek.

But Katrine, have you lost your mind? he said reproachfully.

My mind, Katrine sobbed and sat down on the kitchen chair. I don't have a mind, and you didn't demand it of me either back then when we first met.

Kock turned and left. Katrine was sitting there lonely and crying among the unwashed cups and glasses when the door opened. It was Laurids Toft, Povl Vrist's laborer. Astonished, he looked at her and came closer.

But you're sitting here and crying? he said.

Laurids was a slim fellow with dense, fair hair and a handsome, sunburned face. He went over to Katrine, took her by the chin and lifted her face to the light.

You should dry your eyes and come in and take a whirl, he said. You'll see—your cares will disappear.

I can't dance, Katrine sniffled—you know I'm a married woman.

Of course you can dance, Laurids replied. Who's going to forbid you. — Kock isn't that foolish. I'd much rather dance with you than with any of the girls.

You would? Katrine asked and gave a little smile.

You bet, the laborer assured her. Just come along—you better believe I'll whirl you about so you'll have something else to worry about than sitting here and grieving.

Wavering, Katrine got up.

They can see I've been crying.

Laurids found a washrag, moistened it under the water pump and gently dried her face, which was red from weeping. Katrine let him do it, and when he was done, he bent down and kissed her.

You can't do that, Laurids, she whispered.

Ok, then I won't next time, the laborer said. But I won't promise it for certain.

That evening Katrine whirled around on the dance floor. Kock didn't say anything.

Pastor Terndrup seriously set about implementing his idea and went down to speak God's word to the people at the inn. Kock was surprised when the pastor walked in the door—but the inn was open to everyone. The pastor stood for a moment and looked around and then went to the bar.

The innkeeper, I presume, he said. I didn't know what you look like. It's not every Sunday one sees you in church.

No, Kock answered calmly. The pastor doesn't see me in church. Because I never go to church. That's the story.

Oh well, Pastor Terndrup said. I just happened to be walking by—and looked in. There are various things I'd like to talk to you about if it's not inconvenient for you.

Not at all, Kock answered. If you'd just come with me to my office.

Kock strode ahead of him with dignity into the little room where he had his desk and his books. He offered the pastor a seat and sat down himself and politely extended his hand.

What does the pastor wish? he asked.

The pastor stared a bit confused at him. But Kock sat there deadly serious and enjoyed the situation—struggle and discussion were brewing. The time had passed when he felt honored by clerical company, and he truly wouldn't mince words.

You mentioned before that you never go to church, the pastor said. I trust I'm not intruding when I ask whether you belong to a religious community.

No I don't, Kock informed him. If anything, I must view myself as belonging to the agnosticistic doctrine. But wouldn't the pastor like to smoke?

Kock got up to get cigars, but Pastor Terndrup preemptively put his hands up: Thank you, I never smoke.

It makes the matter a little more complicated that I can't appeal to a religious instinct in you. But perhaps we can talk about it on a general human basis. We live here in a small society, where a set of fixed and invariable moral rules apply, which are based on what surely you, too, would call a serious life-view. But these moral laws, whose significance in any case cannot be denied for the main mass of the parish residents, are violated time and again by things that go on here in the temperance hotel.

What goes on here? Kock asked.

The young people hang out here and throw their money away on foolish amusements. They dance here, and licentiousness and unchaste living follow in the footsteps of dancing. I feel, Mr. Kock—I have the impression you are a serious and right-thinking man—don't you believe that from your bourgeois, moral points of view it's your duty to prevent phenomena that are decidedly disapproved of by most people in the parish?

That's a matter that can be viewed from many sides, Kock said, leaning back in his chair. I'm going to mention an example for the pastor. Let's suppose a Christian missionary is captured by cannibals in Africa, and the morality generally prevailing there demands that he be cooked for soup. Am I then morally obligated to forbear from helping him merely because I'm the only one in the place who has another view of the question concerning the enjoyment of human flesh?

That's comparing apples and oranges, Mr. Kock, the pastor said with irritation.

Not at all, Kock replied. I regard Christianity here in this area as cannibalism, intellectually. I'm an advocate of the greatest possible intellectual freedom, and I'll fight against intolerance wherever it appears. But if you can substantiate your claim with scientific and incontrovertible proof that the young people are harmed by drinking coffee and lemonade and dancing a few evenings a week until 10:30 p.m., then I'll immediately go out and take down my sign.

Since you're not a Christian, we have completely different views of what is of service to the people, the pastor said. For me the point is that even an insignificant transgression can lead to sin and perdition. We humans are not permitted to forget that we have a divine soul.

Scientifically it is of course somewhat doubtful whether one can speak of a soul altogether, Kock said tenaciously. In any event, one can use it only in the concept of psychic function. And as a Darwinist I'd —

Darwinist! The pastor bolted up from his chair. May I ask whether you're an advocate of the monkey theory?

I am, Kock answered. I maintain the conviction that — —

Stop! the pastor shouted. Don't say another word! That you deny the divine is sinful, but you flat out want to make a human being into a monkey—a monkey! The ugliest and most unattractive animal. No further discussion is possible!

The pastor grabbed his hat and hurried through the taproom while Kock accompanied him to the door with exquisite politeness.

The winter was long and ferocious. The frost had eaten deep into the ground and didn't want to let go, and the fjord was frozen over into March. The ice was packed in mountains along the shore, and the sun had no strength. But one night the ice broke up during a crash of thunder. Then suddenly spring was there. The last dirty snowdrifts melted, the rain beat down, and the fields began to green.

Old teacher Aaby shuffled out at noontime when the sun was warm. A new teacher had come. Aaby was a pensioner and lived in a couple of rooms near the church. I've reached biblical age, he said, and scratched the spring-moistened earth with his cane. Biblical age. Oh, yes, I'll probably soon be taking the great journey.

You're still a young man, Anton Knopper consoled him, what's seventy years for you, Aaby, as well as you maintain yourself—after all, you're never sick.

To be sure, Aaby sighed. Sick or not sick. Death will soon call on me. For that matter, it could well come at this moment while I'm standing here talking to you. My heart isn't strong—I've often noticed it—and one day I'll fall down and be through.

Anton Knopper cleared his throat: Of course, a blessed resurrection awaits.

Yes, on the other side of the grave, Aaby said. But you have to go into the grave.

He tottered on, his head bent over toward the ground.

Jens Røn and Tea had had a hard winter. They again had to run up big debts at the coop and borrow from their friends. Tea pinched and saved and was often on the verge of losing her sense of humor. But this time they weren't the only ones struck by bad luck. Povl Vrist was a prosperous man, and he wasn't affected if fishing failed for a year or two, and Anton Knopper had gotten a little money through Andrea and was in clover. He also managed until better times came. But for Thomas Jensen and Lars

Bundgaard it wasn't easy to get enough food for all their children.

Thomas Jensen's manner had become calm—he had always been a gentle man. He didn't complain.

We'll see, he said.

What are you thinking about, Thomas? Lars Bundgaard asked.

All I know is that if we fish well in the spring, then we've been forgiven for our lack of judgment, Thomas Jensen answered. But if we aren't blessed, then it will be probably be demanded of us that we give others the right to come into our waters.

Yeah, that's certainly the way it will have to be, Lars Bundgaard nodded. It will be a heavy loss, but if that's the intention, we must submit.

Povl Vrist had gotten two big seine nets, and he frowned when Mariane told him how the others looked at the matter.

I'm not giving my rights away, he said curtly. Then I'd be a fool for those beggars from the south.

I never thought you would, Mariane replied. But the others believe if Our Lord will help them, they can lay fish traps on a roof and catch larks.

You have a nasty mouth, Povl Vrist said.

— It was a consolation for Tea that others were in straits almost as bad. She could talk to Alma and Malene about how expensive the coop manager's goods were: it was probably because he himself was paid a commission. And she could show off the ingenious patches she sewed on the children's clothing, and harvested well-earned praise for her capabilities.

Tabita sent the money she could do without from her wages. Tabita changed every time she came home for a visit, and one day Tea discovered she was wearing a ring.

But Tabita, she said appalled. What do you have there on your finger?

Oh, it's just a ring, Tabita replied, blushing and embarrassed.

Where did you get it from? Tea asked sternly. I suspect you bought it with your own money. — But take care that vanity not get the better of you.

I do, Tabita said and hurried out into the kitchen. The food was about to boil over.

Many times in the course of the day Tea stole glances at the thin, twisted gold ring on Tabita's finger. In the evening Jens Røn went to bed early and Tabita sat with her mother in the parlor. She was sewing, and the sparkling ring again caught Tea's eye.

You didn't get the ring from some manfolk, did you? she asked. You mustn't hide anything, Tabita.

Tabita didn't answer, but bent deep over her sewing.

I can understand you don't have a pure conscience, Tea said ready to cry. But what will things come to if at your young age you're beginning to act like a fool on the street with menfolk.

I don't either, Tabita whispered.

Yes, but you have a ring on your finger, and you didn't buy it yourself, Tea said. So there can't be any other explanation except that you're up to some love affair. I feel I warned you morning, noon, and night against frivolity. Don't you ever think about that?

Tabita threw her sewing down: If I have to be the way you people want it, it would be better if I hadn't been born at all.

But dear child, Tea said appalled. How can you say such things? You must know your father and I only think of what's best for you, and you better believe the time will come when you'll thank us because we warned you against these temptations. But I'll probably be lying in my grave. Tears welled up in Tea's eyes and she took Tabita's hand.

You know, of course, Tabita, we're pious people, and it's our duty to do all we can to make sure our children can also be saved. And believe you me it's sad for us to notice you withdrawing from Jesus. I've always put my confidence in your having a good disposition. And now I feel you've gotten into some trouble.

Crying, Tabita hid her face in her arms.

I haven't at all, she said. But you people don't understand anything. It's totally different out in the world than you think.

But how can you say such a thing, Tabita, Tea replied angrily. Believe you me I know all about the sinful life people lead in town, and I myself was once young and know that a young girl has to look out for herself. I won't tell your father about the ring—but you have to tell me where you got it from.

I got it—it's a friendship ring, Tabita said.

But who gave it to you? Tea asked. I'm your mother, and I'm obliged to question you. What kind of man is he?

He's a blacksmith, Tabita said. And—we're going to get married once we've saved up enough money.

But dear little child, Tea burst out appalled. Did you get engaged without asking anyone? You're so young. Is he a believer?

No, Tabita answered.

Then you absolutely can't trust him an inch. I wish you'd never gone to the Mogensens' house. They talked nicely to us, but I should have considered the life they led while they were at the hotel. You have to give him back the ring as soon as you go to town.

I'll never do that, Tabita said defiantly. I'm old enough to run my own life.

Tea sighed. She now realized that Tabita had become a grown woman.

But I beg you to take the ring off when you're here at home, she said almost humbly. I'd hate for there to be blabbing about you.

Tabita took the ring off her finger and put it in her bag. Tea didn't talk about the matter any more, but after Tabita had left again, she reflected that she surely should have been stricter toward her. Did she treat her children more mildly than she ought? But on the other hand, Tabita was a smart girl and had never been frivolous. And it meant a lot that she had gotten a good upbringing and heard only pious words in her home. That was a good foundation to build on when the time came for Tabita.

Now Martin was to go out into the world. Jens Røn got a letter from the skipper saying it was time for the schooner to sail. He had been furnished according to their fullest ability with clothing and whatever else was fit and proper. Anton Knopper made him a present of an old sea-chest he had once bought at auction. Martin painted his name in big letters on the lid.

It's solid, Anton Knopper said. You'll be able to use it for many years. Some day, when you're a mate, you may well get one that's more elegant.

But Martin wasn't arrogant: Wouldn't it be good enough? he said. No, I'll have other things to spend the money on. It shouldn't be thrown away unnecessarily.

That's smart, Anton Knopper said. You absolutely have to remember that when you get to port. And remember to put the money and sailor's certificate on top so you can get a hold of it quickly if you're shipwrecked.

Don't talk that way, Tea said terrified. I can't bear thinking something might go wrong.

No, no, Anton Knopper said. You know, it was all just a joke. There's never the slightest danger at sea these days. It's in the winter, in storms. And then the schooner, of course, is carrying wood—it's downright impossible for it to sink.

Yeah, I'll never calm down until Martin comes back home in the fall, Tea said, on the verge of crying. I'd wish for you, Anton, that your boy never feels like going to sea. It's the worst thing in the world to sit at home in eternal anxiety. I felt I'd really gotten away from that when we moved away from the sea. Many was the night I lay awake and listened to the weather when Jens was out there. And now I have to do it all over again.

Martin was undismayed. He strolled from house to house in his fisherman's jacket and said his good-byes. So, you're going away, Martin, Mariane said. Yeah, I'm telling you, you already look like a little seaman. Believe you me the girls will go blind giving you the eye when you come into port. Martin smiled, embarrassed, but Povl Vrist took ten crowns from his wallet. This is for you as a reserve if you should need money, he said.

— In the morning, the day he was to leave, Tea was up early and woke him. In the light of the lamp, which blended in with the gray break of day, Jens Røn read the morning prayer. Tea put a bible at the top of the sea-chest.

You have to read a section in it every single day, Jens Røn said seriously. That way you won't get into any trouble.

Tea took his hand and looked at him with tears in her eyes.

Before you leave us, dear Martin, you have to promise you'll never go dancing or take God's name in vain or play cards. Will you promise us that?

Yes, Martin whispered.

You've been a good boy all your life, Tea said. And if you just stick firmly to Jesus, you'll be fine.

They drank coffee in silence, and the children stared devotedly at their brother, who was sitting in his Sunday best and was about to leave.

Well, it's time, Jens Røn said.

He and Martin picked up the chest and dragged it out onto the road, where the bus would stop.

Be careful when you get into port, his father admonished him. There are wicked womenfolk and wretches who want to lead you to misfortune. And you must always do your duty as your superiors command.

Yes, Martin said in a weeping voice.

Good-bye, my boy, Tea cried and kissed him. They could see the bus.

One by one his brothers and sisters shook his hand. Good-bye, Martin! they whispered.

Martin sat a bit scrunched in a corner of the bus and looked back. Then he rode out into the world.

— Tea felt the boy was closest to her heart, even if that was unjust to the others, and if anything bad happened to him, it would be unbearable. Every day she was on the lookout for the mail to see if there was a letter. And finally a postcard came with greetings. Martin had found the ship and begun to cook. Everything was going well, he wrote. Affectionately, your son Martin Røn.

Tea took the letters from Martin along with her when she went visiting. It was nice to talk to other people about the boy, and Mariane especially was a source of consolation. The children you have! Mariane said. They're gifted and no one can say anything to the contrary.

Yeah, you can talk, Tea answered flattered. Your kids don't lack anything. Aaby wants them to stick to their books.

Come on, Mariane said. That doesn't mean anything. They don't have anything in their heads but fishing, and they lie and root around in the fjord from morning till night. But yours—they want to get ahead—anyone can understand that. And I'm sure Martin is solid, and he'll become something. And Tabita—she's so pretty and capable.

Yeah, Tabita—Tea said anxiously. You must be glad, Mariane, you can keep yours here at home.

I think you and Jens Røn have had bad luck in many ways, Mariane kept at it patiently. But you have such capable kids that no one could demand more. — The other kids will be just as clever—you can almost see it.

But if the conversation turned to other things, Mariane was as sharp-tongued as ever. Now for example there was Laurids. It was rumored he went to the inn as often as there was dancing and busied himself with Katrine more than was decent.

So what, Mariane said in her usual manner. If you were married to Kock, you'd probably also want to dance with the fellows. They say he reads to her from a book in the evening and goes to bed with a book at night. That's no life for a wife.

We know Katrine and know the way she is. But Laurids should consider himself too good for that, Tea said.

He's good at whirling the womenfolk around the dance floor, Mariane replied. You can see that at a glance.

Maybe you'd like to have a whirl around yourself? Tea asked cuttingly.

They sat in the kitchen, and the laborer came in to get his coffee. Mariane turned toward him.

Tea is so taken with you, Laurids, she said. She'd really like to dance with such a young fellow. And you know, they say you've got an eye for the women.

Tea's face turned crimson and she couldn't say a word in response. Was there now going to be a tale that she was looking at the young men? She was about to cry. Mariane discovered she'd been too hard and regretted it.

I'd like to dance with you myself if I can, she laughed, and Laurids wasn't slow—he took her by the waist. They swept across the kitchen floor in a waltz. Mariane hummed the melody, and this shameless sight made Tea feel unwell. Mariane's cheeks took on color, and she carried herself lightly like a young girl and rested securely in the laborer's arms. But she was a married woman, and she was dancing with a fellow you could believe anything about.

Povl Vrist opened the door and stood still at the threshold and captured the situation with one look. His face became hard; he blinked a couple of times, but composed himself.

Well, you're doing a bit of dancing, he said curtly and calmly.

Mariane quickly slipped away from the laborer and laughed a bit out of breath.

Tea didn't believe I could still dance, she said, observing her husband askance. But obviously I can still remember how, even though I'll soon be an old woman.

We'd like to have our coffee, Povl Vrist said and avoided meeting her eyes.

They drank coffee, and Mariane chatted away as if nothing had happened.

So when do you expect the boy back home? she asked.

In the fall, Tea answered and stole a glance at Povl Vrist, who was sitting and frowning. Mariane would come to regret that dance—and maybe it was for her own good.

Then you can have him at home in the winter, Mariane said.

We certainly hope so—Tea made her voice sound melancholy. She wanted Mariane to know she understood what was brewing here.

Povl Vrist got up. Thanks for the coffee, he said, and the two men went back to their work.

Mariane gathered up the cups while they engaged in cheerful small talk. Gloomy, Tea sat in a corner and answered only yes and no. A little later she said good-bye.

So, you're going home, Mariane said.

Yes, Tea answered with a meaningful look. But of course you know, Mariane, if you need help, there's one who'll come just for the calling.

Thanks a million, dear Tea, Mariane laughed. But I hardly think I'll need a midwife right away.




The motorboats pounded the fjord and drew stripes in the shiny, tranquil water. The sun rose copper-red beyond the dark clouds to the east. The planks on the wharf were wet from dew when the fisherman landed.

In the beginning no fish went into the nets, and Thomas Jensen was on the verge of believing the punishment had been imposed on them. But one morning the catch was so big the net could barely be lifted. The exporter stood there for hours weighing and recording in his little book, while singing hymns in a booming voice. And one by one the boats came in so heavily laden they were ready to sink.

That was a big swarm that passed through our waters, Povl Vrist said.

The others nodded—they were in a festive mood. Whatever errors they had committed had been forgiven.

We were doubtless being tested, Lars Bundgaard said.

That was probably the intention, Thomas Jensen replied.

It was a good spring—the herring went into the nets as never before. Jens Røn got his debt paid off, and Tea once again looked at life brightly and spoke about their having the means for a new sofa instead of the old, brown window-seat. Let's move calmly, Jens Røn said, and see if the good times last. But Tea finally got her sofa. It was bought at a used furniture dealer in town and was as good as new with green upholstery and tassels.

— In the spring a familiar guest came—Peder Hygum again got off his bicycle at Thomas Jensen's door. The hawker was gaunt and rumpled, and he cast his eyes down when Thomas

Jensen asked him how he was doing.

Pretty poorly, he said. Yeah, it can hardly get poorer. To be perfectly blunt about the way it is, I went bankrupt and I'm at the end of my tether and I have not where to lay my head.

That's bad, Thomas Jensen said with sympathy and couldn't get himself to ask what would happen with the surety.

But Peder Hygum guessed his thought. The money is lost, he sighed. And it can't be long now before you people will get a letter from the bank about paying. It's terrible I had to bring this misfortune on you.

Alma brought food, and Peder Hygum ate like a hungry wolf.

How are you going to manage? Thomas Jensen asked

Yeah, Peder Hygum said, yeah—

He stood still and resembled a dog that was about to be beaten. But when Alma was out of the room, he said:

The Lord has shown me a way out.

Peder Hygum ran his hand across his sweaty forehead and coughed hollowly.

I better tell you everything, he said. You've been a good man to me and mine, and I want to be honest with you. You see, the business didn't go so well—I didn't get the volume of customers I'd been assured. Then I got the terrible thought that the Lord had taken his mercy from me—after all, I surely know I haven't always been his faithful servant. In my desperation I thought: look at the butcher next door—he swears and drinks and is sweethearts with a married woman. And the shoemaker just across the street has three illegitimate children—one of them with his housekeeper. And both of them are allotted the earth's gifts in abundance, although they don't even say thank you for it. But here you sit, Peder, and have a business with godly books and fight against all sinful impulses in your nature—and still you get poorer day by day and can barely provide food for your family.

But Peder Hygum, Thomas Jensen said horrified. Did you take God to task?

Yes, the hawker cried. Every evening I got down on my bare

knees and prayed for help against the temptations, but I couldn't resist. The devil is shrewd—he sneaks into your heart and confuses all your senses. One day I left home and took to drinking. You have to hear about my steep fall. I caroused away all the money I had, and borrowed more from people who regarded me as a believer. When I returned home one evening from the terrible places where sin wallows in filth, the room was empty. Laura had gone home to her father. Then I converted everything into money and wasn't in my right mind. I staggered about and drank and associated with lewd women.

Peder, Peder! Thomas Jensen said.

I know! the hawker wailed. But now I had to empty the bitter drink to the dregs. I staggered further along the road to perdition. And I ended up in prison.

In prison!—Thomas Jensen bolted up from his chair.

Yes, in the place where they lock up drunken people who are found on the streets. They call it a detention center. I was fined and atoned for it for many days. In prison God once again showed me his merciful face. There was a believing guard who saw my wretchedness and had me placed for some time with good people, and now I know the Lord had his intention when he led me though all that. Now I understand it. I've found the good, pure doctrine. I've become a Baptist.

But Peder Hygum, Thomas Jensen said. Then you've become an apostate.

That's what *you* call it, and I deserve harsh words because I used your money. But along many winding paths the Lord has led me to where *he* wants. God submersed me in the impure puddle of vice so I would understand if I want to be saved, I'd have to be submersed anew in the baptismal font.—

Then you've forsaken our principles, Thomas Jensen said sadly. I never expected that from you.

No, I haven't forsaken, Peder Hygum replied. But God with his own hand has led me to a correct understanding. Oh, I'd give anything so the rest of you could find the way to the right faith.

Let's not talk about this thing any more, Thomas Jensen said. I don't believe in the Baptists' doctrine, and I'm sorry to hear where you wound up. But I don't want to reproach you.

— Peder Hygum stayed as a guest in Thomas Jensen's house for several days and went from door to door among friends and spoke about his conversion. Tea didn't like that talk about God's having guided him through sin and aberrations.

Surely you can understand, Peder Hygum, that God will not lead us out into evil, and you reveal that you have both drunk and committed fornication.

God wanted it that way so I could wind up in the utmost wretchedness, Peder Hygum replied. But now it's all gone by. You know the beautiful hymn:

> Now sin, with reign unbroken,
> No more shall rule my life,
> Since God the word hath spoken,
> That wins for me the strife;
> Baptized, reborn by grace,
> I am redeem'd from evil,
> And have renounced the devil
> And all his works and ways.

I don't take the Baptists seriously, Tea said. But what do you intend to do?

Yeah, a position has been gotten for me, Peder Hygum answered hesitantly. I'll be leader of the Baptists' Sunday school and otherwise be helpful to the pastor.

And you'll get wages for that?

A very small payment, Peder Hygum said. But with thriftiness I can probably exist with my family.

Tea was silent: Judas, too, sold his savior for a small payment. But she was not sitting in judgment. When Peder Hygum departed, no one asked him to come again.

— Tea didn't dare talk with the others about her suspicions—your mouth could easily get you in trouble. But a change was taking place in Povl Vrist, which became more recognizable as time went on. He was taciturn, and his face was gruff and closed. Had something happened between him and Laurids?

Tea pondered, but couldn't find any explanation. People knew Laurids went to the hotel every single evening, and there was a lot of talk about him and Katrine. But was there also something with Mariane? Tea talked to Jens Røn about it. Watch your mouth, dear Tea, he said angrily. After all, ultimately it's none of your business. — You know I'm not curious, Tea replied offended. But I like Mariane a lot, and it would be hard for me if she plunged into aberrations. — When Tea spoke to Mariane, her voice was mild and whimpering, but you couldn't notice anything in Mariane. You couldn't get anything out of her.

— In the evening, when the hotel closed, the young people swarmed at the wharf or in the inn garden. One fellow played harmonica, and there was dancing on the grass. Between the trees you could catch a glimpse of the fjord, the air was sweet and spiced, and the girls hummed while they danced, and snuggled close to the fellows.

One evening a dispute developed between Anders Kjøng and Laurids: they shoved each other and got hot under the collar, rolled around in the flower beds and trampled the heavy, wet earth. But with one rough hold Laurids lifted Anders Kjøng and threw him over and into a bush so hard it cracked.

Now you'll behave yourself, you clown, he puffed.

Katrine came running in from the kitchen.

What's going on here? she shouted.

Anders Kjøng had a hard time getting on his feet and wanted another go at his opponent.

Katrine gave him a push. She was angry.

I won't have this nonsense, she said. How did Anders Kjøng insult you, Laurids?

It was Anders who started it, one of the others said.

Well, you can't control yourself, Katrine scolded him. But I won't have that racket. If you aren't peaceful, then stay away from here.

Anders Kjøng didn't answer, and Katrine turned and went back to the house.

— Katrine's manner had become domineering; she managed

the inn alone. Kock had so many other things to attend to now that he had become editor of the *Joint Governance Magazine* and brought order to the chaos of the time. He wrote articles and held all the threads in his hand, and he was constantly traveling to meetings and was often away for days at a time.

Otherwise he mostly sat in his office and read and wrote, but in the evening he liked to go out and chat with the customers. Kock was no eccentric—he exchanged thoughts even with the simplest folk and didn't look down on anyone. Now here's an article I've written, he said—it deals with rational rule and its principles. Here it is if you feel like reading it.

It's probably above our heads, Laurids said.

Certainly not, Kock said. I've expressed myself in a popular way— you know, it means folksy, everyone can grasp what's in it.

Yeah, I'd like to borrow it, Laurids replied and took the paper. We have to listen to the wisdom we can get.

Anders Kjøng came rushing up to the bar with his hands deep in his pockets. His eyes had an evil glint.

So Laurids is about to read, he said. Now I didn't think *that*'s what he was best at.

You don't think he stands on the same level with you in terms of intelligence? Kock said with an air of superiority.

Maybe he does, Anders Kjøng answered. I've never had much sense either. But I respect Laurids—I know there's something he understands better than you.

What are you driving at? Kock asked firmly.

I'll tell you what I mean, Anders Kjøng said. You're a windbag, and I don't take you seriously in the least.

Katrine came in from the kitchen and stepped over beside Kock.

You can just go your way, Anders Kjøng, she said angrily. No one sent for you.

No, there are others you send for, Anders Kjøng replied and looked at her defiantly.

The other men stood silently and waited to see what would happen. But Katrine stared him in the eyes until he lowered them. Laurids had grabbed a bottle and squeezed it in his hand.

I don't squabble with womenfolk, Anders Kjøng said and turned to go.

He took his hat, but out in the yard Laurids came running after him.

Come in here, he whispered and grabbed Anders Kjøng by the shoulder and pulled him into the coach-stable.

Now I'm going to confide something to you, you oaf, he said hoarsely. Doubtless you've discovered which one of us is stronger. And if you don't get hold of yourself, you'll get a sound drubbing you'll never forget for the rest of your life.

You're surely not the man to give it to me, Anders Kjøng said and freed himself. But I can still see what you and Katrine are planning.

Laurids smacked him across the face and flung him against the wall.

Now I've warned you, he said. If you make the slightest sound to Kock or anyone else, I'll beat you to a pulp. I'm serious.

It's amazing how worked up you are. Now Anders spoke in a more supple way. You obviously don't get a joke. But you're too dumb to get it.

You can call it what you want, Laurids said threateningly. But I'd advise you against any more joking if you don't want your brains bashed.

He turned and left. Anders Kjøng was on the verge of crying. He was always being made a fool of, an insignificant fellow, who acquiesced in threats and accepted a thrashing like a boy. But he'd teach people a lesson. A plan was ripening in Anders Kjøng to go to town and earn money and return as a rich man, who could buy the hotel and every farm in the parish. Then they'd think differently about him. But when he was prosperous, he'd never forget the way Laurids and Katrine had treated him.

— Katrine blossomed, big and blushing-red, with her brown hair like a blast of wind around her head. When there was a ball at the inn, she was seldom off the floor; she smiled graciously every time a man asked her to dance. She had become mild-tempered, and angry words were never on her tongue. Kock nodded: she had grown accustomed to marriage. He viewed her dancing with indifference. Personally he didn't understand what the point of dancing was, but he was tolerant and didn't begrudge Katrine an amusement.

The young fellows stood for hours at the bar and chatted with Kock, who monopolized the talk. He developed his view of all manner of things and advanced decisive proofs. He became ardent and slammed his hands on the bar: that's the way things stood according to the present stage of science. The fellows mostly said yes and no, but willingly received the instruction that flowed their way. And Katrine stood next to Kock, vigorous and broad-bosomed, and managed the whole thing. Whatever happened in the warm summer nights, no one was to forget that Kock was her husband and had made her his wife in his house.


Laurids and Povl Vrist could no longer get on together. Whenever Povl Vrist talked to his helper, it was in a curt and cool tone: Can you do this and that, Laurids, and never a word beyond what was necessary. Laurids acted as if nothing had happened and he had other things to think about. When he came in to get his food, Mariane teased him: you should instead work at the inn since you're there from morning till night. Yes, Laurids answered thoughtfully. But what can I otherwise do to kill time. — No, that's a hundred percent certain, Mariane said, and then you also help Katrine kill time. She may well be hard up in that department. Laurids smiled good-naturedly and let Mariane think what she wanted. When Povl Vrist came in, the conversation stopped—his face was not an invitation to banter.

In the fall Mariane once again felt she wanted to have a radio. On many of the farms in the parish they had already gotten one, and Mariane was full of enthusiasm: it was an invention without equal. Mariane got her wish, and a mechanic was sent for in town, who came and set up the miracle. Because it was a miracle! Mariane was full of joy and praise. Here she was sitting in her own parlor and heard everything from out in the world. Half the town came to visit and put on earphones.

It's a pretty strange thing, Tea said doubtfully; I can't understand how it works. — I don't know anything about it, Mariane replied. But it's the most ingenious thing ever invented: we just turn a knob and we can hear every thing. — Tea listened to music and song and didn't completely like it. It may be nice enough, she said hesitatingly. But as far as I can hear, they're singing strange songs. — Oh, come on, sometimes I can barely keep my feet still when the music is on. — Now that just can't ever be right—that the air has to be filled with dance melodies and lewd music, Tea said with annoyance. No, I wouldn't give very much for that invention. It can only harm people who waste their time listening to it. — But one Sunday Tea heard a sermon and was satisfied. I can hear just so clearly the way the people are walking on the church floor, she whispered. Someone just coughed. Shhh—the pastor is starting and I can hear every word.

Tea became very sad. She'd never have the money for a radio. Really, you will, Mariane said. No, Tea shook her head in a melancholy way. It's not for us, but you and Povl—you'll soon be such big people that the rest of us are nothing by comparison.

The radio was no diversion for Povl Vrist—he was out of sorts. He probably knew he wasn't nearly so smart as Mariane. Without her advice and help he'd never have become a well-to-do man and the biggest fisher there. In everything he'd undertaken he'd asked her for her opinion and quietly followed it. But if Mariane had fallen in love with someone else, then fate could take what it had given: the fish would stay away from his nets, and the storm would destroy his equipment. Then he'd be an unhappy man.

Suspicion gnawed deeper and deeper into him. He used his eyes, caught every smile that Mariane gave Laurids, turned and twisted every word and found a hidden meaning. Indeed, there was surely no doubt any more. Mariane looked kindly on Laurids, who was a young and lusty fellow, and there was nothing to the chatter that went around about him and Katrine at the inn, but was only supposed to throw people off the scent.

Povl Vrist lay sleepless night after night and settled accounts. The traps went into the water, he swung the mallet and let it fall on the post and clenched his teeth. What if he smashed Laurids's head with one blow? In the boat home he sat silently and stared out across the water. The children noticed something bad was brewing and scarcely dared come near him, and Mariane observed him quietly and tried to find out what was gnawing at him. Are you sick, Povl? she asked. No, Povl Vrist said curtly. I think you're changing, Mariane said. We can't remain the same forever, Povl Vrist replied. I'm also not that young any more—surely you know that, Mariane?

One afternoon the two men were sitting and working. Povl Vrist was hewing a post and using an ax with short, sure blows. The shavings sprayed around him. Laurids was disentangling rope from a pile on the floor and hanging it on a spike on the wall. He was crooning to himself:

With joy I lazily
Did spend an hour
Walked through heather in
The summer weather in
The wild rose moor.

A farmer joyfully
I saw appear,
Grain he was reaping in
His son was sweeping in
The roses there.

Now, hear, my dearest one,
What I tell you,
There it stood joyfully
Oh, yes, so peacefully
Violet—blue.

Shut up with that singing of yours, Povl Vrist said curtly. Astonished, Laurids turned and looked at his master; then he set to work again. Now he was softly whistling the melody. Povl Vrist stared angrily at his helper's strong, broad back, and rage welled up in him.

I'll get you to keep your mouth shut, you lout, he shouted and jumped forward a step.

Laurids turned around on his heels and quickly threw himself to the side. The ax whizzed by him and crashed against the wooden partition, where it got solidly stuck in the wood. The laborer uttered a roar, but Povl Vrist was over him like thunder.

The two men staggered about, clinging tightly to each other and with each other's hot breath in their faces. Laurids was taller and more agile, but Povl Vrist's strength was sinewy and compact, and he was wild. He tried to lift Laurids and fling him off, but the laborer resisted with his tough body and stood fast. Snorting like stallions, they stomped in place with slow holds and fast tugs, with their arms wrung around each other's limbs without either gaining power over the other. Their veins protruded from their foreheads, and their knuckles turned white under their grips. Laurids hissed like a cat and bumped his head down on Povl Vrist's face. As he did so he was lifted up and thrown over onto a pile of fish traps.

Povl Vrist rolled over onto him and grabbed him by the throat. He sensed nothing but a desire to finish Laurids off and he bored his fingers deep into the man who was rattling in his throat. But Mariane came rushing in the door and shook his shoulder. She had heard the din from the kitchen.

Povl! she shouted. Come to your senses. You're going to kill him.

Povl Vrist let the laborer go, and Laurids got up.

But why are you two fighting? Mariane asked. She caught sight of the ax and stared at it in fright.

It was nothing, Povl Vrist said and left the shed; Mariane followed him without speaking.

In the kitchen he sat down on a chair. Mariane poured a cup of coffee for him. Her expression revealed nothing.

What did he do? she asked. He's a terrible person.

Oh, I became a little hot-headed, Povl Vrist answered and avoided her look. He was rebellious and took to whistling after I had forbidden him to sing.

You better give him notice, Mariane said. But drink your coffee now. —

Povl Vrist went out to the fjord and emptied the traps. It was odd the way Mariane had taken it calmly. But he wasn't so smart that he could fathom her mind. When he docked at the wharf, Laurids was standing and waiting for him.

His helper walked with him up through town.

What did I do to you? he asked.

You know that better than I do, Povl Vrist answered and looked at him from the side.

I've never heard of trying to kill people because they're whistling, Laurids said. But you'd doubtless prefer me to look for another job.

Yes, Povl Vrist said curtly. You can come in and get your wages this evening.

I can just get it right now, Laurids said. And I'll promise you something you don't deserve: I won't tell people the way you treated me.

Laurids packed his stuff and moved. He settled at the hotel in a little room in the stable and drove out every day and traded in fish. He was a capable man and managed.

— Povl Vrist kept an eye on the way Mariane was taking it. She was the way she always was, and for a long time she didn't talk about what had happened. But one evening they were alone in the parlor, and she said: I think you've become strange, Povl: what is it you're going around and brooding over? Povl Vrist raised his gruff face from the newspaper: A person can always have something on his mind, and are you sure it isn't you who's changed? Mariane was silent for a bit and said bewildered: I'll be blunt, Povl: what you're thinking about me isn't correct. — Didn't you like him all the same? Povl Vrist asked softly. I saw you two dancing together: I can't get over that. — Yes, Mariane said, Laurids is both a clever and handsome man, but I believe you're scarcely in your right mind.

Povl Vrist stuffed his pipe and lit it; his fingers were shaking a bit: If you say there's nothing between you two, then I believe you because I know you tell the truth. But the suspicion—I'll never be able to let go of it. Mariane had tears in her eyes: I never thought things would come to such a pass between us, she said. But I've never taken a fancy to Laurids or any other man—you should know that.

Mariane was silent for a bit, and Povl slowly folded up his newspaper. I don't know, he said, but at times it seems to me the others are right who say we stand in the way of our own happiness. Don't you think we're sitting a bit too high in the saddle? What are you saying? Mariane asked. I don't think we're wronging anyone. Povl Vrist hesitated a little: No, he said. But maybe there's something to what the others say about our playing a dangerous game. I've never had much faith in strict divine worship, but if we were Pious, it would surely never have happened. — You mean I'd never have danced with Laurids that day? Mariane asked drily. — It wasn't exactly that, Povl Vrist said. But, you know, often we do consider whether events might contain a warning sign.

But now Mariane became testy. I wonder: wouldn't Our Lord have other things to do than set fox traps for us? she asked scornfully. And you need to know, Povl, that if you mistrust me, it's a shameful deed. But no matter what you do, you'll never get me to sing hymns and confess my sins in the Mission house.

Mariane rushed out into the kitchen and took to washing up. Povl Vrist sat and drummed with his fingers on the table top; he felt relieved: nothing bad had happened. No, when Mariane got all worked up, he knew her. She said what she was thinking without deceit.

I beg you to forget the words I just uttered, he said, when she stepped into the parlor. — Oh, I've already forgotten it, Mariane answered with a calm smile. But you can't go Pious on me, Povl, no matter what happens.

— Martin came home in the fall and stayed through Christmas. In March he was to go to sea again. Most of his wages he